NIGHT'S BLACK AGENTS
THE ZALOZHNIY QUARTET

BY **GARETH HANRAHAN**
STORY DESIGN **KENNETH HITE**

CREDITS

PUBLISHER: **SIMON ROGERS**

AUTHOR: **GARETH HANRAHAN**

STORY DESIGN: **KENNETH HITE**

LAYOUT: **CHRIS HUTH**

ART DIRECTION: **BETH LEWIS**

COVER ARTIST: **ALESSANDRO ALAIA**

INTERIOR ARTIST: **PHIL REEVES**

GUMSHOE SYSTEM: **ROBIN D LAWS**

PLAYTESTERS: Pete Butler, Linda McNair, Bill Moran, Mike Mullig, Jamie Stefko, Paul Stefko, John Adamus, Craig Spear, Dale Georg, Mollie Carson-Vollath, Andy Vann, Mike Varga, Simon Stroud, Aaron Cattle, Matt Radings, Peter Tracy, Peter Macejka

©2012 Pelgrane Press Ltd. All rights reserved. Night's Black Agents is a trademark of Pelgrane Press Ltd.

CONTENTS

INTRODUCTION	6
THE LISKY BRATVA	**6**
History	6
Josef Lisky	6
Playing Josef	7
Dr. G. D. Dorjiev	7
Playing Dorjiev	7
Areas of Influence	8
Key Assets	8
Mobile Assets	8
Vor Group	8
The Zalozhniy	8
Operatives ("Gastralyor")	9
Reserves	10
Regional Assets	10
LISKY BRATVA ADVERSARY MAP	**11**
THE PHILBY PLOT	**12**
The White & The Black	12
What Are We Looking For, Exactly?	13
Supernatural	13
Damned	13
Alien	14
Mutant	14
Variations	14
Diagramming the Quartet	15
THE OPERATIONS	**15**
THE ZALOZHNIY SANCTION	**16**
EYES ONLY BRIEFING	**16**
The Spine	16
Entry Vectors	17
Outside Leads	17
Inside Leads	17
THE ODESSA JOB	**19**
The Job	19
The Navy Motorboat	20
INFILTRATION	**20**
Tracking the Smugglers	20
Following the Trucks	20
THE WAREHOUSE	**21**
Sneaking In	21
Inside The Warehouse	21
UNDERWORLD	**22**
The Firefight	22
Dorjiev	23
The Guards	23
The Zalozhniy	23
The Russian Sailors	23
Escaping the Warehouse	24
THE CHASE	**24**
Chase Parameters	24
Switching Chases	24
Hazards & Encounters	25

Cornered	26
Out of Sight	26
LEAVING ODESSA	**26**
The Ways Out	26
By Plane	27
By Road	27
By Rail	27
By Sea	27
RUNNING HOT	**27**
The Authorities	28
Supernatural Threats	28
Hunters	28
Operatives	29
The Zalozhniye	29
Interceptions	29
Identifying the Enemy	30
The Lisky Bratva	30
The Zalozhniye	30
Tactics & Responses	31
TRANSNISTRIAN NIGHTS	**31**
MR. HAPPY	**32**
The Bargain	32
IGWE ABESOLI	**33**
The Dacha	33
Bypassing Security	33
The Prodigy	33
Making the Hit	33
DENIABLE ASSETS	**34**
Westward Bound	34
SHADOW OF THE VAMPIRE	**35**
THE SHIPPING ROUTE	**35**
DRAGOVIR VILLAGE	**36**
Arriving in Dragovir	36
The Shipment	36
Enemy Assets	36
Dr. Vathek	36
Virgil	37
Bronislav	37
Threat Response	37
THE MONASTERY	**37**
Approaches	37
The Mountainside	37
The Road	37
The Monastery Up Close	37
Out of the Pit	38
SECRETS OF THE MONASTERY	**39**
THE DEBRECEN GAMBIT	**40**
Identifying Kozorus	40
FINDING KOZORUS	**41**
THE TARGET AND THE TIGER	**41**
The Meet	41
Advance Warning	42
Perhaps too Late	42

Escaping the Trap	42
BURNING THE LISKY BRATVA	**43**
TRADING IN MISERY	**44**
The Human Trafficking Facility	44
Investigation & Reconnaissance	44
Defenses	44
Inside the Camp	45
Taking Out The Camp	45
THE GOLDEN CALF	**45**
Serbian Specialties	45
Investigation & Reconnaissance	45
Getting into the Restaurant	46
The Principals	46
Sergei Rachov	46
Jacob Lengyel	46
Todor Babic	46
Rudi Marko	46
The Deal	46
The Agenda	46
Dealbreakers	47
THE VIENNA RUN	**47**
THE AIRPORT	**47**
The Phone Call	47
The Locker	48
CRASH PRIORITY	**48**
The Foot Chase	48
THE FINAL RUN	**49**
Hitting the Road	49
Reaching Vienna	50
Final Curtain	50
EXIT VECTORS	**50**
Out of the House of Ashes	50
The Boxmen	50
Treason in the Blood	50
CAPSTONE: DR. DORJIEV,	
I EXHUME	**51**
Dorjiev's Forces	51
Killing Dorjiev	51
OUT OF THE HOUSE OF ASHES	**52**
EYES ONLY BRIEFING	**52**
The Spine	52
Old Sins	52
Viennese Blood Opera	54
Entry Vectors	54
Outside Leads	54
Inside Leads	54
PAWNS, BISHOPS AND KINGS	**55**
The Trade Conference	55
Security at the Conference	55
Arkady Shevlenko	55
Playing Shevlenko	56
Investigating Shevlenko	56
The Russian Embassy	56

Shevlenko's Schedule	56
Katarina Volkov	56
Zhenya Mihaylov	57
Sevastyan Popov	57
Taras Kaminski	57
Extra Assets	57
Dr. Ingolf	57
Shevlenko's Schedule	57
Playing Ingolf	58
Investigating Ingolf	58
Anna Shevlenko	58
Playing Anna	58
The CIA Team	58
Albert Carpenter	58
Playing Carpenter	58
Investigating Carpenter	59
The Lisky Bratva	59
The Vampire	59
Playing Thonradel	60
Investigating Thonradel	60
OPENING MOVES	**60**
THE BRITISH CONNECTION	**60**
THE LISKY BRATVA	**61**
INTRODUCING SHEVLENKO	**61**
Contacting Shevlenko	61
Observing Shevlenko	62
The Medical Appointment (2pm)	62
The Mining Seminar (6pm)	62
After The Seminar (7.15pm)	62
ANY OPERATION CAN BE ABORTED	**62**
The Reception	63
Observation Duty	63
The Extraction Plan	63
Abort! Abort!	64
The Van of Dead Men	65
The van escapes	65
The agents catch the van	65
The Hotel Key	66
Clean-Up	66
THE APPROACH	**66**
Shevlenko's Movements	66
The Saudi Prince (Day 2)	66
Meeting with the Vampire (Day 2)	66
The De Beers Meeting (Day 3)	66
Meeting Shevlenko	67
The Old Spy's Confession	67
Meeting Shevlenko Again	67
Shevlenko Reaches Out	67
THE HEART DOCTOR	**67**
Ingolf's Office	68
Breaking Ingolf	68
The Blood	68
The Dead Drop	69
BURNED	**69**
The Hotel Centrale	69
CJH Investments	70
The Lisky Bratva Thugs	70
Interviewing Feinberg	70
VAMPIRE HUNTING	**71**
Investigating Thonradel	71
Police Records	72
Procurement	72
Human Trafficking	72
Local Victims	72
Dealing with the Vampire	73
The Vampire's Prey	73
RESCUE MISSION	**73**
Airport Pick-Up	73
Acquiring Anna	73
The Apartment Block	74
Enemy Assets	74
Block Security	74
The Secret Prison	74
Interrogating Prisoners	74
Mounting A Rescue	75
Undercover	75
Break-In	75
Assault	75
BLOOD OPERA	**75**
The Vienna State Opera	75
The Set-Up	75
The Extraction	76
Getting into the Opera	76
Grabbing Arkady	76
Getting to Safety	76
Countermeasures	76
Unexpected Complications	77
THE CONFESSION	**77**
Final Curtain	78
EXIT VECTORS	**78**
The Zalozhniy Sanction	78
The Boxmen	78
Treason in the Blood	78
CAPSTONE: RUBEDO RISING	**78**
THE BOXMEN	**80**
EYES ONLY BRIEFING	**80**
The Thieves & The Watchers	80
The Spine	80
Entry Vectors	80
Outside Leads	81
Inside Leads	81
THE THIEVES	**82**
The Queen of Thieves	82
Menena Chakroun	82
Playing Chakroun	82
Motivations & Dirty Secrets	82
The Wizard of Locks	82
Massimo Florin	83
Playing Florin	83
Motivations & Dirty Secrets	83
The Beast	83
Keith Lawson	83
Playing Lawson	83
Motivations & Dirty Secrets	83
The Chameleon	84
Arthur Smith	84
Playing Smith	84
Motivations & Dirty Secrets	84
THE MONTAVONS	**85**
THE BLACK SEA BANK	**85**
THE SET-UP	**86**
VISITING THE KOERNERSBANK	**86**
The Meeting	86
Into The Vault	87
The Stranger	87
BACKGROUND CHECKS	**87**
The Party	88
The Clinic	88
Clarique Montavon	88
The Monaco Operation	88
Victor Kozel	88
THE SHIPMENT	**89**
DEATH OF A CHAMELEON	**89**
Contact	90
The Chase	90
Blast	90
The Assassin (Optional)	90
THE OTHER GUYS	**91**
Spying on the Competition	91
The Approach	91
Chakroun's Plan	91
THE MARK	**92**
PLANNING THE HEIST	**92**
Bank Layout	92
Reconnaissance	92
Security Staff	92
Alarms	93
The Routine	93
Vincent Daroud	93
Preparations	93
THE HEIST	**94**
Problem: Getting In	94
Problem: Disabling the Alarms	94
Problem: Security Cameras	94
Problem: The Guards	94
Problem: Getting the Keys	94
Problem: Identifying the Box	95
Problem: Getting Into The Basement	95
Problem: The Vault Corridor	95
Problem: The Vault Door	95
Problem: Inside The Vault	96
IN THE VAULT	**96**
The Philby Box	97
The Other Boxes	97
Getting Out	98
STOLEN ALBEDO	**98**
Buying the Albedo	99
Chakroun	99
Florin	99
Lawson	99
THE SAFE HOUSE	**99**
The Traitor	99
Enemy Forces	100
Moving On	100
RECOVERING THE ALBEDO	**100**
Security Arrangements	100
The Route	101
Running the Hijack	101
At The Bank	101
On The Road	101
At The Airport	101
BANK RUN	**102**
Escaping the Net	102
Getting out of Switzerland	102
Network Connections	102
Fencing the Loot	102
Final Curtain	103
EXIT VECTORS	**103**
The Zalozhniy Sanction	103
Out of the House of Ashes	103

TABLE OF CONTENTS

Treason in the Blood	103
CAPSTONE: KILLING UNCLE JOE	**103**
The Deal	103
Setting Up The Deal	104
The Opposition	104
The Handover	105
Going Deep, Going Dark	105

TREASON IN THE BLOOD — 106

EYES ONLY BRIEFING — 106
The Spine	106
Entry Vectors	107
Outside Leads	107
Inside Leads	107
The Third Party	108

OVERWATCH SECURITY — 109
Weapons Smuggling	109
The Commander	109
Breaking Into The Base	109
The Museum Connection	110

THE MUSEUM RESEARCHER — 110

MOHAMMED AL-KIRKUK — 111
The Confession	111
At Your Door	112

THE MUKHABARAT ARCHIVE — 113
The Archive	113
Finding the Diary	113
We"re Not Alone	113
The Other Intruders	113
The Bell Box	114
Fire in the Stacks	114
The Chase	114
If the Agents Win	114
If the Zalozhniy Escapes	114

THE AL SADEER — 115
The Hotel Shootout	115

TO BEIRUT — 115
The Diary	115
The SIM Card	116

BEIRUT STREETS — 117

THE RECORDS OFFICE — 117

THE KIT KAT CLUB MEETING — 118
Playing Mr. Red	118
The Black and the White	118
Starting Trouble	119

THE EXHUMATION — 119
The Third Party	119
The Soviet Spy	119
The Grave	119
How It All Goes Down	119
Getting into the Cemetery	119
The Gunshot	120
Nikolai's Last Words	120
The Box of Devils	120

KGB BEIRUT — 121

THE ARAB BOY — 122
Getting to Cyprus	122

OLD GHOSTS — 123
Katun	123
Playing Katun	123
The Debriefing	123
After Debriefing	124

KING SAUD'S CITY — 125
The Bedouin	125
Playing Haroun al-Murrah	126
Other Tales of the Cave	126

HAJJ SHAITAN — 127
The Labyrinth of Sand	127
The Thing in the Cave	127
Hunting the Dead	128

TREASON IN THE BLOOD — 129
The Traitor	129
What Was Briefly Yours Is Now Mine	129
Desert Ambush	130
Riyadh Arrest	130
The Mount Doom Gambit	130
Tracking the Traitor	131

LAST TRAIN TO ISTANBUL — 131
The Train	131
Catching the Train	131
On The Train	131
Fighting the Camazotz	132
Final Curtain	132

EXIT VECTORS — 132
The Zalozhniy Sanction	132
Out of the House of Ashes	132
The Boxmen	132

CAPSTONE: THE ALCHEMICAL WEDDING — 133
The Vampire King	133
The Ritual Site	133
Finding the Ritual	133
Vampire Slaying With An Apache Helicopter	133

AGENTS — 136
Roster	136
O'Leary	137
Tanner	138
Whitman	139
Savine	140
Caulden	141
Malach	142
Map – Europe	143
Map – Odessa	144
Map – Vienna	145
Map – Zurich	146
Map – Beirut	147
Map – Baghdad	148

INTRODUCTION

> GET ME SOME OF FEELBEE'S BLOOD. HE'S NEVER ILL.
>
> — IBN SAUD

The Zalozhniy Quartet is a thriller story arc of four missions for your *Night's Black Agents* game. Each of the missions can be played individually, or linked into a campaign in any order. Each adventure includes an optional "capstone" that you can use to turn it into a suitable grand finale. The adventures all take place in Eastern Europe and the Middle East, the old stomping grounds of Communism and the Cold War… and vampires.

On p. 136, you'll find the dossiers for six player characters. You can use these as pregenerated player characters for a new campaign, or replacements if an existing player character (or six!) die at the hands of the Undead. Alternatively, you can use these six as potential allies or foils.

Two common threads run through all four scenarios, one overt, and one hidden: the Lisky Bratva and the Philby plot.

THE LISKY BRATVA

The overt thread is the Lisky Bratva, a major Russian mafiya brotherhood run out of Odessa. Its chief and namesake is Josef Lisky, aided up by his tame necromancer Dofrjiev and backed by his supernatural patrons. Almost every Conspyramid will have a Russian mafiya node: the Russian mob is the universal joint of the modern criminal-paramilitary-intelligence shadow world. The Director can slot the Lisky Bratva into her Conspyramid, reskin it as a gang she already has in her Conspyramid, or even use the Lisky Bratva as an outside player that has uncovered (and begun to exploit) the truth about vampires for its own ends.

The Lisky Bratva appears in all four operations as a dangerous force opposing or shadowing the agents.

- In *The Zalozhniy Sanction*, the agents cross the Lisky Bratva in Odessa and get chased across Europe.
- In *Out of the House of Ashes*, the Lisky Bratva show up in Vienna as servants of a vampire, Simon Thonradel.
- *The Boxmen* involves one of the Lisky Bratva's pawns, the Black Sea Bank of Odessa, purchasing a Swiss bank in Zurich.
- In *Treason in the Blood*, another Lisky Bratva front called Overwatch Security is the major threat during the Baghdad phase of the operation.

HISTORY

The *bratva* (brotherhoods) of the Russian *mafiya* are each ruled by a *vor*. There is no direct translation of that last term, but *thief-in-law* or *thief who obeys the code* is close. The *vor* are an elite class of criminals who follow a strict, unyielding and almost monastic code. They may not ever co-operate with the authorities, they may never take money from a legitimate job, they may not marry or show favor to their families, and they must remain cold and calculating and emotionless to better guide their organization. Few *vor* could keep to the code in the old days, when the Soviet state brutally suppressed criminal gangs; these days, when the line between government official and criminal is so very blurred in the hothouse capitalism of the new era, even fewer bother with the code of the *vory*.

Josef Lisky kept to the code. He went to prison in 1987 and came out twenty years later to find the world had changed. He ran the Lisky Bratva from inside his jail cell, of course — prison is home to a *vor* — but it was not until he walked in the cold outside the gulag that he understood how much it had changed. The old ways were lost, the brotherhood was losing ground on all sides, and he was living on borrowed time. He knew that some day soon, some ambitious underling with no feeling for the *ponyatiya* code would kill him, and the brotherhood would become nothing but wild dogs, drunk on money and power.

To survive, he needed a new *krysha* — a roof, a purpose for the *bratva*. The old rackets of smuggling and organized crime were washed away by the new capitalism, and other gangs had already seized control of protection rackets and the black markets. The Lisky Bratva were out in the cold.

And from the cold, something contacted him.

Today, the Lisky Bratva are agents of the Conspiracy.

JOSEF LISKY

The *vor* is nearly seventy years old, but life in prison made him hard and he could pass for a much younger man.

He has swapped the grey walls of the jail cell for an endless beige realm of airports and hotels; he travels almost constantly, visiting one cell or another of the brotherhood with an entourage of accountants and assassins. If the local gangsters are making quota and obeying the code, he dines with them and moves on. If they fall short, well, someone else can dine that night. He wears shirts that are carefully cut to almost, but not entirely, hide the prison tattoos that mark his rank.

Josef is at heart a traditionalist, a man who still believes in the old code. To be a *vor* is to be a servant; one must put the good of your organization and your masters ahead of your own. He chose to serve his vampiric masters willingly, and his life is theirs to take – or prolong.

Throughout *The Zalozhniy Quartet*, "Uncle Joe" should be a menacing figure in the background, the man who all the gangsters fear. Build up the myth of Lisky in the players' minds. Attribute every clever move made by the Lisky Bratva to his leadership; every bloody atrocity and retaliatory blowback should have his fingerprints on them. Make them fear Lisky – and maybe they'll get a shot at him in *The Boxmen*.

GENERAL ABILITIES: Athletics 4, Hand-to-Hand 6, Health 8, Network 16, Sense Trouble 6, Weapons 10
HIT THRESHOLD: 3
ALERTNESS MODIFIER: +1
STEALTH MODIFIER: +1
DAMAGE MODIFIER: Knuckleduster -1

PLAYING JOSEF

- You've got a core of solid steel. Never accept a failure, never tolerate dissent, never tolerate fear of anything except your wrath. You must be a stern, commanding father to your thieves.
- You owe a debt to the vampires. You are honor-bound to serve them. That doesn't mean you like them, but your honor is the source of your strength. You cannot break your word to them, any more than you could break your own back.
- Pause before speaking. Let the anger build inside you first.

DR. G. D. DORJIEV

No one else in the organization knows where Josef found Dorjiev. No one really wants to know. Some claim he dragged the madman out of some Soviet research facility, while other stories insist that Josef dug Dorjiev out of a mass grave in the Balkans. Wherever he came from, the monstrous doctor is now Josef's attack dog and tame necromancer. Dorjiev will never be a *vor* – he is needlessly cruel and prone to outbursts of murderous anger.

Dorjiev is the Conspiracy's only source of the *zalozhniye* (see p. 8), which makes his position unassailable as long as Josef is alive. Should Josef perish, the necromancer will likely be eliminated by either another rival in the Bratva, or by the vampires, angry at the impudence of a human prying into their secrets. He oversees the Bratva's operations in Eastern Europe from his main bases in Odessa and Transylvania.

UNKILLABLE: Dorjiev cannot die, except in very specific circumstances. He can be reduced to negative Health, but that won't actually kill him, and he'll always regenerate into some form that's capable of movement and action. The agents can make his life very, very unpleasant, but cannot kill him.

ABERRANCE: Unlike a vampire, Dorjiev's still human, so he's got both an Aberrance *and* an Athletics score. Use his Athletics for anything involving physical effort, fitness, and for determining his Hit Threshold. His Aberrance is just there to fuel his Necromancy and other powers.

GENERAL ABILITIES: Aberrance 6, Athletics 5, Hand-to-Hand 8, Health 6*, Network 10, Preparedness 12, Sense Trouble 12, Shooting 6
FREE POWERS: Unkillable (see above)
OTHER POWERS: Necromancy, Magic or Mental Attack
HIT THRESHOLD: 3
ALERTNESS MODIFIER: +2
STEALTH MODIFIER: +1
DAMAGE MODIFIER: -2 (Fist)

PLAYING DORJIEV

- He's Rasputin with a medical degree. Stare at people with an eerie intensity.
- Speak in a throaty whisper.
- Hold one hand across your chest, as if protecting your heart or touching an amulet.

DORJIEV'S DEATH

The zalozhniye literally should not be. They are created from the bodies of those who died untimely, out of the natural order of death. They are aberrations, they are *wrong* at a fundamental level. This gives them their strange relationship with time – because the zalozhniye are "out of order," watches and other timepieces "hiccup" around them.

Dorjiev discovered that this time skip could be exploited for other purposes. He managed to take the moment of his own death and hide it inside the no-time field of a zalozhniy. The zalozhniye are created from those who died untimely, but Dorjiev no longer has a time to die. In effect, the universe no longer contains the moment of his demise, and so he cannot die. He can be maimed, mangled, shot, blown up, but he will always survive, like the mad monk Rasputin…

…unless he's maimed, mangled, shot, blown up or otherwise liquidated within the no-time field of a zalozhniy. His death exists *in potentia* inside that temporal bubble, so he can die within such a field. Therefore, there are three ways to kill Dorjiev:

- Have a zalozhniy kill him
- Kill him when he is in exceedingly close proximity to a zalozhniy
- Kill him when a zalozhniy feeds nearby, and the no-time field expands.

If the agents observe Dorjiev, **Notice** flags his odd habit of never getting too close to his zalozhniye.

NIGHT'S BLACK AGENTS – THE ZALOZHNIY QUARTET

> **P**
> In many sections, the notation "P" is used. P is equal to the number of player characters. So, if the Lisky Bratva have Px20 thugs in Odessa, then they have 60 goons if there are 3 player characters, 100 thugs if there are 5 player characters, and so on.

AREAS OF INFLUENCE

As the conspiracy's local fixers and muscle, the Lisky Bratva has thugs in place in virtually every city from Vienna to Qatar, with the majority of its forces in the former Soviet bloc. The organization's activities reflect the priorities of its masters, so human trafficking and weapons smuggling are primary. The bratva ships sex slaves to Europe and the Middle East, and uses the cash to buy guns and equipment for sale around the Black Sea and the Caspian Sea.

KEY ASSETS

A full accounting of the Lisky Bratva's assets down to the last dollar and the last thug with a gun is pointless — assume that they've got an endless supply of local muscle and competent goons. The important assets are the ones they have in position to affect the events of *The Zalozhniy Quartet*.

A kind Director can let the player characters get hold of this org chart using **Traffic Analysis** or **Criminology**, so the players can mark off the enemy assets as they get eliminated. A cruel Director should keep the players in the dark about what the bad guys still have to throw at them.

The Bratva can call in extra support from its home grounds in Russia and the Ukraine; again, clued-in agents may be alerted to such movements if they use **Traffic Analysis** (or some other method, like **Accounting**) to keep tabs on the flow of money and known members of the Lisky Bratva.

MOBILE ASSETS

Like most Russian gangs, the core of the Lisky Bratva consists of a few leaders and specialists who can utilize local talent for any power plays required on the scene.

VOR GROUP

Josef and his closest advisors and troubleshooters. They fly in to deal with a problematic cell or when Lisky's presence is required. The agents will run into the Vor group in *The Boxmen*, but Lisky could also show up if a cell needs added steel.

- **Josef Lisky:** The *vor* himself. Lisky's too old to be useful in a fight, but he's got strings – and garrotes – to pull around the world.
- **Conspiracy Handler:** Lisky is accompanied by an advisor from the Conspiracy. The nature of this advisor is up to the Director, and should reveal something about the sinister masters. It could be a pale lawyer with a slim black briefcase, a talking head in a jar, a young girl who channels telepathic communications from alien overlords, or one of the true Un-Dead.
- **Accountants, Lawyers and Advisors:** Assume that Lisky can throw any bureaucratic, financial or legal assets he needs at the player characters.
- **Bodyguards:** Lisky travels with three bodyguards (see p.69 of *Night's Black Agents*), all of whom are fanatically loyal to him. These bodyguards are backed up by local thugs drawn from the closest local cell.

THE ZALOZHNIY

The Lisky Bratva has six zalozhniye at the start of the *Quartet,* and a seventh comes online midway through *The Zalozhniy Sanction*. Four of these creatures are with Dr. Dorjiev in Odessa, as only he can reliably control the monsters. The other three are kept in secure containers at various safe locations, and are shipped into the field when necessary — one shows up in Zurich in *The Boxmen,* and another in Baghdad in *Treason in the Blood.* Dorjiev can create more of the creatures, but needs a properly prepared corpse and whatever weird ingredients match the Director's take on the undead.

ZALOZHNIY

In Russian legend, a zalozhniy is a corpse dead "before its time" and refused a proper burial. When the earth spits the body back, it roams the countryside luring the living into premature deaths; when subterfuge doesn't work, it kills them.

These zalozhniye are former enemies of the Lisky Bratva, killed before their time (not hard to arrange) and revived by vampiric (or other) means and controlled by whichever methodology fits the campaign best: implanted chips, vampire blood, magical tattoos, alien mind control, etc. Lisky prefers to reanimate already trained and deadly soldiers, especially former Spetsnaz, explaining the high combat scores: if the agents' ratings in Hand-to-Hand or Shooting are (on average) higher than 13, raise the zalozhniy's ratings to match or exceed them.

Unlike Renfields, they cannot easily pass for human in anything like a good light; they usually wear dark wraparound sunglasses, gloves, and balaclavas or other concealing head and neckwear in the daytime. Uncloaked, they look like what they are – walking corpses, with preserved skin stretched tight over bones, covered in scars and burns from whatever killed them.

They cannot wear watches; clocks hiccup and skip if very near them. This is a side effect of their unnatural, out-of-sequence deaths. The distortion is increased when a zalozhniy murders someone – the effect momentarily expands outwards, causing hearts to skip a beat and disrupting electronics nearby.

In Russian legend, zalozhniye walk the earth for the remainder of their allotted lifespan. A zalozhniy killed before that time comes up returns as a ghost. If this is true of these zalozhniye (for example, in heavily supernatural-themed campaigns), use the ghost lens on the murony (see p. 152 of *Night's Black Agents*).

As in the corebook, abilities and features in italics might or might not be true in all campaigns.

DEATH EATER: For every human the zalozhniy tricks into dying (as opposed to shooting or mauling), the zalozhniy receives 4 pool points in either Athletics or Health. This is the only way a zalozhniy can heal itself back above 0 Health. (For an incredibly tough zalozhniye, also grant 1 *rating* point for each successful trick.) Setting a bomb or booby trap, or poisoning a drink, counts as trickery; agents are at +2 Difficulty to spot such things set by a zalozhniy.

TRUE DEATH: Each zalozhniy has a mortal wound that would have killed them if it where not for supernatural intervention. If they suffer this wound a second time, they are killed outright. For example, a zalozhniy who is "supposed" to die from a stab wound is destroyed if stabbed in the right place; a zalozhniy who was originally destined to die in a burning house can only be destroyed by incineration. Discovering a zalozhniy's true death requires investigation, but if the agents can deliver the right type of attack (often with a Called Shot), the creature is instantly destroyed. See p. 50 for more details on hunting zalozhniye.

UNFEELING: The zalozhniy never becomes Hurt by physical attacks and automatically makes all Consciousness rolls. He can still fight while Seriously Wounded.

GENERAL ABILITIES: Aberrance 13, Conceal 8, Driving 8, Explosive Devices 8, Hand-to-Hand 13, Health 13, Shooting 13, Surveillance 8, Weapons 8
HIT THRESHOLD: 7 (supernatural strength and alertness; Temporal Distortion)
ALERTNESS MODIFIER: +3
STEALTH MODIFIER: +2
DAMAGE MODIFIER: +1 (9mm Makarov PMM pistol), +0 (7.62mm AK-74 assault rifle), +1 (talons), +0 (combat knife), +0 (bite; extended canines) or -1 (fist, kick)
ARMOR: -2 vs. bullets, -1 vs. other (tactical vest); plus Corpse (see *Night's Black Agents*, p. 126) all weapons do half damage; after armor, firearms do only 1 point of damage and shotguns firing shot do only 2 points of damage; car crashes and falls do half minimum damage.
FREE POWERS: Death Eater (see text), Infravision, Temporal Distortion, Unfeeling (see text)
OTHER POWERS: Apportation ("slasher movement"), Mimicry (of friendly voices; as a Mental Attack), Strength (tests mandatory for feats of strength; see *Night's Black Agents*, p. 137)
BANES: Fire, *crucifixes and holy objects* (+0 damage; +1 on face), *Russian Orthodox mass for the dead*; super-science zalozhniy might be vulnerable to a particular chemical compound. See also True Death, above.
BLOCKS: *Consecrated ground, crucifixes and holy objects* for supernatural campaigns; super-science zalozhniye might be blocked by strong electro-magnetic fields.
COMPULSIONS: Obey the Lisky Bratva.
REQUIREMENTS: kill the living (monthly)

OPERATIVES (GASTRALYOR)

In addition to the zalozhniye, Lisky employs a number of human operatives – mainly to counterbalance Dorjiev's influence within the organization. These operatives are based Europe and the Middle East, and all have cover identities that allow them to travel freely. They can show up anywhere.

All the operatives have the following statistics unless otherwise stated.
GENERAL ABILITIES: Athletics 8, Driving 8, Hand-to-Hand 8, Health 10, Medic 4, Shooting 6, Weapons 6
HIT THRESHOLD: 4
ALERTNESS MODIFIER: +2
STEALTH MODIFIER: +1
DAMAGE MODIFIER: -2 (fist/kick), +1 (9mm SIG-Sauer P226 pistol)

THE SNIPER

Uri, ex-Russian army. Family man with a wife and three kids, none of whom have any idea that daddy's an assassin. He has a phobia about injuries to his hands and eyes, so he always wears thick gloves and carries eye protection. **Intimidating** him with the threat of such an injury can dissuade him – but getting close enough to talk to Uri is tricky.
SPECIAL: Infiltration 12, Shooting 12, packing a VSS Vintorez sniper rifle with hollowpoint rounds (+4 damage, thanks to his Special Weapons Training).

THE MARTIAL ARTIST

Rolan, a young Ukrainian street thug with a gift for martial arts. The Lisky Bratva groomed him to be an assassin and bodyguard. He's average-height, wiry, and on lots of amphetamines. His handlers treat him like a fire-and-forget weapon – they point Rolan at a target and let the boy go. **Pharmacy** or **Streetwise** notes the signs of his drug use, and suggests that the best way to beat Rolan is to frustrate him. He doesn't cope well with being confused or baffled.
SPECIAL: Athletics 12, Hand-to-Hand 15, and he'll always use hits that target his foe's joints (see Called Shots on p. 72 of *Night's Black Agents*). Once per session, he can freely refresh 4 Hand-to-Hand pool points, as per Martial Arts (p. 75 of *Night's Black Agents*).

THE GIRL

Maria. Ex-FSB spy, now working for the Lisky Bratva. She's a "swallow" – a female spy trained to seduce targets. Maria doesn't go for the blonde sex-goddess approach. Instead, she presents herself as a pretty, bohemian, slightly nervous student who just split up her the boyfriend and went traveling to get over him – although she'll adapt her story depending on the profile of her target. She's especially good at long-term infiltrations. She might seduce an agent's friend or relative, and wait several weeks for the agent to make contact. She's patient, clever, and absolutely ruthless.

Bullshit Detector won't work on Maria without a very high point spend; it's better to catch her out on an obscure point of trivia with **Art History** or **Urban Survival** (*"so, you lived in Prague? You must know that cafe by the river, where they do the best hot chocolate. Everyone knows that place. What's it called?"*)

SPECIAL: Infiltration 10, Shrink 10, Preparedness 10.

THE DRIVER

Some say he's an ex-fighter jet pilot who lives for the thrill of the chase. Some say he's a former racing driver who took a bribe to run another car off the track. All the Lisky Bratva know is, he's the Driver. He speaks with a thick Russian accent, wears a baseball cap at all times, has bad teeth, and can drive anything from a moped to an aircraft carrier. He's one of the best wheel artists in the world, and specializes in arranging car accidents and intercepting fleeing targets. **Tradecraft** picks up that he considers himself the best of the best, and could be goaded into overextending himself.

SPECIAL: Driving 15, Piloting 12.

THE CON ARTISTS

Henry and David – at least, those are the names they go by these days – have worked together for more than a decade. They are con-men and grifters for hire. Their arrangement with the Lisky Bratva is a purely mercenary one; they need the cash. The con artists are the least dangerous of the various operatives, and never use physical force if they can avoid it. They are masters of disguise and deception, working in tandem to set up elaborate cons. A big **Notice** spend is necessary to see through their disguises.

SPECIAL: Cover 10, Disguise 12, Preparedness 10

THE TORPEDO

In mafia slang, a torpedo is a contract killer. Vasily Cherekov is exactly that. He's an ex-mercenary with a death wish and a very big machine gun. Bombastic and crude, he eschews subtlety in favor of explosives and overkill. **Human Terrain** identifies him as ethnically Georgian, and **Military Science** or **History** can dig up a reference to Cherekov fighting in South Ossetia. Put the two together, and he's got a grudge against the Russian backers of the South Ossetian separatists. Clever agents can use **Negotiation** or **Flattery** to leverage this and turn the Torpedo against the Russian mafiya.

SPECIAL: Athletics 10, Shooting 16. He carries an STG-940, a machine gun favored by the old Stasi, as well as grenades and other firearms. He's got Special Weapons Training in the machine gun, giving it +2 damage.

THE SCULPTOR

A sociopathic surgeon, recruited by Josef Lisky as a weapon of terror. The Sculptor's past was erased by the Lisky Bratva; his new cover identity is named Michel Fleisch. He looks like a kindly old careworn family doctor, but the only thing in his black bag is a selection of scalpels and paralytic drugs.

SPECIAL: Disguise 8, Hand-to-Hand 10, Medic 14, Shooting 10. The surgeon carries a tranquilizer pistol.

RESERVES

In addition to these specialist assets, the Lisky Bratva can drop up Px10 thugs and Px3 thug bosses within 24 hours into any city where they need extra muscle. If cash is the issue, they can lay hands on a million dollars in cash without any problems; bigger sums take only a few days.

REGIONAL ASSETS

In any European or Turkish city, the Lisky Bratva have at least Px4 thugs (use Thug statistics from p. 70 of *Night's Black Agents*) and P thug bosses (use Mafioso statistics from p. 69 of *Night's Black Agents*). They may also have an operative in place, and/or a corrupt police officer or other official who can dump Heat on the agents (and supply P/2 corrupt policemen using the Police statistics on p. 69 of *Night's Black Agents*). Closer to their seat of power in the old Soviet bloc, most cities have Px6 thugs and Px2 thug bosses, and the police are definitely on the take (add P policemen). Assets can be moved from one city to a neighboring one.

LISKY BRATVA ADVERSARY MAP

The Director should feel free to add any specific connections to nodes in her own Conspiracy, ongoing NPCs, or other details to customize this adversary map for her own campaign. She may also want to add more "old vor" at the second tier (especially tied to the Black Sea Bank) to camouflage Akhroyekov's potential to move against Lisky if the time and motive is right (see p. 30 of *The Zalozhniy Sanction*).

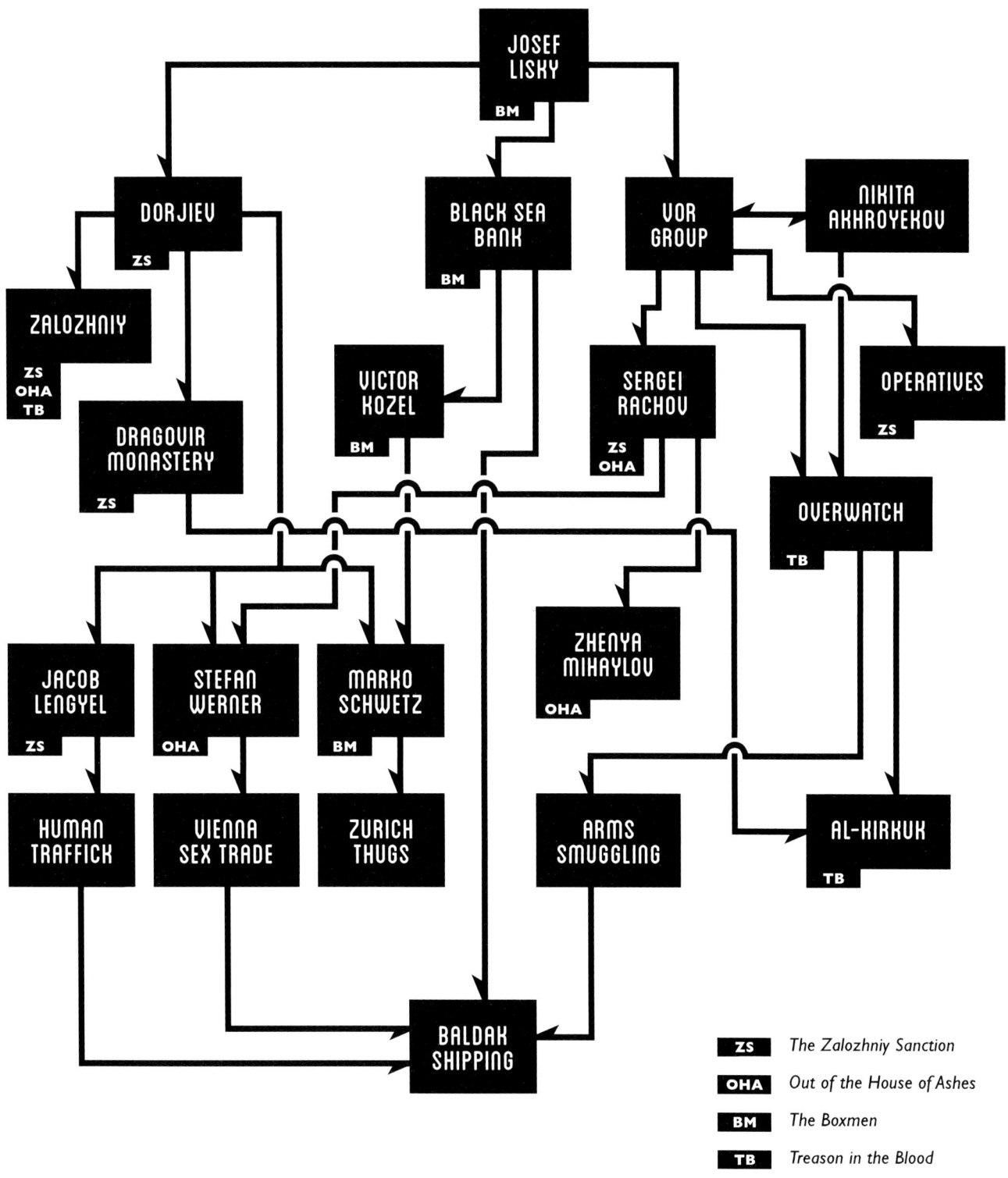

ZS	*The Zalozhniy Sanction*
OHA	*Out of the House of Ashes*
BM	*The Boxmen*
TB	*Treason in the Blood*

NIGHT'S BLACK AGENTS – THE ZALOZHNIY QUARTET

THE PHILBY PLOT

The second major plot thread running through all four scenarios is the White and the Black – and to explains that, we need to go back to two of the most infamous spies and traitors of the 20th century. **Harry St. John Philby** (1885-1960) was an agent of the British Foreign Office working in the Middle East. At the time, the chief aim of the Foreign Office was to safeguard its interests in the Middle East, especially oil, and they intended to set up an Arabian Federation that would be sympathetic to British interests. The Foreign Office's chosen figurehead was Sharif Hussein; Philby secretly supported another Arab leader, Ibn Saud. With Philby's aid and advice, Ibn Saud was able to unify the Arab tribes and became the first king of Saudi Arabia. London saw this as a betrayal, especially when Philby favored American oil companies over the British when selling oil exploration rights to Arabia's vast reserves.

St. John Philby died in Beirut in 1960, and was buried in the Muslim cemetery there (he converted to Islam in 1930). Persistent rumors insist he was poisoned.

Despite his father's fraught relationship with the establishment, St. John's son **Kim Philby** (1912-1988) quickly rose to prominence in the intelligence services. He joined the SOE in 1940, transferred to the SIS (better known as MI6) in '41, was promoted to head of station in Istanbul by '47, and was assigned as the SIS's Washington liaison in 1949, where he had access to the most sensitive information under the UKUSA pact. All that was rather unfortunate, as Philby was also part of the "Gang of Five" – five Soviet spies, recruited at Cambridge in the 1930s.

Two other members of the Gang, Guy Burgess and Roger Maclean, were exposed and fled to Moscow in 1951. Philby was recalled to London and interrogated to determine if he too was a Soviet agent. He managed to conceal his connections to the KGB, but his career in MI6 was largely over. He spent several years as a journalist in the Middle East before he too fled behind the Iron Curtain in 1963. If he expected a hero's welcome in the Soviet Union, he was disappointed – the KGB never trusted Philby, and some believed that he was a deep cover British agent. He died in 1988.

THE WHITE & THE BLACK

St. John Philby was made aware of the existence (or, depending on your campaign) potential existence of vampires during his time with the Foreign Office. He obtained control over two occult items that, combined, are the key to immense power. Using his special knowledge, St. John Philby set up a monstrous scheme. Philby was the trusted friend of Ibn Saud, king of the Nejd (and eventual founder of Saudi Arabia). At a banquet, he covertly dosed Ibn Saud and his sons with vampire blood - but not just any vampire blood. Somehow Philby was able to create a form of hereditary vampire taint, one that would lie fallow, passed from king to prince to prince until triggered by a specific action. When that trigger is pulled, the entire Saudi royal family will become Renfields, under the control of their new, vampiric Master.

Completing Philby's plan requires two separate components: borrowing terms from alchemy, he called them the Albedo and the Nigredo, the White and the Black. He kept the Nigredo with him, believing it could return him to life after he died. The Nigredo was buried with him in the Bashoura cemetery in Beirut, but his resurrection was a failure later. He became a mindless, feral vampiric monster. Both Philby's remains and the Nigredo were moved to a secret location in Saudi Arabia.

St. John intended for his son Kim to carry out the plan after St. John's death, but the younger man lost his nerve and bolted for Moscow, leaving the Albedo in a safety deposit box in a Swiss bank. He revealed the existence of the Albedo and the Nigredo to the KGB during his debriefing in 1963. He intended to convince the KGB to help him put his father's plan into operation, believing that with the correct preparations, he could avoid his father's fate and retain his consciousness through the transformation into a vampire. Fearful of entrusting Kim with that much power, the Soviets stalled, and the secret of the Albedo and Nigredo fell into the undead hands of the Conspiracy.

Combined, the Albedo and the Nigredo make the Rubedo, the Red; they transform the user into a vampire (or, if already a vampire, massively increase

---

NO PHILBY PLOT

Directors who don't want to turn the thriller up to 11 can run these scenarios without the Philby Plot. You will need to do the following:

- Come up with another compelling backstory for Shevlenko in the Vienna operation. Instead of Philby's passbook and the ritual secret, Shevlenko might be able to identify the vampiric backers of the Lisky Bratva.
- Come up with another MacGuffin that the vampires want in the Zurich operation; anything from the Holy Grail to the hyperdrive power core of a crashed alien starship could be locked away in the bank vault.
- Come up with another reason to chase a rival all over the Middle East in the Baghdad operation: either yet another MacGuffin, or a different vampire conspiracy plot taken from your own campaign.

Also, many of the ties and leads from one city to another will be different or nonexistent without the Philby Plot.

INTRODUCTION — THE PHILBY PLOT : THE WHITE & THE BLACK — WHAT ARE WE LOOKING FOR, EXACTLY?

ritual necessary to create the Rubedo, or else the passbook to Philby's Swiss bank account.
- In *The Boxmen,* the agents break into a Swiss bank where Philby left the Albedo in 1963.
- The search for the Nigredo dominates the action in *Treason in the Blood*.

WHAT ARE WE LOOKING FOR, EXACTLY?

Reveal as much of the Philby Plot as late as you can in the campaign: if the agents find the Albedo first, there are only documents pointing toward the location of the Nigredo, but no indication of what the Albedo even is, or that the Rubedo even exists. Only when they find the Nigredo do they find any description of the Albedo and Rubedo, and of the larger plot. If they find the Nigredo first, it's the other way around. The nature of the Albedo, Nigredo and Rubedo elements depend on the nature of vampires in your campaign. Here are some suggestions:

⛤ SUPERNATURAL

For supernatural vampires, look to Middle Eastern mythology.

- The Albedo and Nigredo are two halves of an amulet of Nergal, god of death. Joining them awakens "Nergal's seed" in the blood of the Saudi royals, and transforms the wearer's soul into an ekimmu, an Assyrian astral vampire.
- The formula is derived from Egyptian lore uncovered in the 1890s. The Albedo is a purification rite that wipes away all sin and wrongdoing; the Nigredo is the alchemically distilled essence of Apep, the serpent god of evil. Combining the two, together with a ritual invocation of Sekhmet, goddess of justice, transforms the user into an avatar of fanged Shezmu, god of wine blood and slaughter.

✠ DAMNED

Damned vampires allow the Director to play up the tensions of faith in the Middle East.

the user's power) and give them control of anyone who ate at the King's feast of Eid ul-Fitr in 1931 (or whichever date suits your specific campaign best) and so carries the vampiric taint in their blood. This taint is passed to their descendants, so the master of the Rubedo will instantly gain control of the entire Saudi royal family and most of the other powerful families and factions in Saudi Arabia.

The modern world's hunger for oil far exceeds the bloodlust of the most vicious vampire; control of Saudi Arabia would give the Conspiracy unparalleled influence over the course of history.

Elements of the Philby Plot show up in all four operations:

- *The Zalozhniy Sanction* has no direct connection to the Philby Plot, but the agents can learn vital information if they hit the Lisky Bratva research facility at Dragovir Monastery in Transylvania.
- *Out of the House of Ashes* introduces Kim Philby's old handler, Arkady Shevlenko. He's either got the

NIGHT'S BLACK AGENTS – THE ZALOZHNIY QUARTET

- This first bit really happened: In 1923, Philby collected water from the Jordan River at the spot where John the Baptist baptized Jesus, and sent it off to the British Museum for unspecified "tests of its holiness." Those tests showed him how to keep elder vampire blood in suspension, insulated by the Jordan water. The Albedo is a vial of Jordan holy water (which likely has amazing anti-vampire powers if used on its own); the Nigredo a vial of elder vampire blood taken from Irem, or something similarly demonic. Desecrating the Albedo with the Nigredo, using a specific ritual, brings about the Rubedo. Note that Jesus is the second-holiest prophet in Islam (after Muhammad); this water has the same effect on Muslim vampires or Muslim victims of vampires.
- The Albedo is the holy water that flowed from Christ's side after he was stabbed with the Spear of Destiny; the Nigredo is his mortal blood. Combining the two creates divine ichor, the blood of the living God. St. John stole the relics from the British Intrusives, a group of political agents and army officers based in Cairo, who had obtained them from a temple in Ethiopia.

👽 ALIEN

For alien vampires, look to St. John's explorations of Arabia, and to Soviet psychic-warfare experiments.

- St. John Philby recovered the Albedo and Nigredo from the crash site at Wabar in the deep desert, where an "iron meteor" crashed comparatively recently. Some accounts blame the meteor impact for the destruction of Irem thousands of years ago; other evidence suggests that the impact occurred in 1863 or 1891, as in both years fireballs were seen in the sky over Riyadh. The Albedo is an alien control device; the Nigredo is a computer program that instructs the nanotech assemblers to activate.
- The Albedo and Nigredo are two frequencies that together produce a resonant standing wave that excites the latent vampire DNA in the Saudi royal family. Broadcasting them over a satellite or telephone system will produce the Rubedo. Either the Albedo or Nigredo "package" also includes a syringe full of master vampire blood; inject it into yourself to become a vampire and control the new crop of Renfields.

😵 MUTANT

Mutant vampires hit many of the same keynotes as alien vampires in this context.

- The desert ruins of Arabia are home to a bacterium that transforms its victims into *ghuls*, blood-drinking cannibal horrors with an allergy to sunlight. Tomb robbers and those who dwell in graveyards risk contracting this disease. Philby worked with Karl Twitchell, an American engineer, to isolate this microorganism. He dosed the Saudi royal family with a small amount in 1931; a larger sample of the bacteria forms the Nigredo, while the Albedo is a specially developed culture medium. Place the bacteria in the culture medium, wait a few minutes, then consume.
- In cooperation with an eccentric Russian biochemist, Philby used the blood of the Egyptian vampire bat to synthesize a trinary Renfield pathogen. One part is already in the Saudis' blood; the Albedo and Nigredo are vials of seemingly harmless water teeming with the other two infection vectors. Releasing them into the air at any Saudi airport or government facility will bring about the Rubedo.

VARIATIONS

Many of the details of the Philby Plot depend on the Director's campaign cosmology, and on the specifics of her vampires. For example, if Renfields don't exist, Philby has created some sort of latent vampirism instead. If she has left her options open and her cosmology vague, Philby may have made a one-off discovery, an irreproducible exception: this is probably the best way to handle it regardless.

How, specifically, St. John Philby discovered the vampires and the method behind his plan likewise so depends.

DISCOVERED EVIDENCE IN STATE FILES: Starting with his first posting to Basra in Iraq in 1915, Philby made a habit of copying classified files (or stealing them outright) and saving them to give himself political leverage. When Philby became governor of Jordan in 1921, T.E. Lawrence ("of Arabia") gave him all of

---

ST. JOHN PHILBY'S MOVEMENTS

This basic breakdown provides a list of places where Philby might have discovered the vampire conspiracy, discovered or synthesized the Albedo and Nigredo, and then secreted the Nigredo (if the Director doesn't like the Beirut default in *Treason in the Blood*). Philby's life is not so well-known that the Director can't put him almost anywhere in the Middle East covertly between 1917 and 1955.

Basra 1915-1917
Baghdad 1917
Riyadh 1917-1918; meets Ibn Saud (trip to Jeddah 1917; Cairo, Jerusalem 1918)
Baghdad 1918
London 1919
Baghdad 1920-1921 (trip to Tehran 1921)
Amman 1921-1924 (trip to Damascus, Baalbek, Beirut, Jerusalem 1923; collects holy water from Jordan River)
London 1924 (trip to Jeddah 1924, Aden 1925)
Jeddah 1925-1932 (return to London 1926)
In 1930-1931, Philby serves on Ibn Saud's privy council, rotating between Jeddah, Mecca, and Riyadh.
Empty Quarter expedition 1932 (discovers the lost city of Irem?)
London 1932 (return to Jeddah via Denmark, Hamburg-to-Adrianople including Berlin; meets Hitler)
Jeddah and London 1932-1940
Liverpool and Ascot 1940-1941; imprisoned as pro-German agitator
Wales 1941-1945
Mecca and Riyadh 1945-1953; Philby serves on Ibn Saud's privy council until the king's death
Riyadh 1953-1955
Beirut 1955-1960

his own personal files and notes. Philby served as Ibn Saud's vizier for much of the 1920s and 1930s; he may have found medieval records in Mecca or Medina.

ARCHAEOLOGY: Lawrence's files extended back to Lawrence's archaeological digs at Carchemish and other Hittite cities before the War; Philby was on good terms with every prominent Near Eastern archaeologist, many of whom worked for the British secret service. He explored the Empty Quarter of Arabia, in search of (among other things) the ruins of the lost city of Irem. Philby may have found some inscription, bas-relief, artifact, crashed UFO, or buried vampire that gave him his breakthrough.

INVESTIGATION AND CONTACTS: At one time or another, Philby was a confidant of MI5, MI6, the NKVD, the OSS, and several major oil companies. If any of them had ties to the vampire conspiracy between the 1920s and 1950s, Philby could well have heard of it and put the pieces together himself.

Whether Philby discovered the vampire conspiracy per se depends on the Director's version of the Conspiracy. If vampires simply didn't exist before St. John Philby's death in 1960, then the Director will have to come up with something else Philby might have discovered at any time during the previous four decades that today's vampires want to control.

THE OPERATIONS

As promised, you can run these missions in any order. The most likely route is Odessa-Vienna-Zurich-Baghdad, but you may end up going Zurich-Vienna-Odessa - back to Vienna! -Baghdad with unexpected detours to Moscow and London in between.

Each operation has an optional "capstone," a big finale that wraps up the whole quartet. Use the capstone encounter for whichever mission comes last in your campaign to bring the quartet to a suitably explosive conclusion.

The scenarios assume that the team starts off following up clues from the Lennart Dossier (see *(S)entries* in the ***Night's Black Agents*** rulebook). If that doesn't fit your group, then there are alternative starting entry points for each adventure – and once they're on the trail of the Philby secret, the only way out is through. The Lisky Bratva do not like loose ends.

DIAGRAMMING THE QUARTET

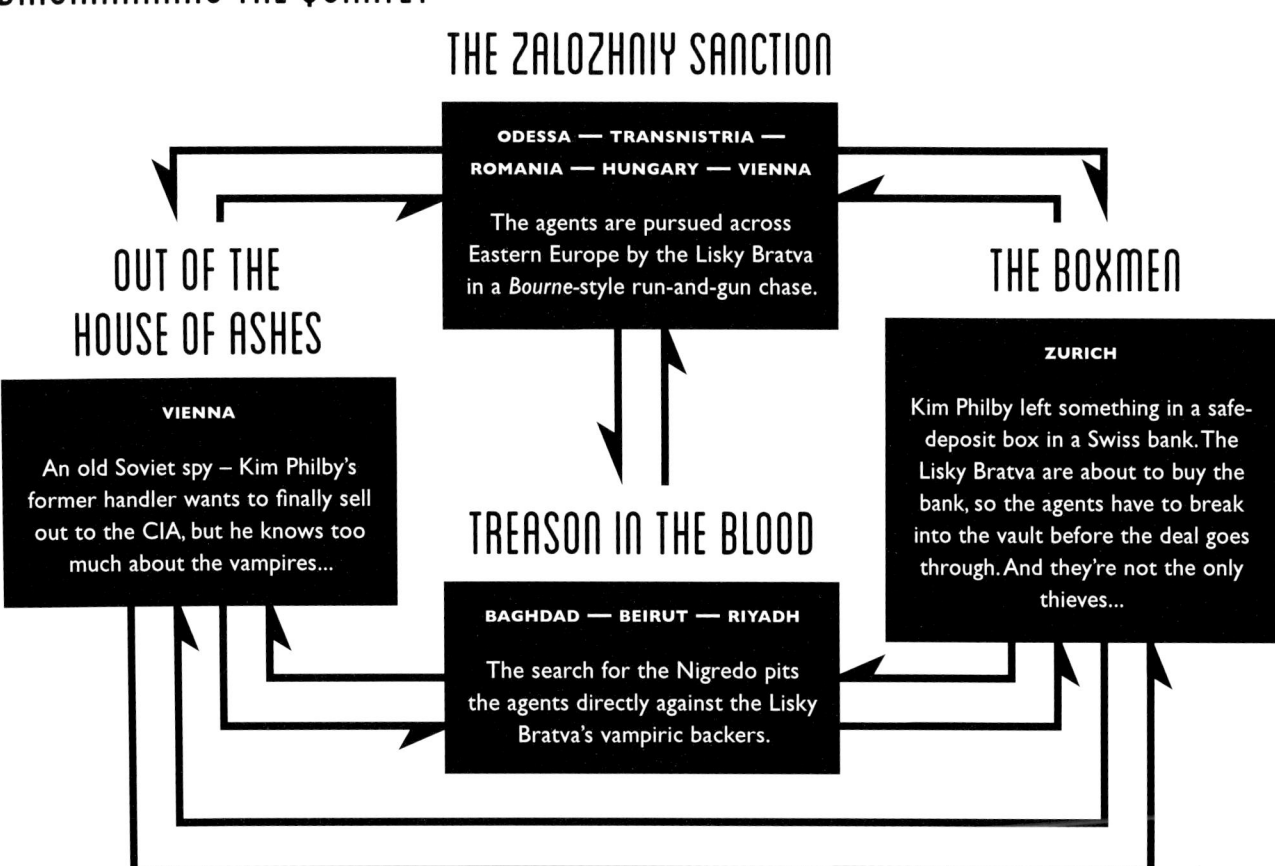

THE ZALOZHNIY SANCTION

This operation is a *Bourne*-style "run and gun." It starts off as a conventional investigation, but rapidly becomes a lesson in why crossing the Lisky Bratva is a very bad idea. When an investigation goes wrong, the agents are pursued by Russian *mafiya* assassins. Their only hope of survival is to make it to the safe city of Vienna. Keep the pressure up at all times as you chase the agents across Eastern Europe. Make that red line on the map a trail of blood…

EYES ONLY BRIEFING

Donald Caroll is an "independent contractor" based in the Crimea, employed to keep an eye on the Black Sea fleet. The Americans, the Russians and the Ukrainians all consider him a moderately reliable informant. He started tracking a gun-smuggling operation based out of Samsun in Turkey six months ago, and has tracked the weapons to Odessa. The agents are sent to identify the next step, by tracking the weapons to a warehouse. They discover that the weapons are just one part of the sinister cargo.

The agents learn enough to realize that the Lisky Bratva are part of the conspiracy, but it all goes horribly wrong. They're pursued through Odessa in a running gun battle, and when they make contact with Caroll, they discover he's been burned too. The Lisky Bratva want them all dead; the agents have to get out of the organization's reach if they're going to survive. Caroll's got a safe-house in Vienna – if they can get there, they've got a chance.

The Lisky Bratva are watching the airports, so it's time for a road (or rail, or boat) trip, taking in a selection of criminal highlights on the way:

THE SPINE

The operation is divided into five smaller ops, each centred on a different city. They're linked in a chase across Eastern Europe in **Running Hot**.

- **Odessa, Ukraine!** The agents work with Donald Caroll to investigate a smuggling ring in **The Odessa Job**. They break into a warehouse, where Lisky Bratva goons ambush them and force them to flee. Caroll's assassinated by a zalozhniy, but he does give the agents the location of his safehouse in Vienna. If they get to **Vienna**, they'll be safe. The road to Vienna leads through **Tiraspol**.
- **Tiraspol, Transnistria!** A country run by gangsters, and one of the biggest markets for illegal weapons in the world. The Lisky Bratva aren't in charge here — if the agents can convince the local warlords to give them safe passage, they can get ahead of their pursuers. In **Transnistrian**

Nights, the agents must sabotage a soccer star's debut to win the favor of a criminal gang leader. He points them at the Lisky Bratva's operations in **Transylvania**, and at a young journalist in **Debrecen**.

- TRANSYLVANIA, ROMANIA! Why are the Lisky Bratva shipping people to an isolated village in the middle of Transylvania? And what happens when the agents get involved? **Shadow of the Vampire** brings the agents to an ancient monastery where they come face to face with the Conspiracy. If the agents survive this optional detour, they come away with vital intelligence about the vampires.
- DEBRECEN, HUNGARY! The Lisky Bratva trade guns and girls for heroin and cash in this post-Soviet city. In **The Debrecen Gambit**, the agents learn that a journalist, Agi Kozorus, knows about the Lisky Bratva's operations in the city. After tracking her down and rescuing her from assassins, Kozorus gives the agents two potential targets — a human trafficking slave camp and a vital drug deal. Hitting either hurts the Lisky Bratva and reduces the forces chasing the agents.
- VIENNA, AUSTRIA! Vienna's neutral territory in the criminal underworld. Once the agents are inside Vienna itself, the Lisky Bratva dare not touch them. All the agents have to do is make **The Vienna Run** - the gauntlet of those last few miles…

ENTRY VECTORS

There are a number of ways into this adventure, from previous ops, from other operations in this collection, or from random chatter. The Director should salt as many leads as she feels necessary, or customize them to suit her campaign.

OUTSIDE LEADS

These leads come from outside this book; from the corebook adventure *(S) Entries* or perhaps from other ops in the Director's previous campaign.

THE LENNART DOSSIER

The Lennart Dossier (from p. 206 of *(S)Entries*, the operation included in the *Night's Black Agents* corebook) may provide leads to Donald Caroll, the Lisky Bratva, or Odessa.

- **Accounting:** The dossier connects the Lisky Bratva's funding to the conspiracy, and suggests that a lot of their cash comes out of Odessa.
- Caroll's mentioned as a source Lennart used when assembling the dossier. **Research** tracks him down in the Crimea.
- **Vampirology:** Lennart describes a string of vampire-related assassinations and suspicious accidents in the dossier — and a recent mob killing in Odessa matches the profile.

OTHER VECTORS

- Caroll contacts the agents; he needs their skills for the final leg of his gun-smuggling investigation.
- **Pharmacy:** Tracking unusual drugs and chemicals puts the agents on the trail of Dr. Dorjiev.

- One of the agent's burned contacts or friends is kidnapped by the Lisky Bratva; they're brought to Odessa before being shipped to Romania. **Electronic Surveillance** lets the agents trace the contact's cell phone, but before they can pin it down, the phone does dead.
- Having previously discovered the connection of the Lisky Bratva to the conspiracy, the agents use **Human Terrain** or **Criminology** to identify the gang's Odessa section as a key node in their operations, and try to burn it. It all goes wrong.

INSIDE LEADS

Intel gathered in other operations in this collection may lead the agents to Odessa and the Lisky Bratva warehouse. If the players don't quite stumble over the right leads in those scenarios, quite often the Director can plant this intel in the mouth (or dead fist, or laptop, or smartphone) of an NPC also on the trail of the Lisky Bratva or of the Philby Plot.

IT'S A TRAP!

If the agents have already tangled with the Lisky Bratva in another operation, then you can up the danger by running this mission as a trap. The Bratva leaked the information to Caroll, knowing he'd call the agents in to help him investigate. Instead of the agents stumbling upon Dorjiev's smuggling operation, they run right into an ambush. If you go for this option, then change the initial encounter in the warehouse to be more of a set-up. For example: the agents find exactly what they're looking for in the warehouse, are drawn into the catacombs, and then the bad guys jump them. In such a case, the agents are saved only by **Sense Trouble**.

SWITCHING CITIES

Swap out the local color, and you can use this operation anywhere in the world. If the agents never go to Odessa, burn them in Cairo or Tbilisi or Berlin and make them run to Vienna. All you need to do is change the names along the way.

If the agents already have a safe house (or a Safety) in Europe, they may run there instead of Vienna. Keep them on track by keeping them on the ground. Air travel lets the agents hop across the world, but if they're forced to travel across country, you can push them towards the encounters in Transnistria, Transylvania, and Hungary, especially if they want to hit back at their harassers. The Lisky Bratva can still try ambushing them when they hit Vienna, or else you can transplant the ambush scene to somewhere near the players' destination.

ODESSA: QUICK AND DIRTY

Bohemian and cosmopolitan, Odessa was the fashionable place to be during the Russian Empire of the 19th century. It was home to a high percentage of the country's Jewish population, although many died in the Odessa Massacre of 1944 and many more emigrated to Israel or America. While the city suffered during the wars of the 20th century, it retains much of its old-world charm. It's one of the biggest ports in the Ukraine, and has taken to capitalism with enthusiasm. The people have a reputation as jokers – and gangsters.

POPULATION
Just over 1 million (a bit smaller than Dallas)

CONFLICT
The Russian rich have used Odessa as their playground for 200 years, and that means money. Several different gangs, including the Lisky Bratva, compete for the city's lucrative vice market.

BACKDROPS
RESORTS & BEACHES: Holidaying families and tourists crowd the beaches of Odessa. The resorts draw a seedier crowd, with lots of drugs and wild parties.

BOULEVARDS: The old streets of Odessa are wide, elegant boulevards; the city resembles Paris in some lights, or Las Vegas in others.

THE POTEMKIN STAIRS: A famous stone staircase, running from Primorsky Boulevard down to the pier. The best known landmark in the city.

ODESSA OPERA HOUSE: The grand old opera house is world-famous, but currently shrouded in scaffolding and sheeting as it undergoes repairs. It's been sinking unevenly for decades.

ST. NIKOLAI BY THE SEA: A small modern church dedicated to the patron saint of sailors; popular among the families of those who work on the docks or on the ships.

ITAKA: A raucous nightclub with a Greek theme; it's built to resemble a classical temple and the nightlife is bacchanalian.

THREE HOOKS
- Catacombs stretch for miles under the city. Anything could be living down there – and come out at night to prey on drunken party-goers.
- Speaking of preying on drunken teenagers, a woman named Diana Semenuha was arrested in Odessa in 2005 for practising witchcraft and vampirism; she lured teenagers and street kids to her apartment, drugged them, and then drained their blood. Some of the blood she kept for her own magical rituals to cure her muscular atrophy, but the rest she sold on Odessa's occult black market.
- Catherine the Great took a personal interest in the establishment of Odessa. Supposedly, she wanted to establish a connection between the ancient Greek colony that once stood there and her modern empire... but what if she sought something specific amid the ruins?

OUT OF THE HOUSE OF ASHES
- **Criminology:** Backtracking the Lisky Bratva's human trafficking ring brings the agents to Odessa.
- **Interrogating** various Lisky Bratva bosses like Stefan Werner point to Odessa.
- **Streetwise:** The weapons used by the Lisky Bratva thugs were bought on the black market; the mafiya's weapon smuggling ring is based in Odessa.

THE BOXMEN
- Documents found in the Koernersbank vault in Zurich point (through **Accounting**) to the Odessa branch of the Black Sea Bank. **Tradecraft** fingers Donald Caroll as a man to talk to about criminal money laundering in that area.
- One of the zalozhniye encountered in Zurich was a French spy, Lili Blaise, who vanished in Odessa. **Research** or **Tradecraft** uncovers the place of her demise.
- **Electronic Surveillance:** Markov Schwetz reports back to Dorjiev.

TREASON IN THE BLOOD
- **Traffic Analysis:** The Lisky Bratva smuggle guns across the northern border into Turkey, then shipped via Samsun to Odessa. Following the trail back leads to the warehouse in Baghdad.
- **Criminology** identifies the Lisky Bratva mercs in this operation, and also pinpoints their headquarters as Odessa.
- Katun can send the agents to investigate Odessa.

THE ODESSA JOB

SCENE TYPE: Introduction
LEAD-OUTS: Infiltration

Donald Caroll is everyone's man in the Crimea. He's American by birth and accent, but he's got a Russian passport. He's based in Sevastopol – as is, co-incidentally, the Russian Black Sea fleet. When the Soviet Union broke up and Ukraine became an independent entity, it took the home port of the Russian Black Sea fleet with it. The compromise is that both the Ukrainian navy and the Russian Black Sea fleet are stationed in the port, and the port facilities are divided between the two.

The arrangement mostly works, barring the odd fistfight, bureaucratic snafu or standoff between warships. Caroll's an information broker and expert on the Black Sea and the geopolitics thereof. He passes information on to the USA about internal politics and port-side gossip, and advises both the Ukrainians and Russians on the US. All three sides find him valuable; none of them trust him in the slightest. Caroll's got a nice *dacha* overlooking Kalamita Bay, and it's there that he meets the characters. They sit in his garden looking out at the waves and the nuclear submarines; Caroll's bikini-clad Russian girlfriend serves them drinks while Caroll barbecues burgers and hot dogs.

He eventually gets around to the point. A few months ago, an old friend from Langley asked him to look into rumors about American-made weapons passing through Odessa. An embarrassing amount of cash and *materiel* has gone missing from Iraq in the last decade, and the CIA's trying to plug some of the leaks.

Some of the stolen weapons were RFID-tagged, and a few month's legwork and bribes brought Caroll's agent to the Turkish port of Samsun. They get loaded onto fishing boats and freighters there, and then are shipped across to Odessa. He's pretty sure that one of the *mafiya* gangs is handling the smuggling — based on the way his man in Samsun was professionally gutted, they're not dealing with amateurs.

To work out exactly who's receiving the weapons, Caroll needs to know where they're going when they reach Odessa. He can't go to Odessa himself – while the Crimea is *technically* part of the Ukraine, in practise it's Russian territory, and he's safe here. There are elements of the SBU (*Sluzhba Bezpeky Ukrayiny*, the Ukrainian secret service) who want Caroll silenced. So, he plans on sitting here eating burgers, while the player characters find the warehouse.

THE JOB

The next arms shipment is coming in on board the *Yelkenci*, a Turkish-owned freighter. The weapons are tagged with hidden RFID beacons; all the agents need to do is follow the freighter's cargo and find out where the tagged crates end up. Caroll expects that they'll be brought to a warehouse somewhere in the north of the city. The team are to infiltrate the warehouse, and

Caroll can provide them with:

- One Russian navy motorboat and six Russian sailors. If the agents want to shadow the *Yelkenci*, or enter Odessa by sea, or if they just feel more comfortable with half-a-dozen hard men who won't ask questions, then they can use this asset. Caroll's called in a favor from a Russian admiral to get the sailors. He doesn't expect the agents to need this level of backup.

STARTING HOT

Optionally, switch around *The Odessa Job* and *Infiltration* scenes. Open the game with the characters sneaking into Odessa in the dead of night, then do a quick flashback to burgers sizzling on the grill at Caroll's dacha while he briefs the team on the mission, then cut back to the infiltration mission.

- Passports and papers (a **2-point Cover** identity only, but enough to get into Odessa if there's a problem with the characters' current names)
- RFID trackers & communications gear. The RFID trackers have a range of around fifty metres in optimum conditions, so the characters should keep eyes on the crates too if possible. Caroll will be right here keeping an eye on things via radio, and will provide support if necessary.
- Cash, in extremely limited amounts.

THE NAVY MOTORBOAT

The boat is piloted by **Kostya** (mid-50s, unnervingly morbid, drinks like a fish); it's got a maximum range of around 200 kilometres on a single tank of fuel. It's normally used to ferry crew back and forth from ships in the harbour, or for inspections, so it can pop in and out of Odessa harbour without attracting attention.

INFILTRATION

SCENE TYPE: Core
LEAD-IN: The Odessa Job
LEAD-OUT: The Warehouse

Sevastapol's around three hundred kilometres from Odessa. How the agents arrived will affect how they leave Odessa, so establish how they intend to get into the city.

- **BY ROAD OR RAIL:** The local police flag down any westerners or anyone acting suspiciously. Using a suitable Interpersonal ability (**Bureaucracy** to explain missing papers, **Cop Talk** to bluff past cops or **Flirting** to distract some bored border guard) lets the characters talk their way past the checkpoint without getting their papers checked. Western agents travelling on Russian, Belarusian, or Ukrainian papers can use **Disguise** (Difficulty 4) to appear suitably post-Soviet. Otherwise, whatever identities they use get flagged by the Lisky Bratva and the authorities once all hell breaks loose.
- **BY AIR:** There's an international airport in Odessa, but there are no direct flights from Sevastopol. If the characters have the ready cash, they can go via another city or charter a flight.
- **BY SEA:** Ferries run from Sevastopol to Odessa. Again, the agents' identities will be flagged if they pass through a security checkpoint.
- **BY MOTORBOAT:** If the agents take Caroll's offer of a motorboat, then they meet Kostya and his stalwart boys in Yuzhne, a port city thirty kilometres up the coast from Odessa. From there, an hour's choppy sailing brings the agents to the *Yelkenci*, while he can have them in Odessa in half an hour. Arriving via boat lets the agents dodge the authorities with **Urban Survival**.
- **SNEAKING IN:** Finally, the characters can take back roads into town, hitch-hike in, sneak through the catacombs and alleyways, and generally keep a really low profile. Again, this requires **Urban Survival**.

TRACKING THE SMUGGLERS

The *Yelkenci*'s a battered old tub that's been bouncing around the Black Sea since the 60s. She wallows in the water under a heavy cargo. Following her's a frustrating experience, as she's so damn slow. She's got a crew of five - all Turkish, all armed. Caroll warns against trying to board her because the Turks are in touch with the Bratva operatives on the shore via radio, so storming the boat risks aborting the whole mission.

The agents can shadow the *Yelkenci* at sea, or just keep watch on Odessa harbour until she arrives.

As the *Yelkenci* approaches, a smaller boat comes out from the harbour and escorts her in. She's a police boat – **Streetwise** or **Criminology** suggests that means the smugglers have their claws in the local police force, the *militsiya*. She docks at berth 22; waiting there are a pair of trucks and eight armed guards. The cargo is rapidly loaded onto the trucks. One of the crew from the boat also boards a truck, while the rest are paid for their delivery with cash. The trucks head into the city at speed.

Using **Electronic Surveillance (Core Clue)**, the team can pick up the RFID signals from the tagged crates. It's the right cargo.

A 1-point **Photography** spend lets the characters get a telephoto look at the cargo as it's being loaded. There are several heavy crates of varying sizes, plus at least one long box that bears a disconcerting resemblance to a coffin.

FOLLOWING THE TRUCKS

It's hard to weave through traffic in a big truck that's loaded with heavy crates, but the drivers give it their best shot, and the stern-faced men with the big guns ensure that most drivers get out of the way. The agents need to follow the trucks to find out where they're going. A **Driving** test is required to keep them in sight (Difficulty 4, or Difficulty 6 if the agent wants to hang back and ensure the guards on the truck don't realise they're being tailed). If this test fails, then the agents can pick up the RFID signals with **Electronic Surveillance**.

The trucks head northeast, on streets parallel to the shore, until they turn into the loading bay of a dilapidated warehouse. The agents immediately spot two armed guards at the door; a 1-point **Notice** spend also alerts them to the guards on the rooftop of the warehouse and the building across the street.

THE WAREHOUSE

SCENE TYPE: Core
LEAD-IN: Infiltration
LEAD-OUT: Underworld

As dilapidated warehouses go, it's quite a nice one, dating back to the 1930s. As the agents have time to prep this assault, break out the rules for Tactical Fact-Finding Benefits (p. 107 of *Night's Black Agents*).

- **Architecture:** There are catacombs underneath most of the city, and judging by the age of the surrounding buildings, that probably includes this warehouse. There may be an alternate entrance from underground that's unguarded. This route avoids the guards on street level. Move the crates from the warehouse level down to the tunnels, so the agents can still pick up the clues from *inside the warehouse*, below.
- **Military Science:** Two guards on the door. Probably more inside. That said, there's lots of cover, and the lighting's bad. It should be possible to either sneak in, or else take the guards out one by one as long as no-one raises the alarm.
  - A successful **Surveillance** test (Difficulty 4) lets the agents watch for other guards. Two more guards on the rooftops. Another two guards patrolling the perimeter. Add in the eight guards from the truck, and that's *at least* fourteen goons. Probably more like twenty – whoever these smugglers are, they've got plenty of manpower.
- **Urban Survival:** There's a police car parked just down the street, but the cops are watching the traffic, not the warehouse. They're obviously here to protect the smugglers, not arrest or stake them out.
- **Criminology:** If the characters get a good look at one of the guards, they recognize the gang tattoos that mark the wearer as one of the Lisky Bratva. A two-point **Criminology** spend might get the character the Lisky Bratva org chart (see p. 11). At this point, though, it is impossible to tell if the Lisky Bratva are actually behind the smuggling operation, or if they are just providing muscle for some other group.

SNEAKING IN

Getting in is easy enough with **Infiltration**. Sneaking past without being noticed is Difficulty 6; the characters can bring this difficulty down with clever schemes and point spends (cutting the power with **Mechanics**, jamming the guards' radios, spotting the patrol patterns with **Military Science** and so on). Alternatively, the agents (plus optional backup) can take out the sentries through equally clever but more violent schemes.

INSIDE THE WAREHOUSE

The ground floor of the warehouse is unguarded. Dozens of mismatched crates lie scattered around the building. Some of them give off RFID signals and are stencilled with English markings, but others have Cyrillic or Arabic lettering.

- The American crates contain, as Caroll suspected, weapons and ammunition. There's also gear like night vision goggles, body armor and other military supplies.
  - **Military Science** or **Traffic Analysis:** According to the tags on the crates, these weapons were destined for the Iraqi militia, and were taken from a depot in Baghdad. Investigating this lead is a lead-in to *Treason in the Blood* (p. 106).
  - **Electronic Surveillance (Core Clue):** Some of the crates here give off RFID signals. Other RFID signals come from somewhere below this warehouse.
  - If the agents want to tool up by grabbing gear from the crates, it counts as 3 points of **Preparedness** that can only be spent on military gear.
- The Cyrillic crates contain food and blankets. Digging around turns up a manifest; **Accounting** or **Traffic Analysis** works out that the "cargo" mentioned are probably people. The Lisky Bratva evidently have their fingers in human trafficking, too. The village of Dragovir in Romania is mentioned as a destination, which leads into *Shadow of the Vampire* (p. 35). Other manifests mention Debrecen, in Hungary, a pointer to *The Debrecen Gambit* (p. 40). A 1-point **Notice** or **Accounting** spend finds a receipt buried amid the papers, mentioning a company called Baldak Shipping.
- The Arabic crates are crammed with books, folders and yellowed papers, mostly in English. Other crates contain plastic-wrapped fragments of clay and stone. **History** identifies the papers as government records dating back to the 1920s and the British Mandate in Iraq; the State of Iraq was under British control from 1918 until 1932. Going through them with **Research** reveals nothing of use – the papers mainly deal with exploration and mapping efforts. There are several handwritten notes in the margins that read "INTRUSIVE." The meaning of this message is obscure. It looks like someone grabbed the contents of some obscure government archive and smuggled them out of Iraq (and that's exactly what happened). A 1-point **Bureaucracy** spend indicates that most of the papers come from the archives of the National Museum of Iraq.
  - **Archaeology** identifies the plastic-wrapped items as fragments stolen from the National Museum of Iraq. A 1-point **Archaeology** or **Languages** spend translates the fragments; they relate to tales of the city of Irem, lost in the deserts of Arabia.

Notice: There is no sign of the coffin-like crate the agents saw being off-loaded from the *Yelkenci*.

Notice or Architecture (Core Clue): Searching around the warehouse reveals a concealed trapdoor leading down.

If the agents decide that finding the guns is enough for Caroll and start to pull out, you'll need to incentivize them to go down into the darkness. A carrot might be two Lisky Bratva thugs emerging from the trapdoor to collect some equipment from the crates. As they work, they grumble in Russian (**Languages**) about "the doctor" and how he's going to deal with "Deniz." That should pique their curiosity.

If you'd prefer a stick, then have another truck full of goons show up. The best place to hide is down in the basement; if they fight, they'll alert the guards outside as well as newcomers.

UNDERWORLD

SCENE TYPE: Hazard/First Reveal
LEAD-IN: The Warehouse
LEAD-OUT: The Chase

The catacombs of Odessa started as quarries. Odessa expanded hugely in the late 18th and the 19th centuries. It was a fashionable city for the upper classes, who demanded houses built out of the local limestone. The network of mine tunnels below grew as quickly as the city above, and today there is a labyrinth of some 2,500 kilometres in the darkness, used by smugglers, partisans, vagrants… and monsters.

The tunnel from the warehouse leads to a larger open chamber, lit by electric lights. As the agents approach, they hear low voices arguing in Russian. One voice is angry, but nervous and fearful. The other is barely audible – it's a scratchy, hoarse whisper.

At the end of the tunnel, the characters find themselves on a small wooden landing, overlooking the larger room. More tunnels lead away on the lower level; the smell of salt water and rot emanates from these lower passageways. The chamber is packed with more crates, like the ones in the warehouse above. There are several dozen armed guards and workers in the room, but their attention is currently focussed on the drama that's unfolding in the middle of the room, not on the player characters.

In the centre of the chamber is a coffin – the same coffin that was recently taken off the *Yelkenci*. **Military Science** identifies it as a standard U.S. Army coffin. It contains the corpse of an American soldier (see sidebar) that Dorjiev intends to animate as a zalozhniy.

The doctor himself bends over the coffin, his face hidden from the agents as he injects a preservative chemical into the corpse's veins.

Next to Dorjiev are two figures. One is a crewman from the *Yelkenci*, a Turk called Deniz. He was the Lisky Bratva's man in Samsun, and they hold him responsible for recent security breaches. He's got about thirty seconds to live.

The other is one of the zalozhniye. It looks almost human in the dim light. Any character with **Military Science** can guess from the figure's stance and physique that it's got special forces training; a 1-point **Diagnosis** or **Vampirology** spend notes that it's not breathing.

Deniz pleads with Dorjiev, promising that he will clean up the problems with the "Baghdad route." The necromancer grunts dismissively and turns back to the corpse.

Faster than the eye can follow, the zalozhniy lashes out and grabs Deniz by the throat. The smuggler is lifted off the ground by the creature's inhuman strength… and then the zalozhniy begins to squeeze. As Deniz dies, the monster feasts.

Everyone feels a moment of… discontinuity, as if their hearts skipped a beat, as if they blacked out for an instant. This is followed by a chorus of electronic beeps, as every wristwatch and mobile phone in the room temporarily loses track of time. This bubble of timelessness expands out from the zalozhniy, so first the guards' phones and watches start chiming… and then the player characters are betrayed by their own gadgets.

And then, suddenly, impossibly, the zalozhniy is right on top of them. That's a 5-point **Stability** test right there.

The agents have an instant to react before the zalozhniy starts mauling them. Shooting the monster is pretty ineffective, as it's a corpse (so guns do only a single point of damage). Hitting it with a flashbang knocks it back off the balcony and gives the characters time to run. If the agents don't react immediately, then the zalozhniy starts off by grabbing one of the agents and trying to Throw him (at the cost of 2 Hand-to-Hand points, see *Night's Black Agents*, p. 76) down into the chamber below for the guards to deal with. If successful, the unfortunate agent takes +0 damage and lands heavily behind a crate.

Once the fighting starts, the Lisky Bratva call in more guards and security assets from nearby. The tunnels are crawling with their goons – **Military Science (Core Clue)** warns that if the characters stay still, they'll get slaughtered.

THE FIREFIGHT

This scene is a race through catacombs, sewers, creepy warehouses and abandoned tenements on the edge of Odessa. Mix up the opposition from location to location – burly stevedores armed with crowbars, armed goons with AK-47s, snipers lurking on rooftops, ex-Spetsnaz martial artists, and the ever-present lurking threat of the undead.

- In the cramped, pitch black (see p. 52 of *Night's Black Agents*) tunnels, the agents can use **Infiltration** (Difficulty 3)

THE AMERICAN ZALOZHNIY

Most of the Lisky Bratva's undead warriors are made from Russian ex-Spetsnaz corpses, but as the organization expands its reach, it needs to draw from a wider pool of recruits. Zalozhniye can only pass for human in restricted circumstances, but they retain the memories and speech patterns they had in life. Acquiring American zalozhniy is one of Dorjiev's current projects. This first American corpse was obtained in Iraq, the victim of a roadside IED. A small hunk of shrapnel cut the carotid artery, but the rest of the body is intact, making it an ideal candidate for transformation into a death-wight.

If any of the player characters have a background in the US armed forces or US intelligence, then the Director can have the corpse be that of an old friend or contact of a player character. The character recognizes his old friend's body when they first enter the underground vault, and the reanimated horror then chases them across Europe. It's a 6-point **Stability** test for the agent who lost a friend.

Alternatively, if the characters have already played through *Treason in the Blood*, then the corpse may be that of a friendly NPC (or even former player character!) who died in that adventure.

COMMENTARY In playtesting, one brave team of spies nearly managed to get wiped out in this scene. Don't let your team meet the same messy end! If the agents don't bug out immediately when the zalozhniy attacks, then throw them around a bit and then give them another chance to run. If they brought the Russian marines, then have the monster chow down on tasty NPC snack food while the agents escape. If they *didn't* bring the marines, then have the marines show up to distract the bad guys if the players are pinned down.

Another playtest group replaced Deniz with a character from *(S)entries*, which tied the two missions together nicely. Look for opportunities to bring back NPCs wherever possible.

---

to escape their pursuers. Remember, all Stability tests in the tunnels are at +1 to Difficulty.

- If the agents are lightly armed, those crates of firearms in the upper warehouse contain heavy weapons to even the odds.
- The catacombs stretch for miles, and it's easy to get lost down here. A 1-point spend of **Architecture** or **Urban Survival** lets the characters navigate. Smuggler tunnels connect to the sewers and the docks, and most of the older buildings in Odessa have at least one concealed entrance to the catacombs.
- The area around the warehouse is a maze of abandoned warehouses, tenements, shacks and alleyways. It's a run-down area of the town.
- The truck from the *Yelkenci* is still parked outside, and the keys are in the ignition.

DORJIEV

The good doctor flees into the tunnels as soon as the firefight starts, taking his three bodyguards (use Bodyguard stats from p. 69 of **Night's Black Agents**) and the coffin with him. **Notice** or **Military Science** spots that the zalozhniy deliberately refrains from making lethal attacks until Dorjiev is clear, and a 1-point **Intimidation** spend reveals that Dorjiev is visibly nervous until he gets well clear of the zalozhniy.

If the agents want to follow him instead of retreating, they've got to fight their way through the guards before chasing him through the catacombs. Once they hit the surface, they glimpse him driving off in an armored van with a Lead of 2 plus the number of rounds the agents spent fighting the guards. Dorjiev has hidden the moment of his death (see p. 7), so he cannot be killed by any means at this point, although he can be severely… inconvenienced. (Throwing a grenade into the van, for example, won't kill him, but it means he might turn up in Vienna as a shambling mess of burnt flesh and shattered bone.)

THE GUARDS

There are a dozen guards (use the Thug stats from p. 70 of **Night's Black Agents**) in the subterranean chamber, plus whatever guards the team didn't eliminate upstairs, plus as many more as you need. The guards fear Dorjiev and his monsters a lot more than they fear arrest, or even being shot by troublesome spies, so they fight fearlessly. They'll try to take the player characters alive at first, but will switch to lethal tactics once the characters fight back.

The guards' priorities are:

- Cover Dorjiev's escape
- Trap the player characters; if that fails then
- Surround the warehouse

In the darkness of the catacombs, the goons are willing to use automatic weapons and lethal attacks. Once the characters escape onto the streets, the thugs have to be a little more retrained – the Lisky Bratva may own the Odessa police, but that does not mean they can get away with full-scale war on the streets. If the agents make it back to the surface and out of the warehouse district, then the Lisky Bratva goons hand over the chase to the local police – at least in public.

THE ZALOZHNIY

The undead monsters are assassins, not brawlers. While they are immensely tough, they can be damaged, and they can only heal by feeding on the deaths of those who died through trickery. Therefore, while the first zalozhniy will pursue the characters through the catacombs, bursting out of the darkness or scuttling along the ceilings like a giant, shockingly white insect, it will flee if it loses half its Health (6 points of damage).

THE RUSSIAN SAILORS

If the agents brought along the six Russian heavies, then the Director should have them killed off by the Lisky Bratva (ideally, by the zalozhniy). The Russians can die giving the agents a

CAROLL'S DEATH

At some point after the chase begins, the agents will contact Caroll or he'll contact them via radio. When he calls, he already knows that everything's gone to hell. He talks to the agents over a headset mike as he grabs his bug-out bag and flees his house.

'Fuck. That warehouse is right in the middle of the Lisky Bratva's turf. They're – COME ON, MARTA – they're big players. Drugs and slave trafficking and worse stuff. If they catch us, we're dead. Fuck.'

There's the sound of a car engine starting as Caroll takes off and starts speeding down the narrow mountain roads above Sevastopol.

'They're onto me here, too. They cut the power to the house a few minutes ago, and there's a chopper buzzing us.'

Tyres squeal as he takes a corner at speed. The characters hear Caroll's girlfriend scream in alarm. He ignores her.

'Listen, I've got a safe house in Vienna. They won't follow us there, it's neutral territory. If you get to Vienna, and I'm not there, then check the airport. Left luggage locker 827, ok? I'll – oh shit.'

There's a loud bang, then a smash as the car runs into a spike strip. The tyres blow out and the car flies off the road, flipping end over end and crashing into a ditch. Miraculously, the radio survives, so the characters get to hear the cacophony of the car crash and the horribly curtailed screams of the victims. There's also a chorus of alarms from their mobile phones. A 1-point **Notice** or **Electronic Surveillance** spend also notices a curious time lag as the zalozhniy time bubble expands out from the point of death.

Caroll just got taken out by the third Lisky Bratva zalozhniy.

A moment later, she picks up the headset and speaks to the player characters through it.

'We will kill you if we can.'

Criminology: If the Lisky Bratva are willing to expend this much time and energy on killing Caroll and the agents, then they're involved in something much bigger that just arms smuggling. Obviously, if you're running *The Zalozhniy Sanction* later in the quartet, then the players already know about the Philby plot and what's really at stake, but otherwise give the players a hint that there's more to discover... if they survive.

MARTA GIVES IT UP

While Caroll is likely killed in the crash, his girlfriend survives long enough to be interrogated by the Lisky Bratva. She reveals that Caroll told the agents about a safehouse in Vienna, and that he mentioned something about the airport train station. The Lisky Bratva know where the agents are going...

CAROLL'S FATE

Optionally, you can bring Donald Caroll back again later in the operation, either as a prisoner or turncoat – or even a zalozhniy. Otherwise, his car is pushed off a cliff into the Black Sea, and the fish dine heavily that night.

---

chance to escape – use them as cannon fodder. Use the Soldier statistics from p. 69 of **Night's Black Agents**. If you have time, and the operation's pacing allows it, let the players run the Russian sailors as they die heroically and messily. If the agents didn't bring the soldiers, then kill them offscreen.

ESCAPING THE WAREHOUSE

Once the agents make it back to street level and get clear of their immediate pursuers, move to **The Chase**.

THE CHASE

SCENE TYPE: Hazard/Chase
LEAD-IN: Underworld
LEAD-OUT: Leaving Odessa

Once the agents escape the warehouse, they need to get clear of their pursuers, and that means a chase sequence. (See the rules on p. 53 of **Night's Black Agents**). Determine their initial Lead based on how clean their escape was – assume 4 for an average escape, 3 if they're scattered and injured, and 5 if they managed to trick their pursuers and got away fairly clean.

The Lisky Bratva has twenty times as many mooks in Odessa as there are player characters, and while they're not all at the warehouse, they can get there quickly.

CHASE PARAMETERS

The pursuers and the abilities used depend on where and how the chase takes place.

The default pursuers are always present; bring in the High-Stress pursuers when the agents' lead is 2 or less, or 7 or more.

To escape, the agents need to get their Lead up to 10.

Remember that characters with high **Athletics** or **Driving** can benefit from the Parkour or Gear Devil cherries.

SWITCHING CHASES

By spending a point from a suitable Investigative ability, the agents can change the type of chase. They can hop out of their stolen car and flee into a crowded nightclub (bluffing their way past the doorman with a **High**

CHASE PARAMETERS

LOCATION	CHASE ABILITIES	DEFAULT PURSUERS	HIGH-STRESS PURSUERS
Catacombs, sewers	Athletics or Infiltration vs Athletics or Surveillance	Lisky Bratva thugs and thug bosses	Zalozhniy
Streets, back alleys, rooftops	Athletics or Infiltration vs Athletics or Surveillance	Lisky Bratva thugs and thug bosses	Zalozhniy
Main streets	Athletics or Disguise vs Athletics or Surveillance	*Militsiya* foot patrols, Lisky Bratva thugs and thug bosses.	Lisky Bratva operative
In a stolen car	Driving vs Driving	*Militsiya* cars	Police helicopter
By boat	Piloting vs Piloting	*Militsiya* boats	Police helicopter
Blending in with the crowds	Disguise or Surveillance vs Surveillance	Lisky Bratva thugs and thug bosses	Lisky Bratva operative

Society spend), then get backstage in the nightclub (using **Urban Survival** to find an unwatched exit) and go parkouring across the rooftops. Each time the characters switch the type of chase, their lead increases by 1.

HAZARDS & ENCOUNTERS
A few sample thrills and spills for each style of chase:

CATACOMBS
- Sudden darkness as the lights go out
- Crumbling wall, about to collapse
- Rusty high-pressure water pipe, ripe to be kicked open
- Drunken vagrants living in the catacombs
- Secret entrance to cellar
- Mysterious underground cinema, art gallery or church

BACK STREETS
- Narrow, trash-filled alleyway
- Side door into the central courtyard of a decaying old house
- Crowd of drunken club-goers spilling out of nightclub
- Drug deal in progress
- Small square with a statue of some long-dead Russian admiral
- Flock of pigeons outside a bakery
- Crazed taxi driver taking a short cut through alleyways

ROOFTOPS
- Row of balconies
- Crumbling tiled roof
- Rooftop garden
- Half-constructed office block
- Onion-dome church roof

MAIN STREETS (ON FOOT)
- Crowded restaurant with tables on the street.
- Religious procession – lots of priests following a banner
- Dozens of tourists disembark from a tour bus
- Nightclub entrance
- Museum or cathedral entrance

MAIN STREETS (BY CAR)
- Slow-moving tourist bus
- Hard right turn down the Potemkin steps
- Narrow cobbled streets leading to a fountain
- Open gate to the docks
- Swarm of taxis block the road

BOAT
- Sudden big wave
- Slowly turning container ship
- Warning buoy near rocks
- Crowded passenger liner with lots of witnesses
- Windsurfers

BLENDING IN WITH THE CROWD
- Drunk and rowdy gang
- Insistent hooker
- Raucous birthday party
- Tour group
- Jewish wedding

HIGH-STRESS PURSUERS

LISKY BRATVA OPERATIVE: While most of the Lisky Bratva's assets in Odessa are just muscle, there are a few talented professionals in town who can be called in to deal with a problem. Pick one of the assassins on p. 9 and throw them at the characters.

POLICE HELICOPTER: Technically, it's a VV helicopter (the VV's are the Internal Troops, the Ukrainian equivalent of the national guard) and the chopper's an ex-Air Force Mil Mi-24, known in NATO circles as a Hind. It's also absurd overkill – the Mi-24's got a 12.7mm Gatling gun (+2 damage, three times per hit) and wing-mounted rocket pods (Class 2 explosive warheads). The chopper won't open fire unless the agents are presenting a clear and present danger to the civilians, or they give it a very clear shot. It will, however, try to force the characters to surrender or run them off the road (or try to capsize them, if they're on the water). The helicopter is not designed for manoeuvring in an urban environment, so agile characters can drive around it. The pilot's got Piloting 6 and Shooting 4.

ZALOZHNIY: The zalozhniy gets ahead of the characters and tries to set traps for them. It might, for example, leave a tempting parked car with the keys in the ignition for them to find, or string a booby-trapped grenade (Class 2 explosive) across a doorway then herd the characters towards it. **Sense Trouble** rolls (Difficulty 4) give the characters advance warnings of these death-traps.

CAUGHT!

Agents caught by the police, as opposed to the Lisky Bratva, are arrested instead of being shot. The *militsiya* may be in the Lisky Bratva's pockets, but they still have to give the illusion of following procedure until the prisoner can fall down the stairs or have some other nasty accident in the cells. The other characters therefore have a small window of opportunity to get the agent out of prison. Doing so requires an identity that can get into prison (requiring a **Cover** check) and then spending **Law** and a skill like **Cop Talk**, **Negotiation** or **Bureaucracy** to either force the police to grant bail or bribe the cops. Either that, or a **Network** contact higher up in the Ukrainian government must beat a Difficulty 5 (remember that spends to spring agents from legitimate custody cost double).

CORNERED

If the agents run out of Lead, then they're cornered by the Lisky Bratva's forces with no obvious way out. Depending on the circumstances, the *mafiya*'s pawns may demand that the agents surrender, or just send in waves of thugs to kill them, or just contain them while they bring in bigger guns like a zalozhniy or three. The Director should give the players a chance to come up with a clever exit strategy to pull their bacon out of the fire. Running out of Lead should hurt – don't let the players get away without spending a few Investigative points or else taking a nasty chunk of damage. The chase then continues with its Lead reset to 4.

OUT OF SIGHT

If the agents hit Lead 10, then they've managed to temporarily throw the Lisky Bratva off their trail – move onto *Leaving Odessa*. A 1 point spend of **Urban Survival** or by a local **Network** contact lets the characters find better shelter somewhere (check into a hotel under assumed names, break into a holiday home, lurk in an all-night cafe) where they can plan their next move. If you haven't done so already, run *Caroll's Death* (sidebar, p. 24).

LEAVING ODESSA

SCENE TYPE: Core
LEAD-IN: The Chase
LEAD-OUT: Running Hot

Finally, the agents have a chance to catch their breath. The Lisky Bratva is still hunting them, so the Director should keep the pressure up. They hear sirens on the streets outside, police knocking at doors, and every eye seems to be following the agents. They need to get out of Odessa. **Criminology (Core Clue)** confirms that Vienna is an "open city" for the Russian mob, neutral turf where peace is enforced. This suggests that Caroll's safe house in Vienna is their best place to lie low; **Military Science** confirms that the agents are severely outnumbered and outgunned. Fighting back means hitting the Lisky Bratva where the agents can actually hurt them – killing goons on the streets of Odessa won't help, but damaging their smuggling routes just might.

The Lisky Bratva's corrupt minions in the militia stick the blame for any firefights or carnage on the agents. The agents are hit with at least Heat +2, plus any additional Heat they picked up during their escape.

THE WAYS OUT

Getting out of Odessa isn't necessarily as easy as getting in was.

BY PLANE

Odessa Central is crawling with police and VV troops, not to mention at least one zalozhniy. Getting past security requires both a **Cover** and **Disguise** test for *each* agent, both at Difficulty 7. Alternatively, the agents can try sneaking past airport security with **Infiltration** (Difficulty 8). If the agents want to bring gear onto the plane, that requires another **Conceal** test at Difficulty 8. Failing such a roll means the agents are spotted by the Lisky Bratva's pawns.

If the characters do make it past security, then there's only one flight to Vienna each day, and there are enemy agents on board (see p. 30 for ways for the Lisky Bratva to block air travel to Vienna). A better option is to take a charter flight to somewhere else (like Debrecen) and head to Vienna by road from there.

Flight time from Odessa to Vienna is about two hours, but flying skips most of this adventure. Use whatever tactics are necessary to get the agents out of the air. (Dorjiev's unnatural weather is a nice low-key way of grounding a passenger plane; for charters, go with ground-to-air missiles…) Getting there is half the fun…

BY ROAD

Renting (**Cover** test at Difficulty 3) or boosting a car is trivial (especially with Grand Theft Auto), and the agents can take side roads out of the city. However, the main road is the motorway north, and that's crawling with police. There are checkpoints and armed patrols all along it; getting past them requires a **Cover** test at Difficulty 6, plus spending points from a suitable Interpersonal ability to bribe or bluff past them. If the agents' total Heat is 4 or more, then the cops insist on searching *every* vehicle; there are massive tailbacks, and the agents must pass **Conceal** and **Disguise** tests (Difficulty 6) to get through the checkpoint in addition to the other tests.

A better option (suggested by anyone who has **Criminology, Human Terrain,** or **Streetwise**) is to take the road to Moldova via Transnistria – it's a criminal hotbed, but the Lisky Bratva are rumored not to have any assets in Transnistria. The checkpoints on that route are also less onerous – a **Cover** test at Difficulty 5 and a nice bribe (1-point Negotiation or Streetwise spend) are enough to get by.

If detected, then it's time for a nice car chase.

From Odessa to Tiraspol is only around 90 minutes (or, the way player characters drive, 60 minutes and a few explosions).

BY RAIL

There are trains from Odessa to several destinations in Russia and Moldova, but there are no direct trains to Europe. The most direct route goes Odessa-Kiev-Budapest-Vienna, but the Lisky Bratva are watching that route like hawks. Getting past security at the train station requires a **Cover** test at Difficulty 6, but that's the easy bit. Every train has a few Lisky Bratva thugs on board, and there is nowhere for the characters to run when they're trapped on board a train.

BY SEA

If Kostya's boat is still available to the characters, then they can get out of Odessa under cover of night. The docks are still full of Lisky Bratva agents, so they'll need to make **Infiltration** tests (Difficulty 6), but at least leaving by sea means they don't have to worry about paperwork. Kostya drops the agents off on the Moldavan coast outside the small town of Mayaky; they can head into Transnistria from there.

COVER IDENTITIES

If the agents had their papers checked when they entered the city, those identities are now burned. Using them will draw unwelcome attention – and since the cops have thrown a ring of steel around Odessa, there's no easy way out that doesn't involve identity checks. The characters need to either use **Cover** to create fresh identities for themselves, or else **Network** or **Streetwise** to find local contacts and buy replacement papers and supplies. Remember that the agents' Heat may screw up such deals.

RUNNING HOT

SCENE TYPE: Antagonist Action
LEADS-IN: Leaving Odessa (Odessa), Deniable Assets (Transnistria), Secrets of the Monastery (Transylvania), Burning the Lisky Bratva (Debrecen)
LEADS-OUT: Transnistrian Nights (Transnistria), Shadow of the Vampire (Transylvania), The Debrecen Gambit (Debrecen), The Vienna Run (Vienna)

For the rest of this operation, the agents are pursued across borders by the Lisky Bratva. It's a chase, but one that takes place over several days and at a much greater distance than a normal car-chase or foot pursuit. The question isn't whether or not the agents can sprint out of the alleyway before the exit's blocked, it's whether or not they can make it to the border checkpoint with a valid exit visa.

This, as if you hadn't guessed, is an Extended Chase (see p. 90 of *Night's Black Agents*). The agents' Hot Lead score starts at 7, minus their Heat on leaving Odessa. (Their official Heat drops by -3 once they cross into Moldova.)

In addition to the assets in each of the locations along the way, throw at least one of the following threats at the agents on each leg of the journey, whenever they fail a Hot Lead test, or whenever the action slows down.

THE AUTHORITIES

The Lisky Bratva have iron control over the Odessa police, but also have bribed members of the police in Moldova (but not Transnistria), Hungary and Vienna. This can cause problems for the characters along the way. Furthermore, any time the agents gain 3 or more points of Heat, their Hot Lead drops by one.

Interference by the authorities works best in Odessa, Debrecen, Vienna or other large cities.

- **BUREAUCRATIC HASSLES:** Paying for permits and bribes to make lengthy paperwork disappear are part and parcel of life on the run, but this time things don't go smoothly. The border guard confiscates the agents' passports to "run them through the computer," all cars are being stopped and sprayed to prevent the spread of potato blight, the agent needs a license to bring his laptop into the country. Whatever the particular bureaucratic quagmire is, it threatens to significantly delay the agents. Spending points from a suitable Interpersonal Ability allows them to talk wtheir way out of the jam, but it's clear someone's making their lives difficult. **Bureaucracy**'s the most useful ability here.
- **FRAME JOB:** The police are given a fake report that contains a description of the player characters and their current mode of transport; it claims that they are part of a dangerous ring of child sex-slave traffickers. The police spot the characters and attempt to apprehend them. These cops are innocent dupes of the Lisky Bratva, so killing them isn't necessary. **Law** gets the agents some leeway to act; they can then discredit the evidence with **Photography** or **Data Recovery**, or gum up the works with **Bureaucracy**.
- **TAP AND TRACE:** The Lisky Bratva manage to get a phone tap onto the agents' current cellphones, or onto the landlines of a suitable location (like the hotel they are staying in). Anyone with **Electronic Surveillance** can notice this tap, but only if they either check the phone deliberately before making a call, or hear the tell-tale click while talking on the phone.

SUPERNATURAL THREATS

Dorjiev's zalozhniy revenants are not the only supernatural horror he can unleash on the player characters. Three of his powers require blood from the player characters – if an agent is wounded or shot, and cannot clean up the spilled blood before the Lisky Bratva get their hands on it, then that agent is vulnerable to Dorjiev's powers. The magical link can be broken by killing Dorjiev, or else by spending **Vampirology, Occult Studies, Diagnosis** or **Chemistry** depending on the nature of the curse. A blood transfusion could dilute or remove the curse, or the agents might need to find somehow who can enact a counter-ritual. A potent vampiric block might also break the connection.

- **BLOOD CURSE:** Dorjiev uses sympathetic magic (or viral contagion, or psychic channelling via the medium of blood) to attack one of the agents. Bloody welts open up across the agent's body; these welts resemble Cyrillic letters. The agent loses 1 Health per day; after 3 days, the message "THE ENGLISHMAN'S PRIZE IS OURS YOU WILL NOT INTERFERE" can be read.
- **BLOOD TRACKING:** Dorjiev can follow the agents via their blood, tracing their movements on a gore-stained map with a razor-sharp pendulum. This reduces all Hot Lead gains by 1. The advantage is that the link goes both ways – the agents can now trace Dorjiev's own movements (or, rather, the movements of the blood sample) with a 2-point **Occult Studies** spend. Dorjiev travels to the Crimea shortly after the agents leave Odessa, spends a day there, then returns to Odessa before moving onto Vienna just ahead of the player characters.
- **BLOOD HAUNTING:** The agent suffers from horrible nightmares. The first nightmare may cause a 1-point Stability test, the second a 2-point test, and the third a 3-point test. In the first nightmare, the agent is buried alive; in the second, he is frozen in the moment of his death, and in the third, Dorjiev comes up to the agent, rips out his own heart, and presses it into the agent's chest. **Shrink** can help deal with Stability losses.

His other two abilities do not need a link to his targets.

- **WEATHER CONTROL:** Either Dorjiev or some elemental force under his control can command the weather. A torrential storm grounds all air traffic, raging waves stop ships from sailing, landslides and floods block road and rail travel. The agents are stuck and must switch to another form of transport.
- **NECROMANCY:** Dorjiev can lend a mockery of life to the dead, allowing him to interrogate the deceased. Merely killing their pursuers doesn't mean a clean get-away – if the agents leave any corpses intact, Dorjiev can still question the dead.

HUNTERS

Send one human operative per player character after the agents, mixed in with a zalozhniy or two. Keep the rest of the zalozhniye for the climactic confrontation in Vienna; the other operatives can be dropped into future operations when you're feeling sadistic.

GOING TO GROUND

When pursued by overwhelming dangers, some players prefer to go to ground and hide instead of running. A quick break at a safehouse to refresh General Ability pools and heal up is fine, but that's it. If the agents start talking about faking their deaths and starting new lives as Croatian sheep farmers, then throw an Operative at them and get them running again. If they stay still, then the Conspiracy can always find them (through supernatural means if nothing else). Running is the only way to survive.

OPERATIVES

The Lisky Bratva's human operatives are described on p. 9. Each of them has a unique approach to dealing with problems, so pick the most appropriate one for the current situation.

- **The Sniper:** Bring the Sniper in if the agents arrange a meeting (like their second dinner with Mr. Happy in Transnistria (see p. 34) or telegraph their location in advance, say by chartering a plane (in which case the Sniper sets up on a rise overlooking the runway, and shoots the pilot first). **Sense Trouble** (Difficulty 7) may give a character a split-second glimpse of sunlight flashing off a rifle scope before the shot is fired. The Sniper can't take out the whole team on his own, so combine the Sniper with a second trap. The Sniper takes his shot, the survivors try to flee before he shoots again – and they run right into a zalozhniy trap.
- **The Martial Artist:** The Martial Artist needs to get close to the agents, and works best when he can engage them one at a time. Obviously, he is especially effective when the agents don't have access to firearms. The Martial Artist might show up as just another passenger on a plane or ferry, or another customer in a restaurant who follows one of the agents to the bathroom. He could also show up at the airport in Vienna (see p. 47).
- **The Girl:** The Girl needs time to work her magic. Instead of attacking the agents directly, she'll seduce one of their contacts or allies, like Mr. Happy or Agi Korozus' hacker friend Tomas (p. 41), and spy on them before sending them into a trap. If any of the agents take an interest in her, she flirts with them; if she gets someone into bed, then she's got a variety of ways to eliminate vulnerable targets. The Girl can also show up as a plant among the slaves in Romania (see p. 36).
- **The Driver:** Obviously, the place for the Driver is on the road, especially the mountain passes of the Carpathians or in the streets of Odessa or Vienna. He drives a vehicle that's somewhat heavier than that of the agents, something with a big reliable engine and plenty of heft. He favors German cars, like Volkswagens – solid, but not flashy. He'll tail the agents for some time, learning their driving patterns (after a day, ha gains a 4-point Driving temp pool to use against them in a contest) and setting up an ambush, and then force them off the road at the worst possible moment – say, by shoving them into the path of an oncoming fuel tanker, or swiping them off a bridge.
- **The Con Artists:** The Con Artists make contact with the player characters through an intermediary, like Mr. Happy or Agi Kozorus. One of them presents as a prospective employer, a middleman, a supplier or some other useful underworld contact who has a grudge against the Lisky Bratva. The other will come in as an antagonist to lend credence to the first con artist's story – if their cover is that one is a supplier who's paying protection money to the Lisky Bratva, then the other shows up as a threatening thug. The con man even reveals some key information about the *mafiya*, like the origin of the zalozhniye, to make the agents trust him. He'll then send the agents into a situation that dumps a lot of Heat on them, like tricking them into breaking into an embassy or a government building in Vienna, or sending them up against the ruling oligarchs in Transnistria. If the Con Artists show up again, they'll switch roles.
- **The Torpedo:** Unlike the other operatives, the Torpedo's not part of the family. He doesn't follow their code. He's a mercenary; deniable, disposable, forgettable. The Torpedo's just passing through this part of the world, and doesn't care about a criminal record or a reputation. Therefore, "overkill" looms large in the Torpedo's vocabulary. The Torpedo shows up with a machine gun and a sackful of grenades, then goes all terminator until he takes down the agents. Transnistria or Debrecen is the best showground for the Torpedo.
- **The Sculptor:** The Sculptor also attacks indirectly. If any of the agent's Solaces are accessible, then she'll target them. Otherwise, she'll isolate and torture useful sources of information like Agi Kozorus, learn all she can about the agents, and then contact the agents to lure them into a trap. "We have your friend – surrender or we will kill him" isn't the most subtle ploy, but it's effective.

THE ZALOZHNIYE

In addition to the zalozhniy who killed Deniz, there is another nearby in Odessa and a third in the Crimea (see *Caroll's Death*). A fourth becomes available once Dorjiev has a chance to turn the American corpse into another monster. So, the agents are pursued by at least two zalozhniye immediately, with another arriving in Odessa a day later, and a fourth popping up at any point after that. The Lisky Bratva can even ship in one of their other three zalozhniye if the situation warrants it, or make more given time and necessity.

Unlike the operatives, who are skilled but only human, the zalozhniye are monsters. Play up their terrible power – have them punch through walls, climb sheer surfaces, explode out of the darkness, crawl across the ceiling. The only advance notice of a zalozhniy attack is when a watch stops ticking…

The zalozhniye gain power when they trick people into dying, so their attacks involve lethal traps where possible, like:

- Car bombs
- Sabotaging trains, planes or boats
- Planting bombs in safe houses
- Poison
- Luring agents into danger with human bait

INTERCEPTIONS

Once is a random encounter. Twice is coincidence. Three times is the Lisky Bratva trying to kill you. As the agents travel from Odessa to Vienna, they may be intercepted by enemy forces en route – maybe by operatives, by zalozhniye, or just by local thugs.

BLOWBACK

The Lisky Bratva's hunt for the agents has wider repercussions. If the agents dig up Network contacts or old friends, hit them with blowback:

- At least one contact should sell the agents out to the Lisky Bratva. He might offer the agents transport or a hiding place, which turns out to be a zalozhniy trap.
- Assets that the agents use in one city can turn up in the next. If the agents got out of Odessa thanks to their friend Mikhail, then Mikhail can turn up imprisoned in the human trafficking camp outside Debrecen.
- You can also force the agents to burn previously trustworthy contacts to get money or other assistance. That old priest in Transylvania may be willing to share his knowledge of the occult with the agents, but he won't be as happy when they steal the jewelled crucifix from his church and sell it for cash.

ON THE ROAD

- Tire-busting spike strip
- Tourists with a broken-down car who flag down help
- Cargo hauler convoy that turns into a roadblock
- Ambush at a gas station
- Sniper shoots out tires

BY RAIL

- Train is diverted to Lisky Bratva stronghold
- Bomb threat forces train to stop and investigate; agents are implicated
- Train is sabotaged and breaks down in howling snowstorm in Carpathian mountains
- Lisky Bratva assassins infiltrate train staff

BY PLANE

- There's a zalozhniy on the wing!
- Unnatural weather forces the plane to divert to another airport.
- Lisky Bratva assassins on board.
- As an idle suggestion, more than seventy Igla surface-to-air missiles went missing after the fall of the Soviet Union. They're man-portable and have enough punch and range to take down a 747.

BY BOAT

- Unnatural weather works here too.
- A Lisky Bratva smuggler pursues the agents.
- The boat is buzzed by an armed helicopter.

IDENTIFYING THE ENEMY

The agents can remember/research/guess a few useful facts about the enemy as they flee across Europe.

THE LISKY BRATVA

Criminology: The Lisky Bratva are one of the Russian *mafiya*; they've got their fingers in everything, but their main businesses are arms dealing, human trafficking, and drugs. The *vor* is an old crook called Josef Lisky. The Ukraine and Russia are their main stomping grounds, but they've got cells all over Europe and the Middle East – basically anywhere within the old Soviet sphere.

- **1-point spend:** There are rumors that one of Lisky's lieutenants, "the Doctor," is trying to push the old man off the top spot. That could splinter the organization – the Doctor's not *brodyagi*, not part of the culture. In fact, if the agents can make contact with some traditionalists within the Lisky Bratva, they may be able to convince them to help the agents deal with the Doctor, assuming he's the same creepy doctor as the agents saw in Odessa.
- **2-point spend:** Nikita Akhroyekov is the most traditionalist of the old *vor* in the Lisky Bratva. Getting his attention and cooperation requires proof of Dorjiev's treason, or providing him something else he wants: the Serbians' drug shipment, for example.

Traffic Analysis + Cryptography: If the agents can get into Lisky Bratva communications (**Digital Intrusion** test at Difficulty 7) then the agents can get an idea of the Lisky Bratva's available assets in the Odessa to Vienna theatre. The Difficulty of the Digital Intrusion test is reduced by -1 if the agents lifted a Lisky Bratva radio from the warehouse (Difficulty 6 **Preparedness** test to retroactively do so). Subtract another point of Difficulty with a 1-point **Electronic Surveillance** spend and a Lisky Bratva cell phone.

- **1-point Traffic Analysis spend:** There are three distinct elements to the Lisky Bratva response. Firstly, they're beefing up security at their operations in Romania and Hungary. Secondly, they've deployed "specialists" to eliminate the agents. Both of those orders came from a mobile source, presumably the organization's leadership. Thirdly, the Odessa section have launched their own pursuit, which seems to be largely independent of the first two responses.
- Getting inside Lisky Bratva communications also gives the agents a temporary pool of 4 points that can be allocated to any intelligence-gathering spends (**Criminology, Traffic Analysis** and so on) or on Tactical Fact-Finding Benefits. This pool is lost if the Lisky Bratva discover they've been compromised and clean house.

Research or **History:** Once they have Dorjiev's name, the agents can dig up more references to the man. He was allegedly one of Ceausescu's doctors, and conducted mysterious medical experiments in an outpost in eastern Romania. This leads into *Shadow of the Vampire* (p. 35).

THE ZALOZHNIYE

Vampirology: The creatures encountered in the Odessa catacombs match tales of the zalozhniye, creatures who died before their time and who now lure others into premature deaths. The zalozhniye were said to feed on the suffering and deaths of others, maliciously glorying in cutting short lives as theirs had been cut short.

- **1-point spend:** Just before he died in a house fire in Amsterdam, a notable expert on vampire lore, Pier Daelman, hinted about a tie between the zalozhniye and Romania. Researching his death turns up one odd clue – after the fire, they found the remains of dozens of clocks in every room in the house, as if he'd become obsessed with the passage of time.
- **2-point spend:** Each zalozhniy has a particular mortal wound. If the agents can recreate these wounds exactly, they can deliver the "proper" death to each zalozhniy.

Diagnosis: A close look at an exposed zalozhniy reveals the presence of wounds that should have been lethal. Some occult force brought them back from the brink of death – or else holds them there.

- A **1-point spend per zalozhniy** lets the agents determine the mortal woulds that can kill the zalozhniy. Mortal injuries include:
  > Gunshot wound to heart, consistent with a sniper shot from a long distance.
  > Gunshot wound to brain, delivered through the back of the neck at short range.
  > Inhalation of mercury fumes.
  > Inhalation of smoke.
  > Cyanide poisoning.

Chemistry (1-point spend): An obscure paper published in a Soviet medical journal in the mid-1980s talks about methods to preserve severely wounded soldiers by treating them with hydrogen sulfide to restrict cell reception of oxygen. One of the researchers is a Dr. G. D. Dorjiev. The description of the technique suggests that it would preserve the tissue, but that it wouldn't keep the brain alive.

TACTICS & RESPONSES

Accounting: Hunting the agents isn't cheap – the Lisky Bratva are throwing a lot of expensive assets into the chase. If the agents can hurt the organization's wallet – say, by disrupting their lucrative trade in drugs and human trafficking – then they won't be able to afford this pursuit.

Criminology: As Caroll said, Vienna's a neutral city – the Lisky Bratva will have to back off and regroup if the agents get there. Otherwise, they'll break their agreements with other criminal syndicates and trigger a major underworld conflict.

TRANSNISTRIAN NIGHTS

SCENE TYPE: Introduction
LEAD-IN: Running Hot
LEAD-OUT: Mr. Happy

Transnistria isn't an internationally recognized country. It's a strip of land on the eastern side of Moldova that declared independence in 1990. The Ukraine doesn't recognize it either, which means crossing the border into Transnistria is a harrowing experience for most visitors. Armed guards demand bribes and tolls, and if they let you cross, you enter a bureaucratic twilight zone, a state of indeterminacy where you are and are not in Moldova. The confusion and danger means that most travellers avoid Transnistria; rail routes take absurd detours to avoid the breakaway state.

Transnistria's population has plummeted since independence. The economy is calcified, so most young people of working age have emigrated to seek employment abroad.

The only real industry in Transnistria is weapons. The country was home to the Russian 14th Army, and when Transnistria broke away, they stayed as a "peacekeeping force" to prop up the local oligarchs. Transnistria is also home to several weapons factories. The country

is run by a golden circle of army officers, ex-KGB, and business oligarchs, all of whom profit hugely from the country's massive trade in illegal weapons. If you want to buy an anti-aircraft missile, or explosives, or want an army's worth of assault rifles, Transnistria's the place to be. Staggering amounts of money pour into this tiny strip of land.

Any agent with **Criminology, Law,** or **Human Terrain** knows about Transnistria's questionable status. They also know that Transnistria's oligarchs are doggedly independent – they permit other criminal syndicates to trade, but they've resisted any takeover attempts with lethal force. Transnistria is (probably) not under the thumb of the Lisky Bratva or their mysterious superiors. Even better, Transnistria does not officially co-operate with the Ukrainian authorities. Once the agents are across the border, the *militsiya* cannot follow them.

Crossing the border means bribery. If the guards suspect nothing, then the agents can get though with **Preparedness** (Difficulty 4) to have cash on hand, or a suitable Interpersonal spend (1-point Negotiation or Streetwise, generally). However, if the agents look like trouble (they're carrying heavy weapons), or like they're *in* trouble (Heat 4 or more), or if their pursuers are close behind, then the border guards are less co-operative. The agents need to give a suitably huge bribe (a half-kilo of cocaine would be ideal, or a few thousand dollars) or somehow convince the border guards not to detain them.

MR. HAPPY

SCENE TYPE: Core
LEAD-IN: Transnistrian Nights
LEAD-OUT: Igwe Abesoli

From the border, it's a short drive to the capital of the breakaway state, Tiraspol. Entering the city is like taking a trip back in time; it's a city-sized gulag of grey concrete streets, rationed supermarkets, and political oppression.

One of the agents (pick someone with a suitable background, or else someone with a high **Tradecraft** or **Military Science** skill) knows a fixer in town, nicknamed Mr. Happy. He's a former army officer, who now runs a cleaning service in Tiraspol. Mr. Happy should be able to supply the agents with anything they need, like fresh papers, medical supplies, weapons, or intel about the Lisky Bratva. (If the players don't seek him out, then Mr. Happy contacts them via some disposable goons and invites them to dinner.)

Research or **Human Terrain** picks up on the fact that Mr. Happy is a fanatic supporter of FC Tiraspol, a local soccer team.

Mr. Happy arranges to meet at one of the best restaurants in town, a Chinese place overlooking the biggest landmark in Tiraspol – the FC Sheriff football stadium. The restaurant is exquisitely appointed and the food is superlative. Mr. Happy has arranged for a private room.

PLAYING MR. HAPPY: He comes across as your favorite eccentric uncle, all smiles and jokes. He's in the middle tier of players in Transnistria – not one of the elite, but he's got a lot of pull as a broker and a fixer. For years, he's feuded with Victor Gusan, one of the most powerful men in the country, former Deputy Head of the local *militsiya,* and owner of FC Sheriff. He appears relaxed and jovial, but **Tradecraft** acknowledges his practiced caution – Mr. Happy enters through a back door of the restaurant, and stays out of sight of any other guests.

THE BARGAIN

Mr. Happy knows the Lisky Bratva want the agents dead. As far as he's concerned, they're walking dead men. Helping them isn't worth his time. **Negotiation (Core Clue)** lets the agents leverage their expertise and reputations by suggesting that they can beat the Lisky Bratva, and maybe Mr. Happy should support the winning team for once.

In response, he gestures towards the window with his chopsticks, where the shimmering palace of the FC Sheriff stadium glows under spotlights. The stadium is absurdly huge and well-appointed; it's a 14,000-seat stadium in a town of around 140,000 people. It looks like an intrusion from the future. Mr. Happy explains that the stadium is home to FC Sheriff, the pet soccer team of a certain gentleman. Now, in two days' time, FC Sheriff will play a friendly soccer match against the other local team, FC Tiraspol. FC Sheriff is considered unbeatable, as they're bankrolled by the oligarch and can buy the best players from across the world.

Happy then hands the agents a copy of the local newspaper. According to a front-page article, FC Sheriff recently bought a seventeen-year-old Nigerian *wunderkind* named Abesoli, a footballing prodigy. This friendly match will be Abseoli's debut in European soccer. Gusan is immensely proud of the boy, and has great expectations of his first match.

Mr. Happy's a lifelong supporter of the other team, FC Tiraspol, and wants to take the wind out of FC Sheriff's sails for once. He wants to ensure that young Abesoli doesn't play in the match tomorrow. So, he needs deniable assets – the agents' mission is to take out Abesoli. Happy doesn't want the boy dead, and above all he doesn't want the hit to be traced back to him. This is, as he puts it, a little joke between friends, between him and Victor Gusan.

- **Bullshit Detector** confirms that Mr. Happy is completely genuine.
- Anyone with **Tradecraft** can guess that this operation is a test of the agents' ability to operate discreetly – if they impress Happy, he'll have more significant work (or at least useful leads and assistance) for him.
- **Criminology** or **Streetwise** suggests that if the Lisky Bratva move into Transnistria, then Mr. Happy won't be happy any more.

He'll be lucky if he's not Mr. Hole-in-his-head. Happy's a potential ally against the Lisky Bratva, if they can convince him to trust them.

- A 1-point investigative **Gambling** spend can dig up a large and unusual bet made on the margin of defeat. If Abesoli doesn't play, then someone (presumably Mr. Happy) stands to make a killing.

If the agents do this little favor for him, then Happy will be very happy indeed. He'll supply them with what they need, and advise them on ways they can hurt the Lisky Bratva.

IGWE ABESOLI

SCENE TYPE: Hazard
LEADS-IN: Mr. Happy
LEADS-OUT: Deniable Assets

Abesoli is staying in a dacha outside Tiraspol, watched over by his FC Sheriff handlers and bodyguards. During the way, he trains in the dacha's gardens. However, he's bored and restless, so he demands to go clubbing in town at night. The agents need to locate Abesoli and prevent him from playing without arousing suspicion.

THE DACHA

The dacha is owned by Victor Gusan, but so is half the country. Finding it is tricky.

- **Photography:** The newspaper doesn't mention where Abesoli is staying, but one of the photos illustrating the article was taken on the grounds of the dacha. Coupling that with some **Research** or **Urban Survival,** or questioning the journalist, Valeria Prochnoyevna, with **Intimidation** or **Flirting** gets the location of the dacha.
  > A 1-point **Photography** spend lets the agent spot the telltale presence of bodyguards lurking in the background. Security is tight around Abesoli.
- If the agents get into the FC Sheriff training ground, then **Electronic Surveillance** or **Digital Intrusion** (Difficulty 2) can be used to get the location of Abesoli's dacha.
- Alternatively, **Streetwise** or **Research** turns up the fact that Abesoli has a special trainer assigned to him. Following this trainer (Difficulty 3 **Surveillance**) brings the agents to the dacha.
- **Streetwise** picks up rumors that Abesoli is a party animal (he grew up dirt-poor in Nigeria, and is now making up for lost time); **High Society** can even get the agents an invite to a popular nightclub where Abesoli is a regular customer. His handlers ensure that he doesn't do anything that would affect his performance on the pitch, but anything else is fair game for the boy king.

BYPASSING SECURITY

The dacha is in the middle of a forest, more than three miles from the nearest village. There is a single approach road, watched by armed guards. The dacha itself is surrounded by a four-metre-tall razor-wire fence that runs through the forest. (Difficulty 6 **Infiltration** to sneak into the dacha over the fence.) At any time, there are two guards at the gate, three more patrolling the house and grounds, and Abesoli is watched over at all times by another guard and two handlers.

- **Outdoor Survival** lets the agents make their way through the forest without being spotted, and identifies a point where trees overhang the razor-wire fence.
- With a few hours' observation, **Military Science** works out the guard patterns. They relax when Abesoli's inside the house; while the gate is always guarded, the gardens are watched only when Abesoli is training outside.
- **Human Terrain** spots the dacha's servants, who live in a nearby village. They're underpaid and almost invisible; bribing them can get the agents into the dacha.

When Abesoli goes to the football stadium or to the clubs, he's accompanied by his bodyguard and his two handlers in one car, and another three guards in a second car. The other guards remain at the dacha. He has a private table in a club attached to the Sheriff Casino.

THE PRODIGY

A year ago, Abesoli lived on the streets in Nigeria; now, he's got a seven-figure salary and is treated like a living god. It's all gone to his head, making him egotistical and entitled. **Flattery** works best when trying to manipulate him, and he's used to women throwing themselves at him with **Flirting**. He's also eager to be the big man, so he can be lured into gambling contests easily. He knows that the upcoming match is the most important of his career, but he believes he's bulletproof and invincible.

He enjoys the attention of fans and groupies. His handlers are less willing to let Abesoli talk to the public, but using **High Society, Negotiation** or a suitable **Cover** gets past them. Abesoli is especially interested in sponsorship deals; he imagines himself as the face of a brand of shoes or cologne, so anyone who might have connections to a big advertising agency (or, better yet, has forged credentials) gets a private audience.

MAKING THE HIT

The agents need to stop Abesoli playing, but without tipping the handlers off that it was a hit. Whatever they do needs to be entirely deniable.

- **Chemistry** or **Pharmacy** can whip up a mild case of poisoning,

if the agents can get the mickey finn into the boy's food or drink (Difficulty 4 **Filch**). To anyone who investigates, it'll look like accidental food poisoning.
- Anyone with **Hand-to-Hand 8+** has the martial arts knowledge to cripple Abesoli temporarily by hitting his knee or ankle. A Called Shot (see p. 72 of *Night's Black Agents*) is needed to inflict the right damage.
- Similarly, giving the boy a nasty case of whiplash from an accidental car crash can work. A well-timed crash (**Driving** Difficulty 5) coupled with disabling cell phones in the area ensures that Abesoli misses the match entirely.

- **Human Terrain** can identify the rural district of Nigeria that Abesoli hails from, which is a region notorious for its superstitions. **Occult Studies** can then be used to prepare a juju fetish to destroy Abesoli's confidence in his ability to play.
- Another option is breaking into the dacha with Infiltration, and then sabotaging Abesoli's equipment.

If the operation is completed successfully, then FC Tiraspol hold their rivals to a historic nil-all draw — which, given the disparity between the two teams, is a wonderful result. The agents can report back to Mr. Happy in *Deniable Assets*.

PENALTY SHOOT-OUT

If the agents fail to stop Abesoli from playing, then FC Sheriff go on to a crushing 5-nil victory. A furious Mr. Happy contacts the agents to berate them, and arranges for another meeting at the restaurant. There, the agent with the best **Notice** spots a new waiter with prison tattoos — and a concealed TEC-9 submachine pistol (damage +1) under his apron. It's a Lisky Bratva assassin (he's got **Shooting 8** and **Health** 8; his other stats are standard-issue thug).

Saving Mr. Happy's life from the assassin convinces the gangster to trust the agents. Move onto *Deniable Assets*.

DENIABLE ASSETS

SCENE TYPE: Conclusion
LEADS-IN: Igwe Abesoli
LEADS-OUT: Running Hot

Once the operation is complete, a very happy Happy contacts the agents again and invites them back to dinner. This time, the whole restaurant is filled with jubilant FC Tiraspol supporters. Happy escorts the agents into a private booth for their conversation. He becomes abruptly serious when discussing the Lisky Bratva.

- So far, the Lisky Bratva have only a minimal presence in Transnistria, but that won't last forever. There were local gangsters in Odessa, men like Victor Karabas, who believed Odessa should be run by the Odessans. He's dead now, shot by the *mafiyas*. Happy will do business with the Lisky Bratva, but he doesn't want them running the place and he doesn't want to end up like Karabas. Anything that hurts the Lisky Bratva buys him more time.

- The Lisky Bratva have a front company, Baldak Transit, that carries shipments from Odessa to Debrecen. These shipments are sometimes weapons, sometimes slaves, sometimes drugs… sometimes other things. Follow Baldak Transit, and you'll find the Lisky Bratva. Mr. Happy can get the agents access to EU transport and licensing databases, or the agents can hack in with **Digital Intrusion** (Difficulty 3). Using **Traffic Analysis (Core Clue)** to trace Baldak Transit movements in those databases leads the agents to *Shadow of the Vampire* (p. 35).
- The Lisky Bratva depends on Debrecen for its drug trade. If the agents can hit the *mafiya* hard there, it will hurt them a great deal. Using **Research (Core Clue)** turns up the name of a journalist, **Agi Kozorus**, who knows more about the Debrecen underworld than anyone else. This leads into *The Debrencen Gambit* (p. 40).

If the agents have made any other deals with Mr. Happy for equipment or supplies, he honors his side of the bargain. He also supplies them with vehicles if they need transportation, and can reduce their Heat by -2 by spreading false rumors about their movements.

WESTWARD BOUND

Getting into Moldova means a bureaucratic headache, as entering via Transnistria means they do not have an official Moldovan entry visa stamp. A **Forgery** spend can be used to fake a stamp; otherwise, the agents are delayed at the border crossing into Romania, reducing their Hot Lead by 1.

If the agents did everything right (seamlessly nobbled Abesoli, kept a low profile in Transnistria, stayed on Mr. Happy's good side) then Mr. Happy can provide them with Moldovan visas giving Cover 4.

SHADOW OF THE VAMPIRE

There are places where evil things sleep in the shadows under the world. One such place is a remote monastery in the Carpathian mountains called Dragovir, and for the last decade, the Lisky Bratva have sacrificed hundreds of victims every year to the things that slumber there.

The monastery is located high in the mountains, accessible only by a snow-bound and treacherous road that jackknifes up the steep slope. Grim stone walls stare out over a barren landscape, and the crumbling ruins of the monastery look like a set for a horror movie. Still, there are a few hardy souls who still live in the mostly-intact central building. The monastery is best known for a strange dry well at its heart.

As part of his research into vampirism and the creation of the zalozhniye, Dr. Dorjiev visited the Dragovir complex and reactivated it, continuing the worship/ritual sacrifice/experiments that were previously carried out there. The Lisky Bratva provide him with support and human victims. The nature of the Dragovir horror depends on what vampires are in your campaign.

✠ Formerly an Orthodox monastery, the monks turned to the worship of Satan when they were besieged by Turks. It is said that one in every seven monks was commanded by the abbot to spit on the crucifix and embrace the power of Hell, so that they might save the monastery's treasures from the enemy. Once the siege was broken, the abbot and his followers were chained to leaden cannonballs and thrown into the pit, Ever since, the monastery has been a weeping spiritual wound, home to dark forces. The monastery was abandoned in the 1970s, when the last monk threw himself from the mountaintop.

🦇 The monastery was built on the site of a much older structure, which was the home of a cult who worshipped vampires. The Church destroyed the cult, but was unable to eliminate their vampiric masters. They were, however, able to imprison the vampires underground. For many centuries, the monks served as jailers for the dead, but eventually began to follow the same dark path as the cultists they replaced. They were purged by a police raid in the 1970s.

👽 The monastery was taken over by Soviet scientists in the 1950s, who erected a satellite dish and a network of aerials and radar stations in the mountains around the monastery. The CIA believed it was a listening post to tap into NATO radio traffic in the Mediterranean, but the locals whispered about the strange lights that used to cluster around the mountaintops in stormy weather. Following a "fireball" incident in the 1970s, research was shut down.

☣ The experiments began in World War II. Scientists from Germany established a secret research centre away from prying eyes in Dragovic, and used Jewish and gypsy test subjects from the Romanian pogroms. When the Red Army rolled into Romania, the NKGB took control of the Dragovir site and scientists. The work continued, with dissidents and other "undesirables" added to the list of victims. The subjects were part of grotesque surgical and mutagenic experiments, which continued until a fire in the 1970s gutted part of the complex.

THE SHIPPING ROUTE

SCENE TYPE: Core
LEAD-IN: Running Hot, Deniable Assets
LEAD-OUT: Dragovir Village

Baldak Transit container trucks travel from Odessa to Dragovir once every few weeks. These containers are crammed with a human cargo. The Lisky Bratva recruits or kidnaps women for the sex trade, potential slave laborers, and even children for use as pickpockets. Not all of their victims make it to the brothels and flesh markets of Europe and Asia. Some are used as sacrifices to the Bratva's sinister masters.

The agents can discover this grisly trade through several possible **Core Clues**.

INTERCEPTING THE SHIPMENT

Each truck is operated by a crew of three, who take it in turns to drive. The crew have firearms concealed in a secret compartment in the truck cabin, as well as a night-vision camera that monitors the prisoners in the shipping container. Standard protocol is for the crew to contact their Lisky Bratva superiors by cellphone at least once per day.

According to the official papers, the truck is loaded with washing machines, and the back third of the truck in indeed crammed with actual cargo. One of the boxes is empty and can easily be moved aside to get access to the hellish inner compartment.

The inner part of the container is a prison for some twenty victims, crammed into a lightless metal box with only minimal food and water, and no sanitation. The floor is awash in urine and faeces. The prisoners have no idea where they are; all are suffering from exhaustion and malnutrition. Ages range between four and forty.

- Following Mr. Happy's tip-off about Baldak Shipping with **Traffic Analysis** indicates that Baldak trucks regularly make deliveries to an isolated village in the Carpathians.
- If the agents still have the RFID tracers from the Odessa job, then they can use **Electronic Surveillance** to search for the crates. Their detector starts beeping when a Baldak shipping truck passes by on the motorway. That truck must be carrying weapons from the Baghdad warehouse – and it's heading for Dragovir.
- **Interrogating** Lisky Bratva operatives or thugs can point the way towards Dragovir.

Getting to Dragovir means driving or taking a train and then a series of buses into the mountains. It's well off the beaten path, but at least it's an unexpected direction. Heading to Dragovir does not affect the agents' Hot Lead.

DRAGOVIR VILLAGE

SCENE TYPE: Core
LEAD-IN: The Shipping Route
LEAD-OUT: The Monastery

Dragovir village is a small community of a few dozen people, located in the valley below the monastery. The real road ends here; the only way up to the monastery is via a stony dirt track that the Baldak trucks cannot climb. Therefore, they unload the human cargo in a field outside Dragovir and then ferry them up by a small bus. The people of Dragovir know that something horrible is going on in the mountains, but the Lisky Bratva have intimidated them into keeping quiet.

ARRIVING IN DRAGOVIR

Dragovir sees only a few dozen visitors every year; there is a small guesthouse in town, mostly for visiting "businessmen." The village is a post-Soviet backwater, with high unemployment. If the agents visit the town openly, they'll be reported to the Lisky Bratva; they'll need to use **Disguise** (Difficulty 4) to blend in.

Human Terrain (Core Clue) suggests that the villagers are terrified of the Lisky Bratva, and identifies one older farmer as a potential leader. Voritz is a stout man with an iron-grey moustache; everyone in Dragovir respects him. He lives on a small farm outside the village, which makes for an excellent staging post. The farm is guarded by four huge wolfhounds; getting past them without being noticed is a Difficulty 7 **Infiltration** test or a 1-point **Outdoor Survival** spend; Voritz calls the dogs off before they kill anyone, although an unwary agent might get a nasty bite. Dog stats are on p. 69 of ***Night's Black Agents***.

Voritz is initially unwilling to talk to the agents, as he assumes they are more criminals from the Lisky Bratva. A suitable Interpersonal ability like **Reassurance** is needed to convince him that he's mistaken. Voritz can outline the Lisky Bratva security forces at the monastery, and the shipping schedule.

If the agents fail to follow up on the Voritz lead, then they'll spot the minibus passing through the town en route to the slave shipment. **Human Terrain** picks up on the sudden rise in tension, suggesting that the minibus is connected to something sinister.

THE SHIPMENT

Four hours before a new shipment of slaves arrives, the Lisky Bratva send a dozen guards down from the mountain in the minibus. These guards prepare the unloading site – a field a short distance outside town. Virgil's minibus waits there until the prisoners arrive at dusk. The prisoners are unloaded and corralled in the field by the armed guards, who wear night-vision goggles after nightfall. The prisoners are then transported, ten at a time, to the monastery via the minibus, with two guards accompanying each load. The drive through the village and up to the mountain takes 45 minutes, so it can take six hours to get a full load "processed."

- **Infiltration** and **Disguise** could be used if the agents want to sneak onto the field as prisoners. It's Difficulty 5 to sneak past the guards; a suitable distraction drops the difficulty by 2.
- **Military Science** or **Electronic Surveillance** can be used to spy on the guards and learn their patterns, so the agents can take them out in the dark.
- The guards have their hands full keeping watch and ensuring that none of the prisoners stumble off into the darkness, so a covert attack could eliminate several guards before the rest notice.

ENEMY ASSETS

There are Px5 guards and Px5 scientists in the monastery, commanded by three or four more experienced and tougher leaders. They've got plenty of firepower. If the Lisky Bratva have advance notice of the agents' presence, then add in one of their operatives, a zalozhniy, or both for added security.

The monastery approach road is watched at all times (the guards use night-vision goggles in the dark). The slopes of the mountain are swept by patrols at least four times a day; patrols also pass through the village once a day. Supplies are brought in from nearby towns once a day.

DR. VATHEK

Dorjiev's assistant and the head of research. Vathek is absolutely terrified of Dorjiev, who has a strange power over him (a curse spell, blood bond, tailored alien virus to which only Dorjiev has the cure). He carries out most of the procedures at the monastery in his master's absence.

- The researcher hasn't slept properly in years. His eyes are haunted, and his body hangs limply as though he was already hanged. He's a man on the edge of collapse, being forced on by Dorjiev's will. He'd kill himself if he had the courage.
- Vathek breaks easily under **Interrogation**. If captured, he'll spill what he knows about Dorjiev and the Lisky Bratva.
- He once tried to murder Dorjiev by dosing him with a lethal poison, enough to kill him a hundred times over. The doctor just smiled and finished his dinner calmly, then told Vathek that he would be punished for his disobedience. That's when Dorjiev established whatever unbreakable hold he has over Vathek.

VIRGIL

The simple-minded driver of the bus to the monastery. He doesn't actually understand that he is bringing people to their deaths.

- Virgil is a local boy from the village. His family were killed by the Lisky Bratva and taken for use as test subjects. He believes they are still alive in the well, and sometimes goes to "talk" to them.
- **Reassurance** is actually the best approach to use on Virgil. He gets aggressive when attacked or threatened, but accepts orders if he believes that everything is ok.

BRONISLAV

Head of security for the monastery. He was once one of the Lisky Bratva's high flyers, but he displeased Josef Lisky, and got effectively exiled to the occult equivalent of Siberia. He drinks heavily, and samples the more attractive sacrifices before handing them over to the dark priests or twisted scientists.

- Lately, he's taken to terrorising the villagers in the valley below. He's rapidly becoming a liability for the Lisky Bratva, and may be eliminated. The assassin could even arrive at Dragovir around the same time as the agents.

- Use Soldier stats for Bronislav; he's an Afghan War veteran. He carries a 9mm Makarov PMM pistol (+1 damage) and a combat knife (-1 damage) everywhere; if he has enough warning, he will armor up (military-grade armor; -3 against explosives or bullets) and grab an AK-74 (+0 assault rifle).
- The best Interpersonal skill to use when dealing with Bronislav is **Shooting.**

THREAT RESPONSE

If the Lisky Bratva suspect the agents or another threat is present, then kill teams of guards led by one of the officers or an operative is dispatched to hunt for them in a 4x4.

If the monastery's overwhelmed, then they hit the panic button. Dr. Vathek starts incinerating any research notes or books of blasphemous lore, and any remaining prisoners are dumped into the pit to get rid of the evidence. In the confusion, the well cover may be removed – see *Out of the Pit*, p. 38.

THE MONASTERY

SCENE TYPE: Hazard
LEAD-IN: Dragovir Village
LEAD-OUT: Secrets of the Monastery

The Lisky Bratva's efforts are centred on the monastery.

APPROACHES

Checking the monastery on commercial satellite imagery using **Data Recovery** gives a general outline of the structure, and the information that there's only one path up the hillside. With a 1-point spend, depending on your vampires, the satellite image shows a weird blur over the courtyard. It's present in every image; in other words, it's not a transient optical or computer effect.

THE MOUNTAINSIDE

Getting up the mountain without being detected is tricky. There is only one path up the hillside, and that's watched. The other sides of the mountain are steep enough to be hazardous in places – anyone with **Outdoor Survival** can make it up without any problems, but other agents must make **Athletics** tests (Difficulty 4) to avoid getting into trouble and attracting attention. Once they reach the upper slopes of the monastery, the agents must make **Infiltration** tests (Difficulty 5) to get up to the monastery without being spotted. (Difficulty 4 if the agents have kept a low profile in the village.)

THE ROAD

The agents can drive up the dirt road, but they'll be spotted instantly.

If spotted, the guards try to turn the agents away, claiming the monastery is government property and is not open to visitors – or they just open fire, depending on whether or not they know the agents are in the area.

If the agents sneak up in Virgil's minibus, they can get past the guards and drive straight into the courtyard through the main gates – the guards don't even bother checking.

THE MONASTERY UP CLOSE

The monastery squats like a stone toad on the mountainside. The main structure is a squat, steep-walled building that contains the church and most of the monastery cells. Gargoyles and strangely distorted statues decorate the exterior. On either side are long low outbuildings. The eastern building has mostly collapsed, while the western side is largely intact. The Lisky Bratva have erected prefabs and tents in the ruins of the eastern side. A smaller chapel completes the quadrangle, enclosing a small courtyard.

- **Architecture (Core Clue):** In the middle of the courtyard is a covered well shaft. This well shaft is guarded night and day.

A palpable aura of decay and death hangs over the place. At night, huge flocks of bats wheel around the monastery's spire.

- **Archaeology/Architecture/ History:** That main section is built like a fortress. Getting in there will be very hard. A better approach would be to circle around the monastery and enter through the western outbuildings or the northern chapel.
- **Mechanic** or **Notice:** No power lines up here, but there's a satellite dish on the roof. There's probably a diesel electric generator somewhere in the outbuildings. Taking that out would disrupt whatever the Lisky Bratva are doing here.
- **Forensic Pathology:** Some of those prefabs are definitely being used for medical research; there are airlocks and disinfectant sprays everywhere, suggesting they're working with a potential pathogen.
- **Data Recovery (Core Clue):** That satellite dish looks like it's connected to a satellite modem. That implies there's a computer system here. If the agents get to that computer, see *Secrets of the Monastery*.

The complex is enormous, and much of it still lies in ruins. Wiring it for alarms would be almost impossible; the Lisky Bratva doesn't believe it's necessary given its remote location. Getting in from the west or north is easy, therefore, but sneaking through the monastery still requires an **Infiltration** test (Difficulty 6). If the agents haven't attacked anyone in town or otherwise drawn notice to their presence, the test is at Difficulty 5: all the guards have -1 Alertness Modifiers until the first alarms sound.

If successful, the agents make it to the computer room without being spotted. If failed, then the alarm is raised and the agents have to run or fight their way out – either way, run *Out of the Pit*.

OUT OF THE PIT

The covered well is the heart of the darkness in the monastery. The victims of the Lisky Bratva are placed in the well. The cover is a heavy steel plate, resembling the lid of a missile silo. A hatch allows the Lisky Bratva access to the horrors below, and they only open it when they have to. Imagine a necropolis crossed with a nuclear reactor crossed with alligator feeding time, and you've got the right vibe. Heavy armed guards prise up the hatch, do what they have to (throw in sacrifices/dispose of experimental subjects/etc) and then slam it shut and count their blessings that it didn't eat them too.

So, there's a pit of horrors ready to devour friend and foe alike. Obviously, this has to open while the agents are sneaking around the monastery. Blowing open the hatch is a great way for the agents to wipe out the Lisky Bratva at the monastery (assuming the agents can get clear of the ensuing carnage). The Lisky Bratva might open the hatch if they're being overrun, or the agents' sabotage might accidentally result in whatever's down there breaking free. Ancient horrors deserve a chance to eat people.

Whatever happens, the agents can use the ensuing chaos to find the computer system and steal data from the Lisky Bratva – or else flee before they're eaten.

The precise nature of the horror depends on vampires in the Director's campaign. In each case, the Lisky Bratva's research should parallel the nature of the Nigredo/Albedo/Rubedo – don't give the game away yet, but hint that they're experimenting with a variation on whatever St. John used on the Saudi royal family all those years ago.

Whatever the horror is, it's a 6-point **Stability** loss.

- ⊕ The pit is used for ritual sacrifices to whatever demonic powers are responsible for loosing vampirism upon the world. The pit is a portal to Hell itself; when opened, flames and sulphurous fumes belch out. The victims are anointed in a ghastly black mass in the main monastery, then chained together and thrown into the pit to be consumed. Spying on this ceremony with **Occult Studies** may give vital clues about the Albedo and Rubedo. When the well is opened, a shambling horde of blackened, burnt zombies crawls forth, linked to one another with red-hot chains. Use the Zombie statistics on p. 154 of *Night's Black Agents*.

- ⛤ A vampiric entity is bound by a tremendously powerful Block built into the well cover; analyzing the cover with **Archaeology** or a similar skill could give a useful clue as to how to stop the zalozhniye. The Lisky Bratva provide this horror with a supply of blood in exchange for power and information. Centuries of imprisonment have driven the creature insane even by the monstrous standards of its kind, so the Lisky Bratva dare not free it. Victims have their throats slit, and are then hung upside-down on hooks just inside the lip of the well. Opening the well frees the creature; the murony (p. 152 of *Night's Black Agents*) is a good model for a blood-hungry *presence* that crawls from the well — the full entity cannot make it past the Block, but its blood-thirst can materialize to prey on the warm lives in the monastery above.

- 👽 The medical experiments at Dragovir are aimed at creating a controllable form of alien hybrid. Thus far, they have been grotesquely unsuccessful — they can turn humans into monsters through exposure to extraterrestrial matter and surgical modification, but the process has so far failed to create a stable form that can survive in our world. The well is a containment facility; the failed hybrids are both protected and constrained by an electromagnetic field; when the cover is opened, crackling electric blue light shines out like a searchlight into the night sky. The interior walls of the well are marked with strange burns, seared into the rock with bursts of impossible radiation. Analyzing these marks with **Astronomy** reveals clues about how the aliens arrived on Earth — maybe the burns depict the constellations of the night sky over Wabar hundreds of years ago. **Photography** may be needed to capture the image. If freed, the hybrid entities swarm out of the containment facility in the well and stumble across the monastery, warping space and time with their weird gravity unless they explode under the pressure of our local physics. The explosion is like a silent nuclear blast that wipes Dragovir off the mountain.

- ⛤ Stacked in the monastery cellars are lead-sealed coffins containing victims of whatever force creates mutant vampires. Organs, blood and tissue from these mostly-dead corpses is surgically transplanted into the prisoners, who are used as living culture media for the vampiric bio-matter. The vampirism eats them from the inside out like a hemophagic tumor. Studying this grisly process with **Forensic Pathology** identifies a potential weakness in the vampiric virus — maybe vampires are vulnerable to a common medication, like blood thinners, or perhaps vampires can be detected with a simple medical test. Once the vampiric element is strong enough, it is harvested to be used in the creation of zalozhniye; the husks of the prisoners are discarded into the mass grave at the bottom of the well. Some of the prisoners retain a little of the unnatural vampiric strength, and rise out of the mass grave as zombies (use the Zombie statistics on p. 154 of *Night's Black Agents*).

SECRETS OF THE MONASTERY

SCENE TYPE: Conclusion
LEAD-IN: The Monastery
LEAD-OUT: Running Hot

Before the monastery is destroyed, the agents have a chance to pick up some juicy clues about the Lisky Bratva, their experiments, Dorjiev, and their connection to the Conspiracy. Pick from the ones listed here or roll your own, but whatever the agents find should both justify the danger of attacking the monastery, and point towards a way to damage the Lisky Bratva and the Conspiracy.

- **Notice:** There's a nameplate on the door of the room where the agents find all these juicy clues. A bloody handprint makes the name hard to read, but picking away some of the gore reveals DORJIEV.

- **CREATION OF ZALOZHNIYE:** A folder of documents labelled RESEARCH PROJECT 4 appears to be bland bureaucracy at first glance, but digging into it with a combination of **Forensic Pathology** and **Vampirology** (and **Languages**, if necessary) reveals that it is actually Dr. Dorjiev's original notes on the making of zalozhniye. It describes whatever method he uses for animating the creatures after their untimely death (necromancy, alien time-slips, a combination of hydrogen sulfide, LSD, conditioning, and the Von Dippel formula), as well as notes on how the creatures grow stronger after murder. Reading this dossier gives the agents a pool of 5 points that can be spent on any test or point spend related to the zalozhniye.

- **BLOCKING THE ZALOZHNIYE:** Related to the above — the agents find information describing a technique for blocking the zalozhniye. It might be a suppressed religious text, a magical compulsion (maybe the creatures are repelled by the ticking of a clock, or grave dirt), or a scientific formula (like a particular

chemical compound or a blast of electromagnetic radiation).
- A dossier on the Philbys, St. John and Kim, highlighting St. John's travels in Arabia, his conversion to Islam, Kim's defection to the Soviet Union and his debriefing by Arkady Shevlenko. It's obvious that the dossier has been actively updated by Lisky Bratva researchers at Dragovir, despite the lack of a clear connection between the vampiric horror in the monastery and the affairs of two dead spies. This dossier gives a pool of 5 points for tests or spends relating to investigating the Philbys.
- The agents find an encrypted hard drive. Breaking it with **Cryptography** turns up some poor-quality digital copies of film footage, documenting Dorjiev's experiments in creating the first zalozhniy. Other videos show bizarre experiments involving victims being blown up or tortured. Analyzing these videos with **Data Recovery** shows odd time jumps and discontinuities, just like the agents experienced in the Odessa catacombs in the presence of the zalozhniy. Buried deep on the drive is one especially strange video.

It shows Dorjiev putting a single bullet in a revolver, then putting it to his head and pulling the trigger five times. The gun never goes off. A close analysis of the video shows there's a time jump between two of the trigger pulls… as if the sixth time the hammer fell, the gun went off, but the moment when Dorjiev was shot never happened. An agent with **Vampirology** or **Occult Studies** could make the leap that Dorjiev managed to somehow exploit the same time-warping phenomenon encountered in that catacomb in Odessa.

THE DEBRECEN GAMBIT

SCENE TYPE: Introduction
LEAD-IN: Running Hot
LEAD-OUT: Finding Kozorus

When the red tide of the Soviet Union retreated from Hungary, it left Debrecen like brutalist concrete driftwood. Parts of the town's endless grey labyrinth are controlled by criminal gangs, and it has become a gateway into Western Europe for drug and sex traffic. Two great invisible rivers of the underworld cross here. The heroin traffic from Albania, controlled largely by the powerful Serbian *Naša Stvar* (literally, "Our Thing," like the Cosa Nostra), intersects with the flow of guns and girls from the east, in which the Lisky Bratva is a major player. In a grim, Soviet-era industrial park on the edge of the city, the Lisky Bratva trade one illicit cargo for another, purchasing heroin and hard cash from the Serbians. This trade fuels the Lisky Bratva's expansion into the West.

It is dangerous to talk too much about the Lisky Bratva. Anyone who does so is dealt with, one way or another. So far, the organization has remained concealed, and few outside the criminal fraternity know anything about their operations.

There is one biting flea at the moment, an irritation that will soon be dealt with. **Agi Kozorus** is a young Hungarian journalist and blogger. Her father was a gangster and career criminal, so she picked up the skills and patois of the underworld at a young age. Her field of expertise is the criminal underworld of Hungary, and in the last two years she discovered the trail of the Lisky Bratva. She's even come to suspect that there is something unnatural about them, and that just whetted her appetite for their secrets.

The Lisky Bratva applied the usual pressures to get rid of her. They bribed her editor, so now she self-publishes most of her work online and writes articles for international magazines. They threatened her with anonymous phone calls, but she grew up surrounded by hard men and criminals, and can swear and intimidate like the most vicious *chainik* (prison bully). They burnt down her flat, but she climbed out a window and escaped, and now she sleeps on an endless succession of friends' couches and cheap hotels. Kozorus is a problem for the Lisky Bratva… and a potentially game-changing asset for their enemies.

IDENTIFYING KOZORUS

Any of these counts as a **Core Clue**:

- Mr. Happy in Transnistria can point the agents towards Kozorus.
- Using **Research, Criminology** or **Traffic Analysis** flags up a series of blog posts and articles written by one Agi Kozorus about crime in Hungary and the surrounding countries. She mentions Josef Lisky and Dorjiev by name, and is obviously knowledgeable about the Lisky Bratva's operations.
- **Streetwise** or **Cop Talk** in Debrecen mentions up Kozorus as a good source — if you can track her down.
- Similarly, a Network contact can send the agents after Kozorus.

FINDING KOZORUS

SCENE TYPE: Core
LEAD-IN: The Debrecen Gambit
LEAD-OUT: The Target And The Tiger

The young journalist moves around frequently to avoid retribution. Her tradecraft is excellent for a layperson; she never sleeps in the same place twice, keeps several unconnected circles of friends, and uses evasive manoeuvres when on the streets. Just knowing her name isn't enough to get in contact with Agi Kozorus. The agents have to put in special effort to find her. Locating her can be considered a **Core Clue** for any of the abilities below; spending 2 points from the investigative ability or 2 points of Hot Lead means that the agents find her sooner (see *Advance Warning*, below), and so have a better chance of saving her in the ambush. If not, they only find her *Perhaps Too Late* (see p. 42).

- **Streetwise:** After a lot of snooping around, the agents meet **Tomas**, an anarchist friend of Agi's. He claims not to have seen her recently, but **Bullshit Detector** tags this as a lie – he's covering for her. if the agents present proof of their *bona fides* and give him a reason to trust them (or force him to talk), then he admits that Agi went to meet an informant at the Debrecen Zoo.
- **Digital Intrusion:** It takes a lot of work (it's Difficulty 8 to do it in time, Difficulty 6 to do it late), and the use of some cutting-edge tools, but the agent is able to get into one of Korozus' email accounts. One of her recent conversations is with an informant inside the Lisky Bratva. From the tone of the conversation, it is clear that Korozus is suspicious of the informant, but she's agreed to a meeting at the zoo. There's a photo of the accountant attached to one of the photos – it's a scan of his ID card from the Black Sea Bank.
- **Cop Talk:** The Lisky Bratva have got their tentacles into the Hungarian police, but the agents are able to identify a trustworthy detective named **Gaspar**. He knows Agi; he thinks she's a fool who'd going to herself killed, but he admires her courage. She spoke to him a few days ago, and asked a favor of him – she wanted to make him to make sure that the uniformed officers in the area around Debrecen Zoo were clean today.
- **Interrogation:** The agents capture a Lisky Bratva goon and find a sheaf of surveillance photos of Agi Kozorus in his jacket. Under interrogation, he admits that a zalozhniy has been dispatched to eliminate the girl. He doesn't know what the plan is, but he does know where – Debrecen Zoo.

Her informant claims to be an accountant in the Black Sea Bank, who has discovered evidence that the Lisky Bratva is laundering money through the institution. He's actually being played by the criminals. They knew someone in the bank was disloyal, so they fed a "barium meal" through the system – an easily traceable piece of intel – that he then passed onto Kozorus. This allowed the Lisky Bratva to identify both the journalist and her source.

AGI KOZORUS

Kozorus grew up surrounded by criminals and gangsters. From her father, she learned the secrets of the criminal fraternity – how to torture a man, how to pick a lock, how to escape prison and how to rule. From her mother, she learned to hate her abusive and cruel father. Korozus is an unlikely journalist, and looks more like an anarchist street thug than a writer with her tattoos and too-big leather jacket, but she makes up with insider knowledge and venomous passion what she lacks in formal education.

She's paranoid and stand-offish, slow to trust anyone. She does have a gift for making friends, which has allowed her to establish her network of allies and contacts. When playing her, give as little away as possible, and treat the agents as useful tools instead of friends until they really prove they are able to help her hurt the Lisky Bratva. Once they do so, they have a friend for life in Agi Kozorus.

THE TARGET AND THE TIGER

SCENE TYPE: Hazard
LEAD-IN: Finding Kozorus
LEAD-OUT: Burning the Lisky Bratva

The Debrecen Zoo was founded in the late 1950s. It's located a short drive outside the city, and covers around half-a-dozen hectares of countryside with animal paddocks and temperature-controlled houses. Harmless creatures like small monkeys roam free within the grounds, but most of the crowds flock to the houses and pens where the more dangerous creatures dwell. Notably, there's the tiger house…

THE MEET

Here's how Agi Kozorus intends for the meeting to go down. She's arranged to meet the informant near the tiger house, in an open plaza where several paths through the zoo cross. It's a high-traffic area, minimizing the risk of foul play if it turns out to be a trap. She'll arrive early and take the small electric train that travels through part of the zoo, allowing her to scope out the meeting site without having to pass through it. If she likes what she sees, she'll then double back and make contact. The informant will pass vital information about the Lisky Bratva onto her. The two will then take separate routes out of the zoo.

Here's what the Lisky Bratva have in mind. They'll allow Agi to spot the informant. Their agents will then move in from all sides. They won't threaten her directly. Instead, they'll rely on the journalist's paranoia. If Korozus feels trapped, she'll try to break out, and the Bratva thugs have left a clear escape route for her – in through the tiger house, where the zalozhniy waits. The monster will first kill one of the staff members, steal a uniform and herd the public out of the house for "cleaning." It will then free the tigers and dose them with a chemical cocktail of adrenaline and synthetic hormones to make them angry and aggressive. When Kozorus tries to escape into the tiger house, she'll be torn apart by the wild beasts – another high-profile "accident" that sends the right message to anyone else who might consider crossing the Lisky Bratva. As for the informant, he'll be grabbed and sent to Dragovir Monastery as punishment for betrayal.

The wild card in both scenarios is the presence of the agents.

ADVANCE WARNING

If the agents find about the meeting well in advance, they can arrive early and spot the Lisky Bratva preparations.

- **Urban Survival:** The agent notices the electric train that runs through on elevated tracks through the zoo. That would be a good way to reconnoitre the area from above. If an agent heads up to the train, **Surveillance** (Difficulty 2) spots Agi Korozus with a high-powered camera, taking long-distance photos of her informant. Spotting Kozorus from the ground is a Difficulty 5 test of Surveillance.

THE ACCOUNTANT

The Black Sea Bank accountant, **Gergely Sandor**, gets captured and eliminated by the Lisky Bratva unless the agents rescue him. If they do so, then a terrified Sandor begs them to help him disappear. In exchange, he tells the agents about the Black Sea Bank, how it is the financial arm of the Lisky Bratva – and how it's recently been ordered to leverage all its assets to purchase the Swiss Koernersbank. See *The Boxmen* operation (p. 80) for more details.

DEAD KOZORUS

If killed, Agi continues the fight from beyond the grave. She suspected that the meeting was an ambush, so she stashed her research notes in an encrypted email account. If she doesn't log back in within three hours of the meeting, her notes automatically get emailed to several friends and contacts of hers, as well as posted on an anonymous webserver. **Tradecraft** lets the agents guess that Agi might have taken such a precaution, and Tomas or Gaspar, as described in *Finding Kozorus* (p. 41), might be recipients of Agi's notes.

The notes include a reference to the human trafficking camp (*Trading in Misery*, p. 44), but don't have the details of the meeting with the Serbians in *The Golden Calf*. Agi's notes also give the agents a 3-point pool that can be spent on any investigation related to the Lisky Bratva's mundane criminal activities.

- **Tradecraft:** There are several people out there in the crowd who are acting strangely. At first glance, they look like ordinary visitors to the zoo, but none of them have kids with them, and they're never going that far from the plaza. It looks like the informant has a floating box of watchers keeping eyes on him.
- **Outdoor Survival:** Something really has the animals spooked over by the tiger house. They're nervous – it's not the presence of predators, it's something else. There's something *wrong* over there that the animals are picking up on.

Agents who arrive early can make contact with Kozorus before the trap is sprung. They've got about twenty seconds to convince her they're not part of a Lisky Bratva trap before she rabbits. **Reassurance** spends coupled with a good story are needed; if Kozorus mistakes the agents for Lisky Bratva, she runs.

PERHAPS TOO LATE

If the agents don't get advance warning of the meeting, then they arrive just as the trap is sprung. They see Agi Kozorus stroll across the plaza towards her contact… then her pace slows as she realizes that something's wrong. Suddenly, eight figures move out of the crowd, blocking her exits. None of them are obviously threatening, but they are all carrying bags or wearing heavy jackets that could conceal weapons. Kozorus turns and heads towards the only exit left to her – the tiger house. Four of the threatening goons follow her; the other four follow the informant as he panics and runs.

If the agents don't act when this happens, then Kozorus gets eaten by the tigers. (Remember to boost the Health and Athletics pools of the zalozhniy when this happens.)

ESCAPING THE TRAP

The Lisky Bratva want to avoid a messy incident, so they'll only draw guns and start shooting when they're out of sight of the public (or if the agents force their hands). Their plan revolves around intimidation and fear, not brute force – at least until the tigers get involved.

Enemy assets on site are:

- At least eight goons, and up to Px4 goons if there are more than four player characters. Most are dressed as tourists,

DRUG-FUELLED TIGER

POUNCE AND MAUL: If the tiger jumps at a victim, the victim gets to make an Athletics test (Difficulty 6, or 4 if the tiger's at 2 or less Health). If the test fails, then the tiger gets to spend Athletics point to boost its damage — every two points spent increases its damage by 1.
GENERAL ABILITIES: Athletics 10, Fighting 8, Health 8
HIT THRESHOLD: 4
ALERTNESS MODIFIER: +3 (keen smell and hearing)
STEALTH MODIFIER: -2 (normally +1, but these beasts aren't in the mood to hide)
DAMAGE MODIFIER: +0 (bite); +1 (claw)
ARMOR: -2 (thick fur)

but a few might be disguised as park staff for extra chaos.
- One zalozhniy, lurking at the tiger house. If the agents disrupt the trap, the zalozhniy goes after them instead.
- Two tigers shot full of drugs, making them extremely aggressive.

Offsite, but available if needed are:

- One corrupt police officer, who'll shunt any Heat generated by the Lisky Bratva onto the agents (up to a maximum of Heat 5).
- More goons. These guys aren't as restrained as the ones assigned to the zoo mission, and are more likely to use deadly force.
- Another Operative (see p. 9).

Kozorus has a safe-house back in Debrecen, but first the agents need to get out of the zoo. Possible chance/combat complications here:

- Panicked crowds of tourists
- Taking a detour through an animal paddock. What vampire espionage adventure is complete without someone getting trampled by an elephant?
- Crocodile pools
- Rampaging tigers
- Zoo staff with tranquilizer guns trying to stop the rampaging tigers
- Exiting through the gift shop

If the agents can't get to Lead 10 by the time they escape the zoo, then switch to a car chase. Kozorus has a motorcycle hidden in the undergrowth just outside the zoo (she never leaves her transport in the open any more, to avoid sabotage).

BURNING THE LISKY BRATVA

SCENE TYPE: Subplot
LEAD-IN: The Target and The Tiger
LEADS-OUT: Trading in Misery, The Golden Calf, Running Hot

If Kozorus is extracted from the zoo successfully, then she brings the agents back to one of her safehouses — a basement flat in a tenement in the worst part of the city. The single mattress works, the electricity usually works, and the internet connection might work. Everything else is a crapshoot. If Kozorus is still jumpy, more **Reassurance** is needed to get her to talk.

Once she trusts the agents, she gives them all the help she can. Specifically, there are two targets which, if hit, would significantly impact the Lisky Bratva.

First, she knows where their human-trafficking ring has its main European distribution node. Packed cargo containers from the east are brought to a grim holding facility near the Romanian border. Those who survived the journey intact are smuggled over the border; she doesn't know what happens to the rest. Hitting that facility would disrupt their trade in misery. She doesn't know its exact location, but **Data Recovery (Core Clue)** coupled with her knowledge of the general area lets the agents find it on satellite photos. They could go there right now if the agents want — but it's a fortress.

Second, a representative from the Lisky Bratva is meeting with someone named **Todor Babic** in four days' time.

Criminology (Core Clue) identifies him as a boss from the Serbian mafia. Presumably, he's here to discuss the continuing partnership between the two organisations. The meeting takes place in an exclusive restaurant, the *Golden Calf*, in the city centre. It's owned by the Serbians.

Attempting either heist slows the agents down. Drop their Hot Lead by 1 if they go after the distribution facility, and by 3 if they go after the *Naša Stvar* meeting. Neither heist is a core scene — if the agents want to press on to Vienna, they can do so, but that means the Lisky Bratva will have more assets to throw at them later in the operation.

NIGHT'S BLACK AGENTS — THE ZALOZHNIY QUARTET

TRADING IN MISERY

SCENE TYPE: Subplot
LEAD-IN: Burning The Lisky Bratva
LEAD-OUT: Running Hot

The drive out of Debrecen is only about 20 kilometers, but no road signs seemingly exist in the area, a leftover gift of the Soviet occupiers, who maintained the whole region as a closed military zone. Finding a specific location requires either a local guide (**Tradecraft** considers this inadvisable), GPS coordinates (obtainable from the satellite imagery with a **Data Recovery** spend), or several hours of driving around in circles.

THE HUMAN TRAFFICKING FACILITY

Calling it a "distribution node" or "clearing house" doesn't do justice to this place. "Concentration camp" paints a more accurate picture. It's located in the abandoned shell of a failed Soviet-era factory, and those who live nearby know better than to ask questions. Trucks cross the border from Romania with their cargo and arrive here. Some victims stay in the camp for only a few minutes before they are loaded into another truck or into the back of a car. Others are confined here for weeks, either because they are too sick to travel, or because there is a delay further down the stream. Others will never leave here at all — the thing in Dragovir is not the only blood-hungry horror that the Lisky Bratva must service.

75% of the victims in the camp are female; most of them are under 20 years of age.

INVESTIGATION & RECONNAISSANCE

Kozorus knows where the camp is, but she's never been able to get close to it. It's heavily guarded.

- **Data Recovery:** The old factory and the surrounding forest gives a lot of cover, but the characters can get a general layout from satellite photos. The main road approaches from the south-east; to the north there are steep hills. It's surrounded by forests and more wasteland.
  - A **1-point Architecture** spend identifies a potential covert access route — a waste pipe from the old factory empties into a nearby river. The agents could sneak up the pipe into the heart of the camp.
  - Another **1-point Data Recovery** spend lets the agents miraculously resolve the photos enough to make out the shadows of individual guards.
- **Architecture** or **History:** That "factory" was certainly an old Soviet-era weapons-assembly facility.
  - **Research** or **Chemistry:** No wonder the place is abandoned — it's a toxic hellhole. Lots of nasty contamination from heavy metals.
  - A **1-point Architecture** spend lets the agents sketch out the floor plans and then (with a **1-point Military Science** spend) guess at the number of guards.
- A 1-point **Outdoor Survival** spend lets an agent sneak through the surrounding wilderness and get a good look at the camp's defences and manpower.
- A 1-point **Traffic Analysis** spend lets the agents monitor both physical and electronic traffic at the base.
- Once the agents have reconnoitred the base, a 1-point **Military Science** spend gives the agents an idea of likely opposition.

DEFENSES

The base is guarded by Px10 mooks and Px2 bosses (*tsekhoviki*, factory bosses). Optionally, throw in another P/2 operative-level bad guys for added toughness. (Alternatively, if the PCs ran into an Operative earlier and didn't kill him, then you can bring him back for an encore). They're all armed and dangerous.

Add in half-a-dozen non-combatant staff, mostly medics. Each of these prisoners is worth $30,000 or more to the Lisky Bratva over the course of a lifetime in prostitution, so the criminals have a vested interest in keeping at least some of them alive. On average, there are between 90 and 200 prisoners in the camp at any time.

Added problems to overcome:

- Bear traps (+2 damage) and tripwires in the surrounding forests – nothing immediately lethal, but crippling and nasty. A **Notice** or **Outdoor Survival** spend gets the team through unscathed; otherwise, it's time for **Sense Trouble** (Difficulty 4) to spot the traps.
- The approach road is equipped with buried claymore mines. **Notice** or **Military Science** spots them in advance; **Explosive Devices** (Difficulty 4) can be used to disarm them, or else **Driving** (Difficulty 5) to get past before they're remotely detonated.
- The camp is patrolled by guard dogs and their handlers. The dogs are used to keep the prisoners in line.

INSIDE THE CAMP

Chain-link fences, crumbling concrete, cavernous empty halls, the acrid smell of heavy metals burning the agents' mucous membranes – and everywhere, the overwhelming atmosphere of despair and suffering. Security is tight, but it's mostly focussed inwards. They want to make sure the prisoners don't escape; protecting the camp from intruders is less of a priority. The prisoners are crowded into shipping containers or the cellars. They stare, hollow-eyed and terrified, out at their captors. Some still delude themselves that they are being taken to a better life in the West, but most of them know they are doomed to a life of suffering and exploitation.

Worse horrors wait below. The Lisky Bratva's backers demand their cut of the human trade. Money is no use to these sinister immortals – they are paid in a different coin. Add a nightmarish processing facility to the basement that mirrors the nature of the vampire in your game. If they are traditional bloodsucking fiends, then some of the prisoners are drained of their blood by stainless-steel surgical leech-machines. If they are alien monsters, then the prisoners are blasted with alien radiation to make them more palatable to their masters. All that's worth a 3-point **Stability** loss.

TAKING OUT THE CAMP

The great thing about a human trafficking camp in the middle of a toxic wilderness, away from prying eyes, is that the agents get to cut loose should they want to break out the guns and the high explosives. If they've got the firepower, they can launch their own little private war. The best approach for this tactic is to sneak in via the underground tunnel, take out as many guards as possible covertly, and then go loud and throw the camp into chaos. Call for **Infiltration** tests at Difficulty 5 to get in without being seen.

Alternatively, the agents can use Agi's media contacts. If they can provide her with photographs, documents and other proof that the camp exists, she can pass it on to international magazines and anti-slavery groups, and from there it will filter through to Interpol. If the camp is dragged into the light, the Hungarian authorities have to take action. However, this won't so much hurt the Lisky Bratva's operations (they'll simply move to another deserted hell-hole in a countryside replete with them) as delay them for a bit.

THE GOLDEN CALF

SCENE TYPE: Subplot
LEAD-IN: Burning the Lisky Bratva
LEAD-OUT: Running Hot

The arrangement between the Serbian Naša Stvar and the Lisky Bratva is up for renegotiation. The Russians have sent two of Josef Lisky's most trusted agents to carry out the negotiations, and Josef himself will finalize the deal by phone.

SERBIAN SPECIALTIES

Korozus knows where the meeting is being held – the exclusive (and mafia-owned) Golden Calf restaurant. Excellent food, even better security.

INVESTIGATION & RECONNAISSANCE

- **Tradecraft:** Whenever there are important guests at the restaurant, a black van parks in the alleyway behind the building. Extra backup for the restaurant's security teams, probably armed guards.
- **Art History:** The owner (well, operator) of the Golden Calf is an art collector and investor, and he's always on the look-out for new pieces. He shows off new acquisitions by hanging them in the restaurant – the agents could use this to smuggle weapons, explosives or bugging devices into the restaurant.
- **Streetwise, Criminology,** or **Cop Talk** spends get the agents the jackets for the four principal negotiators (see below).
- **High Society** can get the agents dinner reservations before the night of the meeting: see *Getting into the Restaurant*, below, for what they might find. Priming the maitre'd with a bribe (**Negotiation**), other incentives (**Flirting**), or a good cover story (**Disguise** (Difficulty 6) to impersonate a member of either the Lisky Bratva or the Serbian mob) makes sure they're on the reservation list the night of the deal as well. Failing that, a 1-point **High Society** spend also gets the agents a table on the night they want.

GETTING INTO THE RESTAURANT

Security is tight – there's a metal detector in the main doorway, some of the staff are clearly ex-military (**Military Science**), and there are security cameras everywhere.

The agents are checked for weapons as they come in; the suave maitre'd politely requires that guests leave any "memorabilia" with the doorman, and anyone who comes armed will be closely watched by the staff. Between the dining room and the street, there's an entrance lobby, a small waiting room and a bar, all of which are guarded – trying to force an entrance is tricky.

There's also a private room upstairs that overlooks the main dining area. That's where the meeting will be held.

Once the agents get a look inside the restaurant, they can use…

- **Electronic Surveillance:** Those security cameras are live – they're being actively monitored, not just passively recording. There are more cameras outside. If the agents are going to sneak around, they'll need to use **Digital Intrusion** (Difficulty 4) or some other form of sabotage.
- **Military Science:** Two guards at the door. Two more at the foot of the stairs. About half-a-dozen staff who might stop an intruder. Up in the meeting room, there are going to be at least four bodyguards. If the alarm is raised, then add in another six guards within seconds.
- **Criminology** or **Human Terrain:** The Serbians like to show off. That means they'll be coming in through the front door, accompanied by an entourage of girls and goons, and they'll spend a few minutes in the bar downstairs before heading up. There'll be a window then.
- **Notice** or **Architecture:** There's a panic room just off the private room.

Sneaking in is virtually impossible. There are three external doors, all of which are watched. The side windows are much too small to be usable; the main windows in the restaurant are bullet-proof. The adjoining buildings are also owned by the Serbians and have similar security.

If there's a threat to the restaurant, then the four principals are escorted out through the kitchens to the back door and that waiting black van. If there's no easy way out, then they head to the panic room.

THE PRINCIPALS

There are four key figures at the meeting.

SERGEI RACHOV

One of Josef Lisky's trusted men, Rachov's a *brodyagi*, a *vor* in waiting. He knows about the existence of vampires, and pretends to be one to boost his reputation among those who know. He avoids sunlight and drinks red wine mixed with human blood. He's in his late 40s, and looks older. Heavily scarred and tattooed, hooded eyes, moves awkwardly from his old wounds.

- **Vampirology:** He's not a vampire.
- Rachov lets his guard down to **Flattery,** especially if it reinforces his self-image as a immortal-to-be.
- Rachov's the most dangerous and sadistic of the four principals.

JACOB LENGYEL

The Lisky Bratva's local head. He's a Hungarian, so he knows he has little chance of rising through the ranks of the Russian-dominated organization.

- **Cop Talk** or **Human Terrain:** Lengyel's paranoid. He worries that the Lisky Bratva will use him as a scapegoat and replace him with someone more to their tastes. He worries that the police are closing in. He worries that the Serbians will cancel the deal and start muscling in on the Lisky Bratva's turf. He worries about his health. Hitting any of those fears with a suitable ability throws Lengyel off.
- He's also the most likely of the four to fold under **Interrogation**, if the agents can convince him they're cops.

TODOR BABIC

The older of the two Serbians, Babic came out of the Yugoslavian civil war with bloody hands and a lot of Milosevic's money. He's a canny bastard, and knows that an alliance with the Lisky Bratva benefits both sides. He squashes his doubts about the Lisky Bratva's supernatural ties, telling himself they're just weird rumors.

- If the agents present Babic with proof about the Lisky Bratva's monstrous experiments at Dragovir, or lure a zalozhniy or other supernatural entity to the restaurant, it will disturb Babic enough to reconsider the deal.
- **Occult Studies** picks up on Babic's subconscious fears. That gold crucifix (spotted with **Notice** in person, or with **Data Recovery** in imagery) isn't just for show.

RUDI MARKO

Brash, tough, arrogant, with an eye for pretty girls. Marko's a talented asset of Naša Stvar, but he's got the discretion of a bull elephant. He's popular among the younger members of the organization.

- **Flirting** gets more attention from Marko that an agent probably wants.
- Marko's also the most hot-headed of the four. If he's pushed (with **Intimidation**) or convinced that someone's mocking him, he flies off the handle.

THE DEAL

Both sides profit from the deal, so while the Serbians have some reservations about their partners, the money's too good to bother with petty concerns like "hey, are these guys just ordinary criminals, or the front for a monstrous conspiracy?"

THE AGENDA

The Naša Stvar want:

- High-quality weapons and sex slaves
- Assurances that the Lisky Bratva won't push into their territories
- Stability and security – no surprises, no problems, just profit
- Access to the Lisky Bratva's money-laundering facilities through the Black Sea Bank. If the agents eavesdrop on the meeting with **Electronic Surveillance**, they'll hear the

bank mentioned several times as a Lisky Bratva asset. Investigating the bank points the agents to Zurich and *The Boxmen* on p. 80.

The Lisky Bratva want:

- High-quality heroin
- Liquid cash that's already been partially laundered

DEALBREAKERS

To disrupt the deal between the Naša Stvar and the Lisky Bratva, the agents need to find some leverage to drive a wedge between the two groups. Possibilities include:

- Making contact with either Marko or Babic and convincing them that the Lisky Bratva are plotting to double-cross them.
- Kidnapping, wounding or incapacitating one of the four principals.
- Offering one of the sides a better deal
- Helping the Naša Stvar to muscle the Lisky Bratva out of Hungary.

THE VIENNA RUN

In the *vorovskoi mir*, the criminal underworld, Vienna is a neutral city. It's a place for meetings, for business, for trade, not for settling accounts. This agreement is observed by every major criminal sect. Only a fool would break the peace of Vienna… but that peace starts at the city limits. The agents will be safe from the Lisky Bratva only when they're inside the city proper. Their enemies have one last chance to stop them.

Before he died on that steep mountain road in the Crimea, Donald Caroll told the agents about his safehouse in Vienna. He kept the details in locker 827 in the airport. Getting to that lock-box should be the agents' first priority.

ALTERNATE TARGETS

If the agents aren't heading for Caroll's safehouse, you'll need to give them another reason to head to the airport. Possible options:

- A zalozhniy captures one of the agents' contacts and uses them as bait
- Rumors that the Albedo or Nigredo is also in the locker
- A suitcase full of Lisky Bratva drug money, stolen by Caroll
- Some other MacGuffin

Alternatively, you can just adapt *The Airport* scene to however the agents arrive in Vienna.

THE AIRPORT

SCENE TYPE: Reveal
LEAD-IN: Running Hot
LEAD-OUT: Crash Priority

Vienna's Schwechat Airport is one of the busiest in Europe. 20 million people pass through it every year, which means 20 million people walk past locker 827 and its secrets. The storage lockers are well away from the main terminal of the airport, directly above the busy train platform that links Schwechat to the city some eighteen kilometers away. When the agents arrive, the left luggage area is empty.

Tradecraft or **Notice:** Yes, actually empty. The Lisky Bratva doubtless have thugs in the airport, and may even have bugged the room, but there's no-one watching it.

When the agents pass through the airport, they spot a lot of foreign dignitaries, here to attend the trade conference (see *Out of the House of Ashes*, p. 52). Be sure to point out one group of Saudi princes, as foreshadowing for the eventual revelation of the Rubedo at the end of the **Quartet**.

THE PHONE CALL

There's a row of payphones near the lockers, and one of them rings suddenly. If the agents answer, they hear a familiar voice – the throaty whisper of Dr. Dorjiev. His message depends on circumstances.

- If this is the start of the **Zalozhniy Quartet**, and your agents are… morally flexible, then Dorjiev makes them an offer. He'll call off the hounds if the agents help him. There is a secret weapon that he wants, something that even they covet. He knows that the weapon was divided into two parts, and that **Arkady Shevlenko** knows more about it. In effect, Dorjiev offers to hire them to obtain the Albedo and Rubedo for him. He's trying to double-cross the Lisky Bratva's masters. It's unlikely that the agents will go down this route (and even less likely that they actually fulfill their end of the bargain), but if they do, Dorjiev will pull what strings he can to reduce the Lisky Bratva's attacks on the agents. He'll also warn them about the impending train crash — it's too late for him to stop his creations, but the advance warning may save the agents' lives.

- If you're running this operation midway through the **Quartet,** then Dorjiev calls to threaten the agents. They've bloodied him from Odessa to Vienna, and now they're going to die. The zalozhniye will crack their bones and feed on their marrow, their suffering will be eternal, and so forth. He'll keep them talking until the train crashes into the train station below.

- If this is the final operation in the **Quartet,** then the agents should have the Albedo and the Nigredo, and just need a chance to put the two together. Dorjiev contacts them to give them a final offer — hand over the secret, and he will spare their lives. If they refuse — and they will — then he hits them with everything he's got left. Run the Capstone encounter on p. 51 once the agents reach Vienna.

THE LOCKER

What the agents find here depends on their Hot Lead:

Hot Lead 6 or more: The agents arrive well ahead of their Lisky Bratva pursuers. The locker is untouched. Inside, the agents find a sealed manila envelope containing:

- The address of an apartment in Vienna, along with house keys.

Urban Survival (Core Clue) lets an agent remember that area of the city and plan a route there.
- The keys to a car in the airport's long-term car park
- $50,000 in cash
- Passports and other documents

Plus, they can get clear of the left luggage area *before* the train crash (see *Crash Priority,* below).

Hot Lead 3–5: As above, but the Lisky Bratva hit the train station while the agents are still in the left luggage area.

Hot Lead 2 or less: The Lisky Bratva got here before the agents. Attacked to the inside of the locker is a small explosive device. Give the agent opening the locker a **Sense Trouble** roll at Difficulty 6. If she fails, the bomb explodes, taking 1d6+6 Health from each agent in the room (treat it as a class 2 explosive, as per the rules on p. 67 of ***Night's Black Agents***).

CRASH PRIORITY

SCENE TYPE: Hazard
LEAD-IN: The Airport
LEAD-OUT: Final Run

A high-speed rail link connects the airport with Vienna. The terminus is directly below the left luggage locker. Right now, a train with more than one hundred passengers is heading towards the airport.

One hundred passengers… and the zalozhniye.

We won't count the driver. He's already dead.

The train ploughs into the station at full throttle, smashing into the barricades with enough force to turn the diesel engine into a bomb. The explosion rips through the platform as the train crumbles and buckles, the rear carriages whipping up and slamming into the concrete roof, cracking it like an eggshell. A wave of fire and debris blasts out of the station.

In the midst of all this carnage, there's a second of unnatural calm. The agents recognize it as the same time-stop bubble that happens whenever a zalozhniy kills a victim, only hundreds of times more intense.

If the agents are in the left luggage area directly above the station, then they have a few seconds' warning. Call for **Sense Trouble** rolls (Difficulty 6). Those who succeed make it out of the left luggage area and up the stairs before the crash.

Those who fail are in the room when the crash happens. The floor of the left luggage area is smashed, dropping agents, lockers and tons of rubble down into the ruined platform below. The agents each lose 1d6+4 Health (Breakfall applies for high-Athletics agents) and they tumble down on the rockslide of twisted rebar and concrete into the hellhole of the ruined platform. Everyone also gets hit by a 3-point **Stability** test (4 points if the agent's on the platform). It's a nightmare. Billowing clouds of concrete dust turn the panicked crowds into blood-stained spectres. The screams of the injured and dying war with the howling of alarms.

The zalozhniye — one for every two player characters — pull themselves out of the wreckage. Unlike the unfortunate passengers and bystanders, the zalozhinye are uninjured by the train crash. Instead, they're massively rejuvenated by it. Their scarred skin glows with power, and they toss huge chunks of debris aside with ease. In game terms, each zalozhniy has 30 points in Aberrance and Health.

Time to run.

The airport is completely locked down; **Urban Survival** points the agents towards the car park and the motorway to Vienna.

THE FOOT CHASE

The agents are in or near a ruined train station, and there are hyper-charged supernatural assassins chasing them. The agents need to get to a Lead of 6 to reach the car park. The zalozhniye move incredibly quickly and have super-human strength, but they're not infallible. The agents might be able to escape in the chaos.

Elements of the chase:

- Fleeing passengers
- Clouds of dust
- Fire suppression sprinklers
- Emergency services – police, fire engines, ambulances
- Storage lockers, back corridors, electrical wiring – the intestines of the airport

Potential point spends:

- **Architecture:** identifies sections of the corridor that were weakened by the train crash and could be collapsed to block pursuit
- **Cop Talk:** convincing the Austrian police to shoot the zalozhniye
- **Tradecraft:** hiding in the crowds of fleeing passengers
- **Urban Survival:** Taking an unexpected route

This is also a great time for the agents to throw down any Blocks they've learned along the way. Sudden escapes can be made at Lead 5.

Every time the agents lose Lead, then one of the zalozhniye gets close enough to take a swipe or swing at them. Play up the absurdly super-charged state of the zalozhniye by having the monsters burst through walls, chuck cars at the agents, or fling player characters off buildings.

If the agents get to the car park with a Lead of 7 or more, then they can get into a car and drive off (stealing a car rapidly requires a **Infiltration** test at Difficulty 5; fail, and you lose a point of Lead). If they only barely make it with Lead 6, then a zalozhniy either grabs the car from behind or lands on the roof – either way, the agents need to ditch the monster before it smashes the car and prevents their escape.

If the agents run out of Lead, then they are surrounded by the zalozhniye. The only way out of such a situation, short of a brilliant and unexpected stroke of genius by one of the players, is for an agent to sacrifice himself and hold the monsters off while the rest flee.

THE FINAL RUN

SCENE TYPE: Conclusion
LEAD-IN: Crash Priority

The zalozhniye aren't the only Lisky Bratva forces between the agents and the safety of Vienna. They've also got conventional forces watching the roads between the airport and the city. The number of these forces depends on how badly the agents hurt the Lisky Bratva.
MINIMUM: Px2 Thugs, P Thug Bosses, all remaining zalozhniye
IF DRAGOVIR MONASTERY STILL STANDS: Add a new zalozhniy
IF THE ROMANIAN CAMP STILL STANDS: Add Px2 Thugs
IF THE NAŠA STVAR DEAL WENT THROUGH: Add P Thug Bosses
IF THE AGENTS' HOT LEAD IS 2 OR LESS: Add P/2 operatives

HITTING THE ROAD

The motorway is choked with traffic. Police helicopters buzz overhead, and emergency vehicles push through the traffic jams. The terrorist attack on the airport means that the bulk of Vienna's police and emergency services have their hands full already, without adding a large-scale firefight between the agents and the Lisky Bratva into the mix.

The final run into Vienna is another car chase. The motorway is blocked with cars, although a small car or a motorcycle could weave its way through. Taking side roads is a better option. The agents need to accumulate a Lead of 10 to reach Vienna safely; if they run out of Lead, then their car crashes and they have to escape on foot.

THREATS & OBSTACLES:

- The Lisky Bratva steal tankers full of airplane fuel and drive them after the agents.

- Snipers on the overpass.
- Narrow country roads with sharp turns
- Zaloznhiye leaping from car to car
- Big Baldak Transit trucks packed with armed goons
- Police cars and helicopters joining the chase

REACHING VIENNA

Once the agents get inside the city limits of Vienna, the Lisky Bratva cease their pursuit. Getting into the city doesn't mean the Lisky Bratva abruptly surrender – if the agents limp over the line, the criminals take a few pot shots at them – but the bulk of the pursuit is called off. (The exception is if this is the final adventure in the **Quartet,** in which case the chance of capturing the Rubedo is worth the gamble. If so, see the *Capstone* opposite, p. 51).

The zalozhniye keep coming. The same monsters from the airport follow the agents into the city. The characters need to find a way to evade or destroy these creatures. Possibilities include:

- **Art History:** There's a Clock Museum in the centre of Vienna, filled with more than three thousand mechanical clocks, all ticking away. When the zalozhniye are nearby, their time-bubbles disrupt ticking clocks. In the clock museum, that means that the zalozhniye cannot hide – the silence of the clocks gives away their presence. The agents can use the clock museum to stalk and kill the zalozhniye, eliminating the creatures' powers of Apportation and their inhuman speed.
- **Occult Studies:** No city in the world is as death-obsessed as Vienna. Some of the greatest graveyards in Europe are to be found here. The quiet dead of many centuries rest beneath the Viennese soil. For the un-dead zalozhniye, such an aura of death drains their power. Their untimely death weighs heavily on them. A zalozhniy in a graveyard loses most of its power, allowing the agents to finally kill the dead.
- **Urban Survival:** Donald Caroll left the agents the location of his safehouse. The zalozhniye captured Caroll before he died. Furthermore, they know that the zalozhniye prefer to kill through trickery. Obviously, the zalozhniye are going to head to the safehouse and plant a bomb there, so that the agents walk into a trap… but if the agents could get across Vienna *before* the zalozhniye, then they could put a trap there *first* and turn the tables on the tricksters.

FINAL CURTAIN

Caroll's safehouse is a surprisingly luxurious apartment in the heart of the city. It's rented in the name of an old college friend of Caroll, but the credentials are rock-solid. There is little chance of anyone tracing the agents here, and any Heat they picked up in the airport run is pinned on the Lisky Bratva. For the first time since Odessa, they can sleep soundly.

SURVIVING OPERATIVES

If any of the Operatives assigned by the Lisky Bratva to eliminate the agents survive this operation, they don't follow the agents into Vienna. Instead, they'll show up in some future operation at the worst possible time.

EXIT VECTORS

This operation uncovers leads pointing to the other operations in this book.

OUT OF THE HOUSE OF ASHES

- There's a international trade conference on in Vienna, so the city is crawling with spooks. This is a good time to do some digging, look up old contacts – or settle old scores.
- **Tradecraft:** Arkady Shevlenko is in town, and the Lennart Dossier fingers him as a potential insider. He might be worth checking out.
- **Criminology:** While Vienna's a neutral city, the Lisky Bratva are interested in the trade conference. Their local kingpin in Stefan Werner.
- Sergei Rachov goes from the meeting in Debrecen to Vienna. Following him leads the agents to the Hotel Europa reception.

THE BOXMEN

- **Accounting:** Agi Kozorus' contact is an accountant with the Black Sea Bank. He (or Agi) can pass on information about the Black Sea Bank's strange takeover bid for the Swiss Koernersbank.
- **Electronic Surveillance:** During the Golden Calf meeting, the Naša Stvar mentioned the Black Sea Bank as being connected to the Lisky Bratva.

TREASON IN THE BLOOD

- **Military Science:** The guns that got the agents into this mess came from Baghdad.
- **Research:** The Philby dossier from the monastery mentions ongoing efforts in Baghdad to steal secret documents related to St. John's early days in the desert. The agents find the name "Mohammed Al-Kirkuk," who's a researcher at the Iraqi National Museum.

CAPSTONE: DR. DORJIEV, I EXHUME

So, the agents are in Caroll's apartment (or another safehouse) and they've got the Albedo and the Nigredo. Did they really think they were going to get away that easily?

Dorjiev wants the Rubedo. It's his ticket to immortality, to control of the Lisky Bratva, to mastery of life and death. He wants out of Lisky's shadow – and more importantly, out of the shadow of the vampires behind Josef Lisky.

Pick one of the agents that was injured by a zalozhniy earlier in the operation, or who was captured by the Lisky Bratva. If none of the agents fit, then go for a valued contact or Solace. The target suddenly doubles over in pain and vomits up blood.

Diagnosis (or another ability, like **Vampirology**) determines that the target is suffering from a magical ritual/psionic attack/alien technology/tailored virus infection/vampiric blood curse/delete as appropriate. Without a cure, the target will soon die in agonizing pain. Medical treatment and drug therapy can delay the inevitable, but only for a few hours. (The victim loses 1 Health per hour; a **Medic** test can slow but cannot stop the rate of Health loss.)

Moments later, the phone rings (or the afflicted target starts speaking with Dorjiev's voice, if that's more appropriate for your campaign). Dorjiev repeats the deal he made at the airport – give him the Albedo and the Nigredo, and he'll relent. The agents are safe from the Lisky Bratva in Vienna, but not from the power of the necromancer. Dorjiev offers to meet the agents in another warehouse on the edge of the city to make the handover – the cure for the Albedo and Nigredo.

- A 1-point **Negotiation** spend forces Dorjiev to let the agents pick the location of the handover. The Prater amusement park is a good choice – public enough to prevent trouble, but with lots of places to hide.
- **Electronic Surveillance** lets the agents trace the call to a cellphone. The cellphone's currently located in a derelict church in a rundown part of the 11th district (Simmering) in south-east Vienna.
- **Streetwise** can also trace the Lisky Bratva to this church – any survivors from the airport chase made their way here.

DORJIEV'S FORCES

He's got whatever forces survived the airport ambush. If the agents eliminated all the zalozhniye, then he's got one last freshly-minted monster with him. Dorjiev's off the reservation for this mission – he's going after the Albedo and Nigredo for his own ends.

The Necromancer is clearly pushing himself beyond his limits. He's waxy-faced and exhausted when the agents finally get to see him. Sometimes, blood droplets well up in his eyes and roll down his hollow cheeks. He's clearly overexerted himself.

KILLING DORJIEV

The only way to stop Dorjiev is to kill him within a zalozhniy time bubble. As the agents should have the upper hand, they can arrange events as they choose. Possible solutions:

- Arrange for the meeting to take place in an open area, and have a sniper standing by, then get Dorjiev close to a zalozhniy.
- Trick a zalozhniy into killing someone, so that Dorjiev's within the temporal bubble.
- If the Rubedo turns its user into a vampire, then Dorjiev will have to die to be reborn as one of the undead. Therefore, he'll have to give up his protected status to use the Rubedo, and the agents can use this window to kill him. This tactic is even more effective if the agents replace the Albedo or the Rubedo with a fake, preventing Dorjiev from completing the ritual.

OUT OF THE HOUSE OF ASHES

Soviet spies, old world elegance, covert operations… and vampires. *Out of the House of Ashes* is the subtle, baroque portion of the quartet. If the agents pull a gun in this operation, they're already in trouble.

EYES ONLY BRIEFING

This operation revolves around the extraction of Arkady Shevlenko, a former Soviet spymaster. The Russians have him, but they're just keeping him warm for the Conspiracy. The Americans want him. So do the agents. The Americans get there first, but the Conspiracy foils their extraction attempt. It's up to the agents to get Arkady out from under the fangs of a vampire…

THE SPINE

The agents kick off their investigation in **Opening Moves**, where they identify some of the players in this drama. There's Shevlenko himself, his four FSB handlers and his Lisky Bratva watchers. They also learn that Shevlenko has a heart condition, being treated by a Dr. Ingolf.

The agents follow Shevlenko to a reception in **Any Operation Can Be Aborted**, where they witness the CIA team trying to extract the Russian. The extraction is foiled by the vampire, but the team learns that one of the CIA team is still out there and **Burned.** The CIA used Dr. Ingolf as a go-between, but he was turned by the Lisky Bratva, as the agents discover when they interrogate **The Heart Doctor**.

From there, the team try **Contracting Shevlenko**. He wants out, but there's a problem. His granddaughter is coming to Vienna, and the Lisky Bratva intend to use her as a hostage, forcing the agents to launch a **Rescue Mission**. They may also go **Vampire Hunting** before the final extraction attempt in **Blood Opera**.

OLD SINS

Arkady Shevlenko was a KGB officer from the day he was recruited in 1955 until he was pensioned off — there was no place for him in the *Sluzhba Vneshney Razvedki* (SVR) that took over the KGB's foreign intelligence duties. Shevlenko had a varied but seemingly unremarkable career. He spent some time in the Middle East in the '60s and '70s, he was attached to the Soviet embassy in the UK in the '80s, and he spent the last portion of his career babysitting other old spies. These days, he's vaguely attached to the Gokhran, a division of the Russian Ministry of Finance that deals with the sale and purchase of precious stones. The Russian government wheels him out to various state functions and foreign trade conferences.

There are a few curious elements to Shevlenko's career that hint of darker connections. He was in Beirut in 1960 at the same time that St. John Philby died of a heart attack shortly after collapsing at a club (where the waitress who served him and Kim Philby was heard to exclaim in horror, "God! I've poisoned him!"). During the '70s, he spent six months in prison in Iran, and was freed by the events of the Revolution in '79, having been arrested for the "attempted theft of historical relics."

Later, back in Moscow, he was assigned as Kim Philby's final handler. The KGB always treated Kim as a valued agent, despite his insistence that he was a KGB officer, not an asset. (Kim always maintained that he was recruited as a full officer by Arnold Deutsch in 1934, and that therefore he was a full member of the KGB prior to his recruitment by British intelligence.) By the 1980s, Philby's intelligence on British and American espionage was years out of date, but he was still considered an authoritative source on British culture and thinking, as well as several *other* topics. Shevlenko ran Philby's final debriefing in 1988, just before Kim Philby died.

In that terminal briefing, Philby confessed his last secret to Shevlenko, initiating him fully into the Philby plot. He told Shevlenko about the Albedo and the Nigredo, and the preparations St. John had made in Riyadh in 1931. Perhaps Kim intended that his friend Arkady should put the plan into operation, or maybe he wanted Arkady to sabotage it so the Conspiracy could never obtain the Rubedo… or perhaps he just unburden himself of that last secret.

He passed on two other items to Shevlenko. One was a talisman or weapon of mysterious origin that acts as a potent Block, preventing the vampires from compromising Shevelenko directly. The second was a vital part of the plan. If you're running this operation before *The Boxmen*, then Philby gave Shevlenko the Koernersbank Passbook to Deposit Box 1274, a document that allows the bearer to claim the contents of that safety deposit box. If you're running this after *The Boxmen*, then Philby gave Shevlenko something equally valuable, like knowledge of the ritual to create the Rubedo or the location of Gertrude Bell's diary.

VIENNA: QUICK AND DIRTY

Capital of Austria, one of the great cities of Europe. After World War II, it was divided into zones like Berlin; after 1955, Austria was established as a neutral country, which made Vienna an ideal home for international institutions — groups like the UN, OPEC and the International Atomic Energy Commission have offices here, and the city's hosted many key summits and treaty negotiations. It's famed for its architecture. The city's divided into 23 districts. The river Danube runs through the city.

POPULATION
2.4 million (Slightly smaller than Chicago)

CONFLICT
Vienna's a hotbed of international intrigue and espionage; it's the spook capital of Europe. The conflict here happens at a remove — deals and agreements made over coffee in a quiet restaurant lead to bloodshed and suffering half a world away. Vienna's a calm eye in the geopolitical hurricane.

BACKDROPS
HOFBURG PALACE: Formerly home to the Habsburg dynasty, now the official home of the Austrian president. The sprawling palace complex also contains numerous museums, government buildings, conference venues and tourist attractions.

UNO CITY: Officially, it's the Vienna International Centre, but most locals call it UNO city. It's a complex of buildings north of the Danube, home to the United Nations and other international bodies. UNO City is extra-territorial, with its own police force.

ZENTRALFRIEDHOF: One of the biggest graveyards in Europe, containing more than three million bodies. It's an interdenominational graveyard. The Zentralfriedhof covers 2.4 square kilometers, so it's easy to get lost amid the graves…

THREE HOOKS
- In the 1950s, a group of occultists with fascist sympathies met in Vienna in the studio of Wilhelm Landig. There, they developed the concept of the "Black Sun," a mystical symbol that promised to revive the energies of the Aryan race, taken from SS ceremonies and from a floor mosaic in Wewelburg Castle in Germany. The Landig group also investigated tales of hidden power under the polar ice caps, and claimed to have contact with the secret Antarctic base established by the Nazis in 1938. The "Black Sun" could be code for the Nigredo.
- The "Angels of Death" were a group of four nurses who killed at least 39 people, and possibly as many as 200 over a four-year period. They worked the night shift at Lainz General Hospital. A patient asked one of the nurses, Waltraud Wagner to end her suffering with a morphine overdose. The nurse complied — and soon developed a taste for killing. She recruited three other nurses and led the group. Initially, most of their murders were mercy killings, but later they eliminated annoying or troublesome patients and killed according to their whims. Maybe there were an unusual number of dark-haired Hungarian women among their victims…
- Rumors filter through espionage circles — stories of other displaced spies like the agents, wild tales about vampires, about a world-wide conspiracy, and about organizing to fight back. Are there other people out there who are also fighting the Conspiracy — or is this a honey trap to lure the agents in?

Shevlenko hid this second item in Vienna; he's kept the talisman on him ever since.

VIENNESE BLOOD OPERA

For most of the last twenty years, the FSB (Soviet state security) have kept close tabs on Shevlenko. The Conspiracy wanted him kept safe until they were ready to move on the Philby plan. Now, that time has arrived. They intend to get Philby's secret from Arkady. Most of the FSB agents watching Shevlenko have no idea about the existence of vampires or the Conspiracy – they're just following orders.

Shevlenko knows the conspiracy is coming for him. He suffers from a degenerative heart condition, and receives treatment from a specialist in Vienna, a **Doctor Ingolf**. Through Ingolf, he made contact with the CIA and passed on enough information to pique their interest. The CIA plans to extract him. He's sent for his one surviving relative, his granddaughter **Anna**, to meet him in Vienna. She'll be extracted too.

Meanwhile, the Conspiracy has its pieces in place too. Due to events elsewhere (like their work in Baghdad, or in reaction to the agent's actions), they are now ready to force Shevlenko to talk. In the past, this has proven difficult. The talisman protects Shevlenko from supernatural compulsions, his inconveniently weak health means physical persuasion won't work, and he's too stubborn and clever to be persuaded to help the Conspiracy. In the past, the only leverage that worked was using Shevlenko's family against him, but his wife is dead and his son died in a suspicious plane crash. They're running out of people Shevlenko cares about.

The Conspiracy has dispatched a vampire to Vienna to watch over Shevlenko and find a way to make him give up Philby's secret. They've already compromised Dr. Ingolf, so they know about Arkady's schemes with the CIA. The Conspiracy intends to foil the extraction, acquire Anna, and show Shevlenko that he has nowhere left to run.

ENTRY VECTORS

There are a number of ways into this adventure, from previous ops, from other operations in this collection, or from random chatter. The Director should salt as many leads as she feels necessary, or customize them to suit her campaign.

OUTSIDE LEADS

These leads come from outside this book; from the corebook adventure *(S) Entries* or perhaps from other ops in the Director's previous campaign.

THE LENNART DOSSIER
- The Dossier mentions Arkady Shevlenko, although Lennart was unable to determine if Shevlenko was part of the Conspiracy or an enemy of the vampires. **Research** puts Shevlenko in Vienna right now, as part of a trade conference.
- **Vampirology:** The Dossier mentions a strange incident in 1994, where a man was found drained of blood in an alleyway in Vienna. The Dossier identifies the man as Boris Vali, a former Soviet spy. Vali's death was never made public.
- **Bureaucracy:** Several documents obtained by Lennart via the CIA can be traced back to Shevlenko, hinting that he's leaking information to the Americans.

OTHER VECTORS
- **Traffic Analysis:** Eavesdropping on Lisky Bratva/Conspiracy traffic points to a "significant asset" – probably a vampire – coming into Vienna soon. This could be a chance to injure the Conspiracy by taking out one of the immortals.
- **Accounting** or **High Society:** There's a big trade conference on in Vienna soon. Vampires are drawn to big money and power as surely as they're drawn to blood.
- **Criminology:** Vienna's a free city, neutral territory for the criminal underworld. It's a good place to hide out – or to gather information about the Lisky Bratva.

INSIDE LEADS

Intel gathered in other operations in this collection may lead the agents to Vienna, Shevlenko, and the trade conferencee. If the players don't quite stumble over the right leads in those scenarios, quite often the Director can plant this intel in the mouth (or dead fist, or laptop, or smartphone) of an NPC also on the trail of the Lisky Bratva or of the Philby Plot.

THE ZALOZHNIY SANCTION
- The agents end up in Vienna after the events of *The Zalozhniy Sanction* with an intimate understanding of the importance of the Lisky Bratva to the Conspiracy. Investigating Lisky Bratva activity in Vienna will soon point the agents at Shevlenko.
- **Criminology** and some shoe leather lets the agents identify Werner as the Lisky Bratva's kingpin in town.
- After spotting him in Debrecen, the agents might track Sergei Rachov to Vienna and the opening reception at the Hotel Europa.

THE BOXMEN
- Box 1274 was owned by Kim Philby. **History** or **Research** or **Tradecraft** identifies Shevlenko as Philby's final handler.
- Marko Schwetz was contacted by Stefan Werner, urging him to complete the bank buyout as soon as possible now that the Lisky Bratva had Shevlenko in hand. Shevlenko's here in Vienna.

TREASON IN THE BLOOD
- Nikolai's documents identify Arkady Shevlenko as his superior in the KGB.
- **Tradecraft:** There are rumors in the intelligence community that St. John Philby was poisoned by a Russian agent, and some people finger Shevlenko.

PAWNS, BISHOPS AND KINGS

Before we get into the meat of this operation, let's discuss the major players and the environment.

THE TRADE CONFERENCE

For the four days of the scenario, Vienna is home to an international trade conference. The city's full of corporate executives, government officials, journalists, spooks and hangers-on. Officially, the theme is "*commerce in a multi-polar world*"; in practise, it's an attempt by bankrupt western governments to borrow money from cash-rich nations, mainly the Saudis and the Chinese, mixed with corporate deals with developing-world governments. Play up the Saudi involvement wherever possible, to foreshadow the final revelation of the Philby Plot. The agents keep running into delegations of Saudi princes, or hearing about the wealth of Saudi Arabia.

During the day, conference delegates attend meetings, seminars and round-table discussions at venues throughout the city. The real business gets done in the evenings, in bars and restaurants and hotel lobbies.

SECURITY AT THE CONFERENCE

The Austrian *Bundespolizei* want this conference to go smoothly. They've called in extra police from other cities to help deal with the expected crowds of protestors, not to mention the added risk of street thieves, kidnappings and potential terrorist attacks. If you're running this operation after *The Zalozhniy Sanction*, then security is sky-high after the terrorist attack on the airport train. There are police cars everywhere in Zurich, and they've got both WEGA (*Wiener Einsatzgruppe Alarmabteilung*, the local equivalent of SWAT) and EKO Cobra (Austria counter-terrorism forces) on alert.

In game terms, any Heat gained for violence, explosions, or anything that might be connected to terrorism is **doubled** while in Vienna. Furthermore, the agents must roll for trouble from Heat every day, instead of once per session or once per operation. That's four Heat rolls over the course of the operation – and if the agents do draw the attention of the authorities, throw the special forces at them (use the special police stats on p. 70 of **Night's Black Agents**).

ARKADY SHEVLENKO

Arkady Shevlenko looks like death. He was born in 1934, and grew up amid the hardship and devastation of World War II. He was the youngest of six brothers, but was the only one to survive the war. He ended up in a state orphanage for a few years, and was recruited by the KGB when he was 21. For the last twenty years, he's suffered from a mysterious heart ailment that requires regular treatments by coronary specialists, notably Dr. Ingolf of Vienna.

His illness hasn't slowed Shevlenko down, or stopped him drinking. His mind is still sharp despite his age, and he has enough favors and friends in the Russian government to keep his cushy position in the Gokhran. He pretends to be senile when it amuses him; it makes people underestimate him, and lets him get away with mischief.

PLAYING SHEVLENKO

- You're old and tired and half-drunk all the time. Cultivate an attitude of fatalism.
- Never exert yourself. It's dangerous.
- You only care about two things – your granddaughter's safety, and hurting the Conspiracy.
- You wear the talisman that Philby gave you around your neck; grip it as tightly as you can with your frail, liver-spotted hands, and never let it go.

GENERAL ABILITIES: Athletics 3, Hand-to-Hand 2, Health 4*, Network 20, Preparedness 10, Sense Trouble 12, Shooting 4
HIT THRESHOLD: 3
ALERTNESS MODIFIER: +0
STEALTH MODIFIER: +1
DAMAGE MODIFIER: -2 (Fist)
*Shevlenko's in very poor Health; he loses 1 point of Health whenever he has to make an Athletics or Hand-to-Hand test.

INVESTIGATING SHEVLENKO

The agents can dig into Shevlenko's past through research (digging through microfiches of old Soviet newspapers and government archives, internet searches) or questioning sources (retired spies, journalists, underworld contacts). Offer the players the chance to spend an extra point of an ability like **Tradecraft** or **Urban Survival** or use a Cover when enquiring about Shevlenko; if they *don't* take such precautions, then they may be flagged by the FSB as a potential threat.

Virtually any of the Academic clues can also be found with **Research,** but it takes a lot longer.

- **History (Core Clue):** Arkady Shevlenko was a KGB field officer for most of the mid-50s until the 1970s; he spent the 80s as an agent handler, debriefing old assets like **Kim Philby**, and has since moved to the Gorkhan division of the Finance Ministry.
  › 1-point **History** spend: Shevlenko was, it is said, the last person to debrief Philby. The two were friends, and it's rumored that Philby confided in him. The famed spymaster **Yuri Modin**, the controller for the Cambridge Five from '44 to '55, said that Shevlenko was probably the only man who really knew where Philby's ultimate loyalties lay.
  › 1-point **Research** spend: Shevlenko's wife died in 1990. His son Piotr died in a plane crash in '95; anyone with **Piloting** who reads the report can tell it stinks of sabotage. His only surviving relative is his granddaughter, Anna – and she seems to have dropped off the grid entirely.
- **Tradecraft (Core Clue):** The KGB split into the SVR (Foreign Intelligence) and FSB (Domestic Security). As an ex-KGB general, Shevlenko's certainly got a dedicated FSB team nursemaiding him. He's staying at the Russian embassy, and that place is a fortress.
  › Spending 3 points from **Tradecraft, Electronic Surveillance, Photography, Notice, Traffic Analysis** and/or **Urban Survival** (or a few **Surveillance** tests) lets the agents observe Shevlenko long enough to identify the four key members of his bodyguard team (see below) and learn his patterns.
- **Diagnosis (Core Clue):** Shevlenko's a sick man, suffering from a heart condition. Any stress could be lethal for him. There is a doctor in Vienna who specializes in exotic heart problems, a **Dr. Ingolf.** Shevlenko's one of his patients.
  › **Pharmacy**: Wild speculation but… Shevlenko's symptoms could be the result of poison, probably something related to digitalis. Oddly, his symptoms also match those of St. John Philby, who died of a heart attack in Beirut in 1960. Of course, Shevlenko had heart problems for around twenty years, and he's in his late 70s now; one doesn't need to look for poison when old age would explain everything.
- If the agents have photographs of Shevlenko (**Network,** a 1-point **Tradecraft** or 2-point **Research** spend), a 1-point **Notice** or **Data Recovery** ("let me zoom in on this") spend spots that Shevlenko always wears a necklace or talisman of some sort around his neck.

THE RUSSIAN EMBASSY

Arkady's staying at the embassy, and there's next to no chance of getting him out of *there*. Any extraction of Shevlenko will have to be done while he's out in Vienna. The agents may be able to arrange a meeting with Shevlenko inside the embassy.

SHEVLENKO'S SCHEDULE

Obtaining a copy of Shevlenko's public schedule is easy with **Bureaucracy, Research** or **High Society.** He's dining out in style on the Finance Ministry's dime. In the schedule, private meetings and events are in *italics*.

THE FSB HANDLERS

Shevlenko's accompanied at all times by an entourage of four FSB agents, who are his handlers, nursemaids, bodyguards, drinking buddies, personal assistants or jailers depending on his mood. While only one or two of them may be physically at Shevlenko's side at any given moment, the others are never far away. Use the Bodyguard statistics from p. 69 of *Night's Black Agents* for the four.

KATARINA VOLKOV

The leader of the group, and rather frustrated with having to babysit a senile old diplomat. She has little patience for Shevlenko, and considers him a dead weight that's dragging down her career. She's extremely competent and thorough, when she controls her temper.

- Officially, she's Shevlenko's personal secretary.
- Using **Bureaucracy** to frustrate Volkov is the best way to throw

SHEVLENKO'S SCHEDULE

DAY	EVENTS
1	Meeting with Dr. Ingolf. Dr. Ingolf warns him of the planned CIA extraction tonight. Speech on mining prospects in Central Asia (Vienna International Centre) Reception (Hotel Europa) CIA attempt to extract Shevlenko.
2	Second meeting with Dr. Ingolf Meeting with Saudi prince Meeting with vampire.
3	Round table discussion with gem manufacturers, chaired by De Beers (Russian Embassy) Anna Shevlenko arrives in Vienna and is kidnapped by Lisky Bratva.
4	Attending gala opera/conference closing ceremony (Vienna Opera House) Shevlenko surrenders Philby's secret to the vampire.

her off her game. She's sick of cleaning up Shevlenko's diplomatic incidents and little problems.

- **Cop Talk** is the best way to speak to her if the agents want a favor, if they present themselves as Austrian police or some other representatives. Volkov won't give anything away, but she appreciates professionalism.

ZHENYA MIHAYLOV

Young and pretty, most observers dismiss Zhenya as arm candy for a lecherous old man. Her fellow agents have an equally low opinion of her – they know she's a trained FSB bodyguard, but assume that she got through the training on her back. In fact, Zhenya's the most dangerous of the four bodyguards. She's the Conspiracy's agent in place, here to spy on Shevlenko and ensure he doesn't escape.

- Her cover is that she's Shevlenko's nurse.
- **Tradecraft** shows that she's underplaying her skills.
- She's used to men **Flirting** with her, and plays into it. Any agent who tries seducing her may think he's succeeded, but it will turn out to be part of her plan.
- **Intimidation** on its own doesn't worry her, but when coupled with **Vampirology**, it can convince Zhenya that her cover's blown and that the agents know she's part of the Conspiracy.
- Optionally, Zhenya might be a Renfield.

SEVASTYAN POPOV

The most junior of the four officers. Popov's massively overworked, as both Mihaylov and Kaminski dumped most of their duties on him. He's eternally behind schedule and buried under a mountain of paperwork. Dying in the line of duty would be a sweet release for him.

- If the agents try to schedule a meeting with Shevlenko, or try to arrange an interview, or have any official questions, they'll be diverted to Popov.
- Either **Flattery** or **Negotiation** works well when dealing with Popov.
- Trying to use **Intimidation** on him is exactly the wrong strategy – he might come across as a nebbish, nervous dogsbody, but underneath that, he's a trained bodyguard. Push him, and he'll push back with unexpected force. **Bullshit Detector** picks up on the steel beneath the harried bureaucrat.
- Officially, he's an aide from the Gorkhan.

TARAS KAMINSKI

He's the group's attack dog. He's the only one who is obviously a bodyguard; six and a half feet of muscle and brute force. He's obviously ex-military.

- He's very good at hurting people; Kaminski's Health and Hand-to-Hand should be higher than those of the average agent.
- **High Society** is the best ability to use to bypass Kaminski; he can deal with violence and danger, but he fears jeopardising his career by offending someone powerful.

EXTRA ASSETS

In addition to those four dedicated bodyguards, Shevlenko is protected by other staff from the Russian embassy if there is not already security present. For example, when Shevlenko meets with Saudi prince Sattam, he brings along another four bodyguards from the embassy. However, when attending a public function, he relies on the existing security and does not bother augmenting it.

- **Traffic Analysis:** The agents can locate Shevlenko by eavesdropping on Russian security radio traffic.

DR. INGOLF

Lukan Ingolf is a respected heart specialist, who runs a private medical practice in the centre of Vienna. A lifelong vegetarian and tee-totaler, he's an ascetic contrast to many of his clients. He divides his time between Austria and the United States, and is considering moving his practice there. The CIA recruited Ingolf as a spy five years ago; many of his clients are rich Eastern European and Russian oligarchs. Initially, all they wanted was a copy of his client list, but he was also used as a communications channel between Shevlenko and the CIA. Now, the CIA are using him to arrange Shevlenko's extraction.

The Conspiracy traced Shevlenko's leaked information to Ingolf, and turned him. He is terrified of the vampires; they gave him a sample of vampiric blood, and it shattered his faith in a rational, ordered universe.

NIGHT'S BLACK AGENTS – THE ZALOZHNIY QUARTET

PLAYING INGOLF
- Speak slowly and cautiously; never commit yourself to anything.
- Keep your hands clean. Be fastidious about hygiene.
- Swallow nervously. Hold your body stiffly.

INVESTIGATING INGOLF
- **Diagnosis** or **Forensic Pathology**: Ingolf's a well-known specialist in coronary medicine.
- **Bullshit Detector** picks up on Ingolf's nervousness.
- Accessing US immigration records with **Digital Intrusion** or **Bureaucracy** turns up the fact that Ingolf's on a CIA watch list, and he's had trouble getting entry visas at the most inconvenient times. Lately, though, all these problems have gone away.

ANNA SHEVLENKO

Arkady's only surviving relative is Anna Shevlenko. She hasn't seen her grandfather in years, although they stay in touch through occasional postcards and emails. Her father's death scarred her, and she and her mother fell out years ago. Arkady supported her through college by sending her money from one of his secret bank accounts, but has tried to keep her at arm's length for her own safety.

Anna is a graduate student of political science and history, although her studies have come second to partying and nightclubs in the last few years.

PLAYING ANNA
- Life is short, and people die when you least expect it. Live in the moment.
- Get into arguments easily.
- Check your cellphone obsessively.

THE CIA TEAM

A five-man team is in Vienna to extract Shevlenko. Most of the information he passed onto the CIA through Ingolf was low-grade material, intended solely to establish a relationship with the Americans. Now, Shevlenko has shown that he knows something about the Conspiracy, and the CIA want him.

The leader of the five-man CIA team is **Charlie Green**, an experienced spook with a strong Texan accent and a rapidly receding hairline (both of which he can conceal perfectly when under cover.) If any of the agents have connections to US intelligence, they may know Green; he's got a reputation as a reliable man, but something of a latent cold warrior who joined the Company thirty years too late. He is the sort who would launch a semi-sanctioned extraction mission, just to annoy the FSB.

Green and three other members of the team are going to die before the agents ever get to them. The last member of the team is **Lynne Feinberg**, the team's bagman. She ends up burned and on the run after the botched extraction in *Any Operation Can Be Aborted* (p. 62).

ALBERT CARPENTER

Albert Carpenter is the MI6 station chief in Vienna. Middle-aged, rotund, bearded, and usually seen wearing a grotty green plastic raincoat. Carpenter's on the outs with his superiors back in London, so his career has stalled him in Vienna. He's been station chief here five years, and it looks like he'll be station chief here until he retires.

CARPENTER'S GAME

Carpenter's function in the operation is to point the agents at the CIA extraction attempt, so they know that they've got to extract Shevlenko themselves to get Philby's secret. If you want, you can have him toddle off into the night after Day 1.

If you keep him around, though, you can use him as a source of help, a dispenser of hints or a source of paranoia for the players. What's Carpenter up to?

- He's pointing the agents at the Conspiracy to drive the vampires out of Vienna
- He wants Philby's secret for himself – he's going to steal it and sell it to the highest bidder
- He wants Philby's secret for himself – he's going to create the Rubedo and fulfil the dream of that other great British eccentric agent, St. John Philby.
- He wants Philby's secret for British intelligence, putting the genie of the Philby traitors finally back in the bottle
- ◐ In a **MIRROR** game, Carpenter's secretly a servant of the Conspiracy. He shows the agents the botched extraction in *Any Operation Can Be Aborted* (p. 62) to subtly warn them off further investigation of the Conspiracy, and reports everything they do to his vampiric masters.
- Even more ambitiously, what if Carpenter's secretly a vampire? In fact, he could be the vampire who made Simon Thonradel, and show up in the *Rubedo Rising* capstone as the ultimate villain if you're not using Anna Shevlenko.

ANNA AS PAWN

If this is the last operation in the **Quartet**, then you can use Anna as the Conspiracy's backup plan. In this scenario, Anna's a sleeper agent, possibly even a brainwashed Renfield. The operation proceeds as normal, including Anna's possible kidnapping by the Lisky Bratva, but her real goal is to smoke out Arkady's allies and locate Philby's secret.

One of the agents knows Albert Carpenter. He runs Vienna as his personal fiefdom, and knows everything that happens in the city. Out of courtesy, Green warned Carpenter about the upcoming extraction of Shevlenko.

PLAYING CARPENTER
- Never run, never speak hurriedly. Give the impression you're always three steps above everyone else.
- Never neglect creature comforts. Every meeting with Carpenter is in a nice restaurant or a good pub – and you're buying.
- Lean on an umbrella, stroke your goatee.

- Play up the English stereotype — everyone's "old boy" or "dear girl," and vampires simply aren't cricket.

INVESTIGATING CARPENTER
- **Tradecraft** or **Streetwise:** He's very well connected in Vienna.
  - 1-point **Tradecraft** spend: He's *suspiciously* well connected. There are rumors that he has an unspecified arrangement with the Russian GRU (Russian military intelligence), and that's why London doesn't trust him.

THE LISKY BRATVA
Mafiya assets in place in Vienna are as follows:

- PX4 Thugs, PxThug Bosses, all of whom are a bit more subtle than the average Lisky Bratva goon. They know that starting trouble in Vienna is a very bad idea.
- **Stefan Werner:** The Lisky Bratva's local kingpin is Stefan Werner. Four years ago, Werner was a lieutenant in one of Austria's home-grown crime syndicates; he overthrew the old boss with the help of the Lisky Bratva. It is only in the last few months that he has come to realize how devilish that bargain was. The vampire is his first exposure to the supernatural, and it's terrified him. He's baby-faced and nervous, looking more like a harried student than a crime boss, and he's always worried that one of his own followers is going to remove him the way he removed old Mathias. He's always on the look-out for ways to prove that he's got what it takes to run the operation, which means displays of cruelty and bloody punishments for those who cross him.
  - A 1-point **Streetwise** spend lets the agents identify Werner through rumor and informants. A **Criminology** spend can do the same through police records.
  - Someone talented in **Intimidation** can tell that Werner's faking his confidence. Once the agents know he's in over his head, they can offer him a lifeline with a **Negotiation** spend. If the agents can remove the vampire without implicating Werner, he'll restrain the Lisky Bratva.
- **Sergei Rachov**, one of Josef Lisky's lieutenants. Sergei also crops up in *The Zalozhniy Sanction* (see p. 46). He's here to facilitate the vampire's activities in Vienna (and also works as a decoy for any would-be vampire hunters).
  - If the agents eliminated Rachov in *The Zalozhniy Sanction*, then replace him with **Vitez**, a greasy, cold-hearted Hungarian who normally oversees human trafficking operations.
- **Kontrollinspektor Orban:** is a mid-ranking police officer assigned to security for the trade conference. He's on the Lisky Bratva's payroll. He can move up to 5 points of Heat from the Lisky Bratva to the agents, as soon as he has a valid description or identity to pin on them.
  - **Cop Talk** or **Criminology** spends can identify Orban. From there, the agents can either bring him down by establishing a clear link between him and Stefan Werner, or else turn him with an **Intimidation** spend.

THE VAMPIRE
The Conspiracy wants Philby's secret, and the time has come to force Shevlenko to talk. To force the old spy to confess, the Conspiracy has dispatched one of its own — a full-fledged vampire travelling under the identity of **Simon Thonradel**. The write-up below assumes a standard Linea Dracula vampire. If you've got a more exotic take on vampires in your campaign, either adapt Thonradel to suit or use him as the vampire's host/puppet/dimensional focus/alternate identity/decoy as needed. (If you do replace him with another vampire, remember that he needs to have Strength and Vampiric Speed at the very least to take out the CIA team in *Any Operation Can Be Aborted*.)

Count Thonradel — to give him his proper title — was created in the mid-19th century. He pretends to be the spoiled heir to old European money, a bored Eurotrash trust fund kid. He claims that his great-grandparents moved to France in the 1920s, taking their fortune with them. He seems arrogant, boorish and irritating, which is exactly how he finds humanity. He amuses himself by playing to the worst traits of the stupid mortals who surround him.

NIGHT'S BLACK AGENTS – THE ZALOZHNIY QUARTET

GENERAL ABILITIES: Aberrance 26, Hand-to-Hand 15, Health 15, Weapons 13
HIT THRESHOLD: 7
ALERTNESS MODIFIER: +3
STEALTH MODIFIER: +3
DAMAGE MODIFIER: +3 (sword), +1 (bite; extended canines), or +0 (fist, kick)
ARMOR: -1 (tough skin); Unfeeling
FREE POWERS: Drain, Infravision, Regeneration (all damage from physical weapons regenerates at the next sunset; can regrow limbs or eyes in a year)
OTHER POWERS: Addictive Bite, Apportation (into any place holding his native earth or any room he has been invited into), Clairvoyance (assigns or those he has bitten), Cloak of Darkness, Dominance, Infection (those who drink vampire blood only), Magic, Mesmerism (eye contact or voice), Necromancy, Send to Sleep, Spider Climb, Strength, Summoning (rats, wolves), Turn to Creature (bat, wolf; only at sunset or midnight), Turn to Mist, Vampiric Speed
BANES: beheading, stake to the heart, sunlight (prevents use of all vampiric powers)
BLOCKS: cannot enter a room without being invited (embassies don't count), crucifixes and holy objects, running water, wild roses
COMPULSIONS: kill and drain a fallen enemy
DREADS: crucifixes and holy objects, garlic, mirrors
REQUIREMENTS: drink blood, must sleep in his native soil each night

PLAYING THONRADEL

When he's undercover as a human:

- Annoy the players. Come across as a rich idiot who deserves to be taken down a peg.
- Carry a drink at all times. Complain loudly about how boring everything is.
- Smirk a lot. Be insufferable.

When he's a vampire:

- Stand up straight. Look down on the players.
- Thonradel's a predator. He unsettles everyone around him. Glance at the player's necks, sniff the air, lick your lips subtly.
- Smile, and show your teeth. You're invincible and immortal

INVESTIGATING THONRADEL

- See *Vampire Hunting* on p. 71 for details on investigating Thonradel.

OPENING MOVES

SCENE TYPE: Introduction
LEADS-OUT: The British Connection, Introducing Shevlenko

There's an undercurrent of tension in Vienna. Everywhere the agents look, they see signs of added security. More police on the streets. Brand-new security cameras, bolted to the side of baroque old buildings. Burly men in dark suits, tailored to hide the bulge of shoulder holsters. Big cars with tinted windows, rolling in convoys down the rain-wet streets. It's spook central.

On the street, outside a big hotel, the agents spot a news team reporting on the first day of the trade conference. The reporter talks about the hopes for the conference, how the business leaders and politicians of the world have gathered here to shape trade policy for the next decade.

The opening scenes should be driven by the agents — what do they want to investigate?

THE BRITISH CONNECTION

SCENE TYPE: Core
LEAD-IN: Opening Movies
LEAD-OUT: Any Operation Can Be Aborted

One of the agents knows **Albert Carpenter.** Ideally, bring up this connection in response to **Network** or some other spend. If the agents want local information or supplies, then suggest Carpenter as a reliable source. He's MI6, but sufficiently independent from London to be involved in side deals. Carpenter suggests meeting in a rather nice restaurant that's only a short walk from the Vienna International Centre in the early evening.

At the dinner, Carpenter probes the agents. He wants to know what they are doing in Vienna, do they intend to cause trouble, who or what are they looking for and so on. If he's on good terms with his contact among the agents, then his questions are friendly ones, with an undercurrent of "*how can I help?*" Otherwise, he's clearly marking his territory for the agents, and making sure they don't do anything stupid. Using **Tradecraft** or **Reassurance** to establish they can be trusted is a good move at this point for the agents.

Possible topics of conversation:

- **ARKADY SHEVLENKO:** He knows Shevlenko. The old goat is in Vienna for the conference all right. He's staying at the Russian embassy, surrounded by FSB minders. He's speaking at some mining seminar this evening, at the VIC. Co-incidentally, it's just a short walk from the restaurant if the agents want to attend. The Russian embassy should have his public schedule.
- **THE LISKY BRATVA:** Vienna's a neutral city, and the Lisky Bratva obey this truce. They're involved in the local vice industry, but not to a significant extent. He hasn't crossed paths with them.
  > If the agents press him and spend a **Network** point, he'll identify Stefan Werner as the local head of the organization.
- **THE TRADE CONFERENCE:** It's a terrible bore. He's rushed off his feet, making sure that the English weapons merchants only flog missiles and bombs to the right sort of corrupt developing-world governments, as opposed to the wrong sort of corrupt developing-world governments.
- **VAMPIRES:** "Nonsense, dear boy. No such thing." **Bullshit Detector** can't read him.

After dinner, Carpenter asks his contact (or the agent with the highest **Tradecraft** rating) for a favor. Would they terribly mind accompanying him to an appointment this evening? He'll pick them up from wherever they are staying. It may take a few hours, but it just involves a little stake-out. This offer is a **Core Clue,** and leads to *Any Operation Can Be Aborted.*

THE LISKY BRATVA

SCENE TYPE: Alternate
LEAD-IN: Opening Moves (or whenever the agents check in on the competition)
LEADS-OUT: Introducing Shevlenko, Rescue Mission

Criminology or **Streetwise** identifies the Lisky Bratva's main operation in town as human trafficking.

- 1-point **Criminology** or **Streetwise** spend: Stefan Werner is the local kingpin. They can track him down, but not before this evening's events. See *Rescue Mission* for more.
- **Traffic Analysis:** The agents need to get hold of a Lisky Bratva cellphone or some other route into their network before they can start in on **Traffic Analysis**. Using **Digital Intrusion, Filch** or **Infiltration** works perfectly well.
  > A 1-point **Traffic Analysis** spend picks up the rumor that a senior figure in the Conspiracy is in town. There are mutters about a "special delivery."
  > **Tradecraft (Core Clue):** The name "Shevlenko" crops up a few times. The Lisky Bratva are watching this Russian diplomat closely.

INTRODUCING SHEVLENKO

SCENE TYPE: Core
LEADS-IN: Opening Moves
LEADS-OUT: Any Operation Can Be Aborted, The Heart Doctor, The Approach

Shevlenko's got a busy schedule for day one of the trade conference, with two public appearances. In the evening, he's presenting a seminar on mining and gemstones, and then he's one of the guests at an exclusive cocktail reception at the Hotel Europa. Before all that, he has an appointment with Doctor Ingolf.

CONTACTING SHEVLENKO

Trying to contact him through official channels gets the agents through to Popov (see p. 57). He tells them that Shevlenko has no time for appointments today, but that he is speaking at a mining seminar that evening.

- **(Core Clue) Bureaucracy** gets a copy of Shevlenko's official engagements for the conference.

- **High Society** or **Flattery** convinces Popov to reveal that Shevlenko is attending a reception at the Hotel Europa after the seminar.
- **Negotiation** coupled with a convincing cover story gets Popov to arrange a meeting between Shevlenko and the agents at the Russian embassy tomorrow. The cover story must relate to Shevlenko's official position in the Gorkham.

OBSERVING SHEVLENKO

The agents can put Shevlenko under surveillance, picking him up whenever he leaves the Russian embassy. **Urban Survival** lets the agents get in place quickly enough to spot Shevlenko when he leaves for his doctor's appointment; otherwise, they pick up the tail when Shevlenko leaves the embassy to go to the mining seminar.

Call for **Surveillance** tests (Difficulty 4). If successful, the agents keep Shevlenko under observation without being spotted by his bodyguards. If the test fails, then that agent is spotted by the bodyguards. The FSB mark the agent and remember his features, but do not take action unless the agent appears threatening.

- **Tradecraft** or **Military Science** identifies **Volkov** as the head of Shevlenko's security detail, and Kaminski as the obvious bodyguard.
- **Notice** also picks up on the fact that Popov and Mihaylov stick close to Shevlenko and are armed, although they could be aides, not handlers.
- Eavesdropping on Shevlenko, either by getting up close to him or using **Electronic Surveillance** and a directional microphone, gets a long Russian diatribe about his heart.

THE MEDICAL APPOINTMENT (2PM)

Dr. Ingolf's practice is located in a townhouse in the centre of Vienna. Shevlenko's accompanied by his four handlers and another four guards from the embassy when he goes to the appointment. All three entrances to the house are guarded — getting in while the Russians are there is impossible. **Research** or **Diagnosis** identifies Ingolf as a cardiac specialist **(Core Clue)**. For more on Ingolf, see *The Heart Doctor*.

THE MINING SEMINAR (6PM)

Shevlenko's seminar is held in the Vienna International Centre, which is the one of the United Nation's headquarters in Europe. Several major organizations are also based out of the VIC, including the International Atomic Energy Agency. The seminar is closed to the public, but a successful **Cover, Disguise** or **Infiltration** test (Difficulty 4) gets the agents inside. The room is crowded with trade conference delegates, including a group of Saudi investors. Shevlenko works the crowd, and even greets the Saudis in fluent Arabic (**Languages**). He mentions that he learned Arabic from the son of Haji Abdullah — **History** identifies that as a name used by St. John Philby, father of Kim Philby. A 1-point **Notice** spend picks up on the body language of Shevlenko's handlers — none of them pays attention to the conversation with the Saudis, suggesting none of them speak Arabic.

The seminar goes into detail on the geology and politics of Central Asia, with special reference to Afghanistan. Shevlenko knows his stuff, and it is clear that his age has not dulled his mind. (If your campaign's vampires have a Middle Eastern or Central Asian origin, then **Vampirology** picks up on some coded warning in Shevlenko's lecture.)

AFTER THE SEMINAR (7.15PM)

After the seminar finishes, the agents can grab two minutes with Shevlenko under the watchful eyes of his minders. They can arrange a meeting for the following day with a suitable ability (**Negotiation** is the obvious choice, or **Accounting**, or **Military Science** or **Chemistry** – anything that can be tied to Shevlenko's role in the Gokhran. The old spy has Popov sort out the details of the meetings. **Bullshit Detector** suggests that Shevlenko was hardly listening and would have agreed to a meeting on any topic. (Shevlenko thinks he's going to be extracted by the CIA tonight, and that he'll be in Washington by this time tomorrow.)

If the agents drop hints using **Vampirology** (and are clued-in about real vampires, not just Hollywood monsters), then Shevlenko instinctively grabs his protective amulet and insists on meeting the agents tomorrow. He adds that if he can't make the meeting tomorrow "due to ill health," he'll certainly track them down in the future.

High Society (Core Clue) gets the agents an invitation to the reception after the seminar in *Any Operation Can Be Aborted*.

ANY OPERATION CAN BE ABORTED

SCENE TYPE: Core
LEADS-IN: Introducing Shevlenko, The British Connection
LEADS-OUT: The Approach, Burned, The Heart Doctor

The Hotel Europa (*****) sits in the middle of several acres of parkland at the edge of Vienna. It was built as a mansion in the mid-19th century before becoming a hotel in the 1950s. In addition to the main hotel, there are several smaller buildings on the grounds. These former stables and groundskeeper lodges were converted into private houses or extra accommodation. The hotel caters to the ultra-rich, and is a favored venue for dinners, balls, fundraisers and political functions. You need **High Society** just to get past the door.

Arkady Shevlenko's attending the champagne reception at the hotel tonight. The reception is for delegates to the trade conference. Security at the hotel is extremely tight — the guests are a heady mix of oligarchs, bankers, corporate CEOs and politicians. The CIA intend to extract Arkady Shevlenko from the party tonight.

There are three ways for the agents to enter this section:

- **Guests at the Reception:** Agents who know about the reception in advance can get an invitation with **High Society** (possibly coupled with **Network, Forgery** or **Flattery**).
- **Sneaking into the Reception:** If the agents follow Shevlenko from the mining seminar and don't prepare in advance, then they can still sneak into the reception with **High Society** and a 1-point spend from **High Society, Flattery** or **Negotiation**, or a test of **Preparedness** ("Of course I already obtained an invitation"), **Filch** ("of course I just now obtained an invitation"), **Disguise** ("I work at the hotel") or **Infiltration** ("I am a ninja").
- **In The Car with Carpenter:** Ideally, one or more agents take Albert Carpenter up on his offer – see *Observation Duty*, below.

THE RECEPTION

Agents in the hotel can mingle or observe the reception. Shevlenko's in the middle of the crowd, drinking mineral water when his handlers are watching him and swigging champagne when they turn away. The old spy is clearly excited, and his enthusiasm bubbles over into the rest of the reception. Getting close to Shevlenko is tricky, as there's a crowd of other guests around him at all times.

The agents also note the hotel security's unobtrusive but thorough security presence. They also have paramedics standing by, in case any of the guests fall ill.

Spice up the reception with a few added encounters:

- *'So, who are you and what do you do?'* Probe the agent's cover stories. They can deflect suspicion with **Flattery** or **High Society**, but agents without these skills who can't think of a suitable substitute may get into trouble.
- If any agents have connections to finance or politics (or just pick someone with a really high **Network**), then that agent runs into a former contact, **Naomi Delani**, a senior researcher at the World Bank. The agent last met Naomi back when they were working for their former employer, before their descent into darkness. Naomi was a good friend back then – does the agent jeopardize cover by acknowledging her. (If the agent does re-establish contact with Naomi, she's a free 4-point **Network** contact with connections in politics and finance in both the US and Africa).
- Both **Simon Thonradel** and **Sergei Rachov** are at the reception. **Vampirology** spots Rachov immediately, thanks to his mode of dress and demeanour. Spotting Thorondel requires a **Notice** spend to spot the out-of-place young man.
- There's a roulette table off to one side of the ballroom, for any agents with **Gambling**.

If any of the agents gets too close to Shevlenko, the lovely Zhenya Mihaylov runs interference. She'll flirt with any male agents, and complain about being hit on by drunken businessmen with any female agents. Either way, she'll try to uncover why the agents are interested in Shevlenko. **Flirting (Core Clue)** or **Flattery** lets the agents get a few minutes with Shevlenko. The diplomat appears drunk (**Bullshit Detector** picks up that he's feigning it), but promises to meet with the agents at the Russian embassy. See *Meeting Shevlenko*, p. 67. (If the agents don't suggest a meeting, have Arkady make the offer.)

After an hour, the party expands into the gardens of the hotel, as delegates slip off down the moonlit paths for private conversations or to have a breath of fresh air. Shevlenko meanders into the garden in conversation with various delegates. His four handlers follow him like four mismatched shadows. **Streetwise** or **Notice (Core Clue)** lets the agents keep him under observation. Move onto *The Extraction Plan*.

OBSERVATION DUTY

Meanwhile, away from the glittering lights and the string quartet, Albert Carpenter and any agents who accompanied him sit in a small car parked outside the high stone walls surrounding the hotel grounds. From their vantage point, they can see one of the back gates of the hotel, and can make out the lights of the hotel in the distance. Between the gate and the hotel is an old stables, now converted into a guest lodge. Carpenter has a thermos flask of tea and a foil-wrapped packet of sandwiches packed next to his binoculars.

He'll explain what he and the agents are doing here over tea *after* they give their word that they won't interfere. (If the agents mention they need to talk to Shevlenko, then Carpenter promises that he'll arrange it *after* the operation. Old Arkady will be much more talkative then.)

- Friends of his from Langley are carrying out a "little job" here tonight. They gave Carpenter advance warning of the operation as a professional courtesy, "UKUSA and all that."
- **Tradecraft (Core Clue):** An extraction of this sort would usually involve a cleaner who remains behind to erase any evidence of the operation. This cleaner wouldn't be part of the main team; they're probably waiting in reserve somewhere, monitoring the operation remotely. This clue informs the agents of the existence of a fifth CIA agent, *Lynne Feinberg* (see *Burned*, p. 69).
- The action should be kicking off soon. Carpenter plugs a little black box into the car's radio, and tunes some dials. The agents hear Russian voices over the radio – Carpenter's hacked into the radio channel used by Shevlenko's handlers.

Move on to *The Extraction Plan*.

THE EXTRACTION PLAN

The CIA intend to get Shevlenko tonight. Green and another CIA agent are waiting in the old stables at the far end of the gardens, dressed as hotel staff. Two other agents are parked nearby, in a fake ambulance.

During Shevlenko's meeting with Dr. Ingolf this afternoon, they briefed him on the plan. Here's how it's supposed to work:

- Shevlenko wanders into the garden, and heads in the direction of the old stables. His handlers follow.
- Shevlenko complains about feeling ill, and says that he wants to go back to the embassy. He sends one of the handlers to bring the car down to the back gate of the hotel grounds.
- That handler heads back to the hotel to fetch the car. He'll be delayed by the hotel valet, who's been bribed by the CIA to stall the handler.
- Shevlenko's condition worsens, so he sends another handler back to fetch the hotel paramedics.
- The CIA start jamming the FSB's radios and cellphones.
- Green and the other disguised agent show up at Shevlenko's side, claiming to be paramedics sent by the hotel. They carry Shevlenko into the stables. They examine him and claim that he needs immediate hospitalisation.
- The fake ambulance arrives. In the confusion, the handlers are made to think that Shevlenko's loaded onto the ambulance, but in reality he's switched with a dummy. This is the riskiest part of the operation, and Green suspects they'll end up stunning one or more of the remaining handlers with tasers or thiopental injections.
- The fake ambulance departs, drawing the remaining handlers away in the FSB car, which should have arrived from the front of the hotel by this point.
- Shevlenko is revived and leaves with Green in the CIA's van, which is parked at the back of the stables.
- The fake ambulance arrives at the nearest hospital, where the FSB discover they've lost Shevlenko. By then, he should be well on the way to a CIA safehouse.

There are two factors that the CIA haven't taken into account. The first is the player characters. The second is the vampire.

ABORT! ABORT!

Assuming the agents don't intervene, everything goes as planned at the start. Shevlenko convincingly portrays a man in acute distress; Popov runs off to get the car, only to be stalled by the bribed valet; Volkov goes off to fetch the paramedics from the hotel, and Green and the other CIA agent show up to help Shevlenko back to the stables. The fake ambulance shows up…

… and then the killing starts. The vampire followed Shevlenko to the stables, and can tell that his "heart attack" is a fake using supernatural senses. The vampire proceeds to slaughter the four-man CIA team using superior speed and strength. Shevlenko watches in horror as his CIA would-be rescuers are killed by the vampire before his eyes. Miyhalov keeps Kaminski from getting involved.

The agents' involvement depends on where they are:

- **In Carpenter's Car:** The agents hear the Russian transmissions over the radio until the jamming starts. Carpenter nods with satisfaction, and points his binoculars towards the old stables. The agents see Shevlenko being carried into the stables… and then there's the distant sound of gunshots. The jamming stops. **Preparedness** (Difficulty 3) lets the agents pull a pair of thermal-vision binoculars out of a black bag, which lets them see the carnage in the stables.
- **At The Reception:** Agents at the reception who didn't follow Shevlenko into the gardens may use **Notice** to spot that Simon Thonradel and Sergei Rachov are missing. They then hear shouts and shots echoing across the garden. The hotel security staff move to secure the building – unless the agents sneak out towards the stables immediately, they'll be locked inside the Hotel Europa.
- **At The Stables:** If the agents try to head to the stables, then they need to make it past both Shevlenko's other bodyguards (Mihayov and Kaminski), who try to stop anyone from interrupting the vampire. Any agent who makes it into the stable building becomes a target for the vampire. Stopping Thonradel without a plan and preparation is unlikely to succeed – show the unfortunate agent just how dangerous an angry vampire can be. If they get really lucky and manage

to drive Thonradel off, then it's up to the agents to explain the four dead CIA agents in the stables.

THE VAN OF DEAD MEN

After killing the CIA agents, Thonradel throws their bodies into the CIA's van, which is parked at the back of the stables. He then drives off at high speed, racing past Carpenter's car.

If the agents pursue the car, run it as a chase sequence through the dark, rainy streets of Vienna. The CIA van starts with a Lead of 4, and escapes at 7. Potential hazards:

- *Politzei* squad cars
- Slick rain puddles
- Narrow alleyways
- Heavy traffic

THE VAN ESCAPES

The van evades the agents – and then smashes through a crash barrier on the river-side and plunges into the Danube.

The agents arrive too late to spot the escaping vampire, but do arrive before the police arrive. Swimming out to the sinking van lets the agents find a clue – floating amid the wreckage is a plastic key-card to a hotel room with **Notice (Core Clue)**. See *The Hotel Key*, below.

THE AGENTS CATCH THE VAN

If the agents catch up with the van, much the same thing happens – only this time they get a clear look at the vampire as he escapes by leaping out of the van as it

---

BLOWBACK

There are three major sources of Blowback in this operation – the Lisky Bratva, the Vampire (both part of the Conspiracy, but at different levels), and the Russian FSB.

FSB BLOWBACK

The FSB are sinister, unreformed-KGB spooks, but Vienna isn't their home turf and they're not going to start an international incident. The risk of serious blowback from this source is low (but if the agents mistake the Conspiracy for the FSB, things could get complicated).

- **HARASSMENT:** Sinister phone calls to the agents' hotel or cell phone, complete with heavy breathing or disturbing electronic screeches.
- **BREAK-IN:** The FSB break into the agents' hotel room or car. This is done purely for the intimidation factor, to show that it can be done. They might alter settings on electronic gadgets, hide alarm clocks (set to go off in the dead of night) or move personal items – nothing actually damaging or dangerous, just really unsettling. (Of course, if the agents have illegal items in their hotel rooms, then a simple break-in could escalate into much worse trouble).
- **ADDED HEAT:** The Russian embassy complains to the Viennese police. Add a point or two of Heat to the agents' total as long as they stay in Vienna.

- **THREATS:** Taras Kaminski and a few leather-jacketed FSB goons from the embassy go on a hunting expedition. They find a lone agent (or a friend or contact) and threaten him.
- **ELIMINATE SHEVLENKO:** If it's clear that multiple hostile forces are trying to extract Shevlenko, then Volkov may decide that the old spy has outlived his usefulness, and eliminate her boss rather than let anyone else have him. She'll try to terminate Shevlenko immediately after the opera on Day 3.

LISKY BRATVA BLOWBACK

The Lisky Bratva are wary of breaking the peace in Vienna, so they'll only escalate their response if the agents are getting too close to Philby's secret.

- **INCREASED SURVEILLANCE:** The Lisky Bratva put out the word to the criminal underworld that they're looking for the agents. The player characters are followed on the streets, and their location is reported to the Lisky Bratva. This may increase the difficulty of any **Surveillance** tests, or force a 1-point levy onto any **Streetwise** or **Urban Survival** spends (increasing the cost of the spend by 1, reflecting the interference caused by the Lisky Bratva).
- **PLANT DRUGS:** The criminals plant a block of heroin amid the agents' possessions, in their car, or in a hotel room, then tip-off the police.
- **CAR BOMB:** As an extreme measure, the Lisky Bratva can bring in an assassin (or even a zalozhniy).

Sense Trouble (Difficulty 5) for advance warning, and **Explosive Devices** to disarm.

VAMPIRE BLOWBACK

Simon Thonradel's main duty is to watch over Arkady and ensure no-one else gets their hands on the old spy, but he can take a quick break to make the agents' lives hell.

- **INCREASED HEAT:** The vampire kills someone (maybe a girl matching his victim profile, provided by the Lisky Bratva) and dumps her exsanginated body in the Danube. **Forensic Pathology** can provide clues about the nature of the vampire, but the immediate problem is the increased police presence throughout the city, which raises the Heat even more.
- **DEAD BODY:** The vampire kills someone (a useful contact of the agents, Lynne Feinberg, Albert Carpenter, or even poor Popov) and dumps their body somewhere the agents will find it. It's partially a warning to back off, and partially a frame-up – the police show up just after the agents find the body.
- **AMBUSH:** The vampire attacks one of the agents and attempts to kill him in a way that looks like an accident – he might throw the agent off a rooftop in a "suicide," or throw a car into the Danube just like the CIA team.

smashes through the river-side barrier, then scaling a sheer wall like a fast-moving lizard. If the agents made it into the reception, they recognize Simon Thonradel; otherwise, **Photography** lets them grab a quick picture (assuming vampires can be photographed in your game).

They can also retrieve the hotel key that leads them to Lynne Feinberg.

THE HOTEL KEY

Cryptography or **Data Recovery (core clue)** lets the agents discover that the hotel key is for room 204 in the downtown Hotel Centrale. This leads to *Burned* (p. 69).

CLEAN-UP

Volkov knows that *someone* tried to kidnap Shevlenko, but doesn't know who is responsible. As soon as she recovers Shevlenko from the stables, she crams him into the back of a car and drives hell for leather for the Russian embassy. The agents have a brief window to check out the stables before the police swarm in. No bodies are found in the stables, and while there are signs of a struggle, there is no blood or other forensic evidence. The only witness to the vampire attack was Arkady Shevlenko.

If the agents never pick up the hotel key, then you can use Albert Carpenter to point them at *Burned*. **Bullshit Detector** picks up that he knows more than he's saying about the CIA; pushing him with **Negotiation (Core Clue)** makes him reveal he knows where the CIA were staying and that there's a fifth team member still out there. In exchange, he wants the agents to make the whole incident vanish. If the Russians find out that the Americans were trying to grab Shevlenko, it would massively ignite tensions between the Russian Federation and the western powers.

THE APPROACH

SCENE TYPE: Core
LEADS-IN: Introducing Shevlenko, The Heart Doctor
LEADS-OUT: Vampire Hunting, Rescue Mission, Blood Opera

After the aborted extraction, Arkady Shevlenko is back in the FSB's tender care, and now Volkov and her team are on guard. Finding out what Shevlenko knows got just a lot tougher.

SHEVLENKO'S MOVEMENTS

Despite the incident at the Hotel Europa, Shevlenko insists on carrying out his other engagements — after a visit to Dr. Ingolf in the morning of Day 2. Ostensibly, this is a check-up to ensure that last night's attack and exertions did not cause further damage; the real reason is that Shevlenko wants to use his channel to the CIA to get further instructions. At the meeting, Ingolf lies to Shevlenko, claiming that he's heard nothing new from Green or the CIA.

If the agents follow Shevlenko with **Urban Survival** or **Electronic Surveillance (Core Clue)**, he leads them to Dr. Ingolf's practise. See *The Heart Doctor*, p. 67.

THE SAUDI PRINCE (DAY 2)

Shevlenko meets Saudi Prince Sattam at the Russian embassy in the afternoon of Day 2, to discuss the sale of certain gemstones held by the Gokhrana. The meeting has no covert significance, unless you want to drop in coded messages to the Conspiracy and the Philby Plot. For example, if one of the components came from Wabar or the River Jordan, then Shevlenko could mention surveying in the Rub al Khali desert or water rights along the Jordan.

MEETING WITH THE VAMPIRE (DAY 2)

On the evening of Day 2, Thonradel and Sergei Rachov visit the Russian embassy. They're escorted up to Shevlenko's rooms by their agent, Zhenya Mihayov. There, Shevlenko is informed of the conspiracy's plans for him. The talisman prevents Thonradel from killing Shevlenko personally, but it won't protect Anna. Neither will the CIA. The vampires know everything — there is no escape from them. Shevlenko will give them Philby's secret, one way or another.

Vampirology spots something odd about Thonradel as he leaves the embassy (flinching away from sunlight, hissing at the shadow of a cross cast by a nearby church, or just sensing the presence of the agents from a distance and looking straight at them. If the agents follow Thonradel, he visits the Museum of Art History (see *Vampire Hunting*, p. 71).

THE DE BEERS MEETING (DAY 3)

Shevlenko reluctantly attends a meeting in the Russian Embassy on day 3, to discuss the international jewel trade with various gem manufacturers, jewellery wholesalers, governments and non-governmental organizations. The agents can use it as cover to meet with Shevlenko or to scope out the Russian embassy. A suitable **Cover** (Difficulty 5, Difficulty 4 with a **High Society** spend) gets the agents into the meeting. Security at the embassy is much, much too tight to even contemplate an extraction.

The meeting itself has nothing to do with the Lisky Bratva or the Conspiracy, but during a coffee break, two bankers discuss the upcoming takeover of the Swiss Koernersbank by the Black Sea Bank. Shevlenko overhears them — the news clearly shocks and terrifies him so much that he has to take more heart pills immediately. **Bullshit Dectector** picks up on the moment when his mask slips.

MEETING SHEVLENKO

With **Negotiation** and a good cover story, the agents can arrange a meeting with Shevlenko at the embassy. Check the agent's Cover after the meeting; if the test fails, then the FSB or the Lisky Bratva flag the agent as a threat (see *Blowback,* p. 65).

Either Volkov, Popov or Mihayov is also present at any meeting. To speak freely, the agents need to find a way to get Shevlenko on his own. A suitable Interpersonal spend (**Bureaucracy** for Volkov, **Flirting** for Mihayov, **Negotiation** for Popov) works, as does faking an incident or a phone call. Alternatively, the agents can use **Languages** to converse in Arabic, which none of the handlers speak.

Once he's not being watched, Shevlenko points to a decorate lamp while droning on about mineral reserves. **Notice** finds a listening device concealed in it, while **Electronic Surveillance** disables it. (A 1-point spend lets the agent adjust the microphone so it's still recording, but it's so distorted that no-one can make anything out, thus averting suspicion while ensuring privacy). Disabling the microphone lets Shevlenko speak openly and spill his core clues.

THE OLD SPY'S CONFESSION

Shevlenko waits for the agents to make the first move – they need to prove they are aware of the real situation, and that they aren't part of the Conspiracy. Using **Vampirology, Reassurance** or **Tradecraft** helps, as does mentioning the CIA extraction. (If the agents pretend to be CIA, that also works.) Shevlenko explains the situation:

- He wants to defect. In exchange, he offers a secret entrusted to him by Kim Philby on Philby's deathbed – a secret that *they* want more than anything else.
  > So far, he's been protected from the vampires thanks to something else Philby gave him, but he can no longer rely on it. Its power is fading.
  > **(Core Clue)** His granddaughter Anna is flying into Vienna tomorrow. She must be protected too. (See *Rescue Mission,* p. 73).
  > **(Core Clue)** He's a virtual prisoner in the embassy. The only opportunity to extract Shevlenko will be at the opera on Day 4 (see *Blood Opera,* p. 75)
- He doesn't know how the vampires knew about the extraction at the Hotel Europa, but one of them attacked the stables.
  > He can describe the vampire. If the agents know **Simon Thonradel**, they can recognize him from the description. If they don't, then the description coupled with **Research** or **High Society** or **Notice** (for those who attended the reception) give this clue, leading to *Vampire Hunting* (p. 71).
  > Dr. Ingolf was his contact with the CIA. (See *The Heart Doctor,* p. 67).
  > He believes he is being watched by the vampire, and tells the agents that any attempt at extracting him will fail unless they can deal with the vampire and its agents first.

MEETING SHEVLENKO AGAIN

The agents can arrange multiple meetings with Arkady, but the risk of detection grows. Increase the Difficulty of Cover tests by +1 for each meeting after the first.

SHEVLENKO REACHES OUT

If your players refuse to make the first move and need to be pushed a little, then Shevlenko can make the initial contact. He's heard of the agents through his underground sources, and knows that they have the talent to extract him. He contacts the agent with the best **Tradecraft (Core Clue)** through a suitable cut-out (or via Albert Carpenter) and invites them to a meeting at the Russian Embassy under the cover of official Gokhran business. During the meeting, he'll make reference to some legendary operation that the agent was responsible for (*"the FSB know you're behind the Minsk assassination"* or *"tell me, is it true you are the woman who wrote the Emerald Dossier?"*).

THE HEART DOCTOR

SCENE TYPE: Core
LEADS-IN: Introducing Shevlenko, The Approach
LEADS-OUT: Burned, Rescue Mission

Dr. Ingolf's medical practice is an unlikely setting for international occult intrigue. It's located in a converted townhouse in a quiet, upmarket respectable street. His neighbors are mostly other doctors, bankers, financiers and smaller embassies and consultancy firms. Ingolf has three other doctors working with him, as well as a staff of eight – including his formidably Teutonic secretary, **Frau Steiner.**

Getting an appointment with Ingolf at short notice requires **Negotiation** or a **Forged** referral from another doctor. Alternatively, they can follow Ingolf home (he's married, with two young children) and intercept him there.

Optionally, if the agents follow Ingolf, they may spot him making a dead drop report to Sergei Rachov (see *The Dead Drop,* below).

When speaking to Frau Steiner, a 1-point **Flattery** spend makes her compliment the agents on how polite they are, not like that "awful man" who called earlier in the week. She describes **Sergei Rachov**.

NIGHT'S BLACK AGENTS – THE ZALOZHNIY QUARTET

INGOLF'S OFFICE

Getting access to the office requires making an appointment with Ingolf, then distracting or incapacitating him in some fashion. Alternatively, breaking into the doctor's office requires an **Infiltration** test (Difficulty 4).

- **Diagnosis:** Looking at Shevlenko's medical records, the damage to the spy's heart is at least partially self-inflicted. He's been poisoning himself.
  > **Tradecraft:** Possibly, he wanted to preclude physical or chemical interrogation – any attempt to pressure Shevlenko to confess would likely kill the man.
- **Research** turns up information on Ingolf's problems with US entry visas.
- **Electronic Surveillance (Core Clue):** Office phone records show several recent calls from the Hotel Centrale. All of these calls went directly to Ingolf, whereas almost every other call went through his secretary. There's also one direct call from a mobile phone, made on the morning of day 2. Ingolf never answered it. This phone belongs to **Lynne Feinberg**. See *Burned*, p. 69.
  > **Traffic Analysis:** There was a flurry of calls before and after Shevlenko's appointment yesterday, as if Ingolf was being briefed or coached.
- **Chemistry** or **Forensic Pathology:** There's a small laboratory adjoining Ingolf's office. His sample of vampire blood is kept there, locked in a safe. See *The Blood*, below.

BREAKING INGOLF

If the agents try a subtle approach, they run into a wall – Ingolf doesn't discuss his patients with other patients, and he certainly doesn't discuss his covert dealings with the CIA or the Lisky Bratva. **Bullshit Detector** picks up on his nervousness and can tell that he's lying, but if the agents want him to talk, they need to establish their power over him and hit him with **Interrogation**. That means putting Ingolf in a situation where he can't walk away and can't refuse to answer questions; they'll have to either kidnap him or lock him in his office and ensure he can't call for help.

Interrogating Ingolf forces a confession.

- The CIA recruited him as a channel to Shevlenko.
- **Occult Studies:** Shevlenko wore a strange talisman at all times, even during medical examinations or scans.
- **Tradecraft:** The CIA had a five-person team, led by Charlie Green and based out of the Hotel Centrale.
  > They contacted him via telephone and told him to tell Shevlenko that the extraction would take place at the Hotel Europa, via the gardens. Shevlenko was to lose as much of his entourage as possible, then fake a heart attack. Ingolf provided him with a pill to mimic the symptoms.
  > He has not heard from the CIA since then, but he's deliberately ignored any potential contacts from them. His role in this is done; he just wants to go home to his family and forget all this.
  > There were only four people at the Hotel Europa operation; there must be a fifth man still out there. If the extraction operation was Charlie Green's idea and not officially sanctioned by the company, then that fifth agent is burned.
  > **Bullshit Detector (Core Clue):** He's holding something back about this fifth agent. If pressed with **Intimidation** or **Interrogation**, he admits that he knows her name, or at least her cover name. It's **Lynne Feinberg**. He's already passed this information onto Rachov – he didn't tell the agents because he fears they'll blame him for her death. Rachov will certainly want to remove any loose ends.
- **Interrogation (Core Clue):** Ingolf was contacted by **Sergei Rachov** a month ago. Rachov told him that his masters knew about Shevlenko and the CIA, and that they wanted him to continue passing on information between the two – but he would now also report everything to Rachov.
  > He can describe Rachov.
  > He contacts Rachov via a dead drop – he leaves taped messages at a particular waste bin in the city centre. See *The Dead Drop*, below.
  > Rachov convinced him to defy the CIA by showing him something terrible. He gave Ingolf a vial of blood, and told the doctor to analyze it. Dr. Ingolf is a world leader in the fields of coronary and circulatory diseases. He is an expert on blood – and that vial was like nothing he had ever seen. Whoever created such a thing is far more powerful than mere governments. See *The Blood* for more details.
  > The blood shattered his faith in an ordered world. It made him feel like a medieval alchemist confronted with an atomic bomb. He is sorry he was forced to betray Shevlenko, but what can he do, in the face of such terrible, unknowable power?

Play up Ingolf's reaction to the blood. It was the perfect method to turn him – the Lisky Bratva effectively showed him God in a vial, and the only rational response was to change sides and serve them.

THE BLOOD

Rachov gave Ingolf a vial of vampiric blood, taken from Simon Thonradel. The vial is kept in his laboratory, locked in a safe (**Mechanics, Difficulty 6** or **Explosive Devices, Difficulty 4** to break in; using plastique may attract attention). Dr. Ingolf's research notes are also in the safe.

Diagnosis, Chemistry or **Forensic Pathology** is needed to comprehend the scientific notes. Their content varies depending on the nature of vampires in your campaign, mixed in with plenty of speculation and pseudoscience. Drop in lines like:

- Genetic markers for Gunther disease (congenital erythropoietic porphyria)
- Clear evidence of hyper-viscosity;

> ### THE FEINBERG OPTION
>
> If the players lose track of their objectives, or misinterpret key clues, then you can use Feinberg or her CIA superiors to nudge them back on course. Either Feinberg finds the PCs and asks for their help salvaging the operation, or some old ally of a CIA-connected PC makes contact and points them at Feinberg. You can then segue back into Burned.

diluting a sample with plasm temporarily reduced viscosity down to 1.9 centipoises, but viscosity returned within 24 hours suggesting ongoing serum protein production in the sample
- Previously unknown forms of t-cell present, similar to cytotoxic t-cells.
- Spectrography shows presence of heavy elements, including iridium and sulphur

There is also evidence hinting towards a weapon that can be used against Simon Thonradel. This can be a weakness specific to him, or a general Block or Bane for all vampires in your campaign. For example:

- **Silver:** Accidentally touched sample with silver cufflink; sample demonstrated immediate adverse reaction, destroying 50% of cells
- **Garlic:** Blood tests are positive for strong reaction to diallyl disulfide
- **Ultraviolet light:** Exposure to UV light in laboratory severely damaged sample
- **Extreme cold:** Attempted to freeze portion of sample for later study; complete cell death occurred at sub-zero temperatures due to formation of ice crystals within anomalous blood cells
- **Blood Thinners:** Attempted to counter hyper-viscosity with heparin blood thinner; results were unexpectedly adverse.

Finding Ingolf's research on this topic lets the agents develop a countermeasure for use when *Vampire Hunting* (p. 71).

THE DEAD DROP

Ingolf communicates with the Lisky Bratva by dropping digital tapes into a particular trash bin near his practise. The doctor regularly dictates patient notes and diagnoses into his voice recorder; he also uses it to record reports for the Lisky Bratva and to tape conversations with the CIA team. Agents who put the trash bin under observation see that the tapes are collected by a young man in street clothes. Following the young man requires a **Surveillance** test at Difficulty 6; if spotted, he bolts and leads the agents on an urban chase. The Lisky Bratva courier has **Athletics** 7. Successfully trailing or chasing him leads the agents to the apartment block on Veronikagasse (see *Rescue Mission*, p. 73).

BURNED

SCENE TYPE: Alternate
LEAD-IN: Any Operation Can Be Aborted, The Heart Doctor
LEAD-OUT: The Approach, Rescue Mission

The last member of Charlie Green's CIA team is **Lynne Feinberg**, a junior analyst specializing in Eastern Europe. She is the least experienced member of the team in field ops, so she remained back at the team's base, the Hotel Centrale, while the rest went to the Hotel Europa and the botched extraction of Shevlenko.

According to the plan, Feinberg was to wait at the hotel until she got a confirmation phone call from Green; she was then to initiate a clean-up operation, erasing all records of the CIA operation. She was then to move to another hotel, wait until Day 3, then collect Anna Shevlenko and get her on a plane to the United States, fulfilling Green's promise to Arkady.

She sat by her phone, waiting for that call, until she saw the first news reports of a traffic accident. Realizing that her team was dead and the operation was a failure, she went to a back-up plan. She hastily cleaned the hotel rooms, then went to escape and evasion to throw off any pursuers. Finally, she contacted her superiors, only to discover that Green's operation was off the books. As far as the CIA is concerned, she's gone rogue and is considered burned. If her involvement in the "attempted kidnapping" comes to light, they'll disown her.

The only way for her to get back into the Company's good graces is to bring in Shevlenko and the intelligence that Green promised.

THE HOTEL CENTRALE

The Hotel Centrale's an anonymous block of concrete, catering to weekend-break tourists and business travellers on a small budget. It's entirely bereft of charm or character. The CIA team rented three adjoining rooms on the fourth floor.

Tracing the calls to Ingolf's office with **Electronic Surveillance** points the agents to the phone in room 406. Alternatively, **Data Recovery** on the key retrieved from the crashed van brings the agents to that room. The room has already been hastily cleaned – there's a smell of disinfectant in the air, suggesting that every surface has been wiped clean of fingerprints. The waste-paper bin is out on the balcony, and its half-full of ashes – Feinberg incinerated any documents that could connect the room to the CIA.

Searching the room turns up a Vienna phone book. Feinberg accidentally left a biro in the book, marking the last page she had open – a list of financial investment firms with offices in Vienna. **Accounting (Core Clue)** (or a background in the CIA, or some research) flags one of the companies, CJH Investments, as a CIA front company. After being rebuffed by her superiors in Washington, Feinberg headed for CJH to ask for help.

CJH INVESTMENTS

CJH is a small investment firm that focusses on the developing world. It has offices in the heart of Vienna's financial district on Börsegasse. The CIA contact officer there is **Nelson Selig** – brusque, professional, a teflon-coated personality. He was already irritated at Green's cowboy extraction operation, which Selig thinks is cold-war-era nonsense; the fact that Green botched it and ended up with four CIA agents drowned in a river makes it all much worse. He keeps Feinberg waiting in the CJH lobby for several hours before finally telling her that he can't help her. She's burned – she's on her own. If she heads back to Langley for a debriefing, maybe someone will take pity on her, but he can't help her while she's in the field in Vienna.

If the agents head to CJH investments, they spot Feinberg in the lobby or leaving the building. Unless the agents stop her, she walks down towards the nearest subway station, intending to vanish in the crowds.

THE LISKY BRATVA THUGS

The agents aren't the one people looking for Lynne Feinberg – thanks to Dr. Ingolf, the Lisky Bratva are also on her trail. To break Shevlenko's spirit, the Lisky Bratva must eliminate any straw of hope that he could cling to. Feinberg must be eliminated.

She's followed by a number of Lisky Bratva Thugs equal to the player characters, plus one Thug Boss (for a bigger challenge, upgrade the thugs, or add in an Operative or even a zalozhniy). They follow her down the street and into the subway station. There's a long underground walkway between this particular street-level entrance and the station itself, and unfortunately for Feinberg, it's empty right now. There are no witnesses.

Unless the agents intervene, the Lisky Bratva trap Feinberg in the tunnel, knock her out, and then carry her through an employees-only service passageway that leads back to the street. They throw her into a car and drive her off to the Lisky Bratva apartment block on Veronikagasse.

If the agents do intervene, you've got a fight scene.

- There's a study iron handrail dividing the two sides of the walkway, perfect for smashing people's heads.
- Stairs at one end of the tunnel, escalator at the other, both ripe for throwing goons down.
- Bring the thugs in waves – start with two following Feinberg, then two more waiting in the tunnel, and then add reinforcements.
- Capturing and **interrogating (Core Clue)** a thug points the agents at the Lisky Bratva apartment block in *Rescue Mission* (p. 73).

INTERVIEWING FEINBERG

Tradecraft coupled with a convincing story (or Albert Carpenter's endorsement) convinces Feinberg that the agents should be listened to. She's clearly strung out and exhausted – this is her first time in the field. **Reassurance** and the promise of assistance gets her talking. Obviously, she's more forthcoming to ex-CIA or other American intelligence agents. She has no idea that vampires exist, although she did hear Green use the term when discussing Shevlenko's leaks. She assumed it was a codeword.

- Feinberg can fill the agents in on the extraction and the CIA's interest in Shevlenko, if the agents haven't figured it out already.
- **(Core Clue)** She remained behind to collect Shevlenko's granddaughter, Anna, who's flying in on the evening of Day 3. She has a passport and ticket for Anna to get her to Washington.
- The team considered a second possible extraction plan for Shevlenko – he's attending the closing ceremony at the opera on Day 4. They considered trying to smuggle him out then, but Green went for the Hotel Europa smash-and-grab instead.

- Of course, any further attempts to extract Shevlenko are doomed unless the agents can identify whoever killed the CIA team, and work out a countermeasure.
- She wants to get Shevlenko's intelligence data to buy her way back into the CIA, and to protect Anna Shevlenko from any backlash for the botched extraction. If the agents help her, she'll owe them. See *Rescue Mission*, p. 73.
- Optionally, Feinberg may have intel that points the agents towards another operation. She may know that the Lisky Bratva run Overwatch Security in Baghdad (*Treason in the Blood*, p. 106) or introduce the agents to Donald Caroll in the Crimea (*The Zalozhniy Sanction*).

FEINBERG'S FATE

Without the agents' intervention, Feinberg is picked up by the Lisky Bratva on day 2. Her fate after that depends on the cruel whims of the Director – she might get drained by Simon Thonradel, or killed to throw Heat on the agents, or just show up as a prisoner in the apartment on Veronikagasse.

VAMPIRE HUNTING

SCENE TYPE: Alternate
LEAD-IN: Any Operation Can Be Aborted, The Approach, Rescue Mission, The Heart Doctor
LEADS-OUT: Rescue Mission, Blood Opera

Before the agents have a hope of getting Shevlenko's secrets, they need to deal with the threat of his vampiric protector, Simon Thonradel.

If the agents did not get close enough to identify Thonradel as the vampire, there are other ways to determine his identity:

- **Data Recovery/Electronic Surveillance:** Security camera footage from the Hotel Europa shows that Thonradel left the reception shortly before the attack
  - Of course, if vampires don't show up on cameras in your game, then the absence of Thonradel is the clue.
- Shevlenko can identify Thonradel as a vampire after he meets him on day 2.
- **Urban Survival/Vampirology:** If the agents follow Sergei Rachov, they may spot him in conversation with his master.
- **Traffic Analysis/Streetwise:** Breaking into some secure Lisky Bratva communications shows that Baldak Shipping brought a "special cargo" into Vienna on the same evening that Simon Thonradel arrived and hit the nightclubs.

INVESTIGATING THONRADEL

- **High Society** or **Research** identifies Thonradel as the heir to old money. A few gossip and tabloid stories paint him as something of a playboy, but he's largely invisible to the media. There's just enough material out there to give Thonradel a convincing legend.
  - A **Research** or **Photography** spend notices that some of the news articles are fake. Someone is planting news stories to create a cover for Thonradel.
  - **Accounting** connects Thonradel's money to the Black Sea Bank.
  - **Urban Survival:** Tracking Thonradel after he leaves the Russian embassy leads the agents to the Museum of Art History.

Edit the clues below depending on vampires in your campaign. For example, if vampires are a more recent phenomenon, then change the portrait to a photograph from a tabloid magazine and compress the period of Thonradel's killings. Non-human vampires might prey on a particular bloodline, or people with a particular genetic condition, or those born on a particular day.

- **Art History:** Thonradel reminds the agent of a portrait that once hung in the Vienna State Opera, but was moved for protection during the way and is now stored in the Museum of Art History. Its origin is uncertain, but it dates back to the 1860s. It is entitled "*The House of Ashes*," and depicts a young nobleman embracing a woman while a mansion burns in the background. It's traditionally taken as an allegory for the decline of the nobility in the Austro-Hungarian Empire.
  - The man in the painting bears an uncanny resemblance to Simon Thonradel.
  - A few scattered script pages on the ground by the woman indicate that she is an actress – a profession associated with scandalous women.
  - The woman in the painting is dark-haired with green eyes and a heart-shaped face.
  - **Human Terrain:** From the woman's dress and hairstyle, she's Hungarian.
  - **Occult Studies:** Talking to the museum curator (or local paranormal experts) turns up a legend associated with the painting – it's said to be haunted by the ghost of the actress, who was murdered soon after marrying the young nobleman.

Thonradel has a psychological predilection for a particular sort of prey – he murders women who remind him of his former lover. (Give this clue to the

> **OPTIONAL: MAKING IT PERSONAL**
>
> If your group can swallow a big co-incidence, and you want to up the thriller stakes, then have one of the agents match the profile of Thonradel's victims. Have one of the spies be a dark-haired woman with a Hungarian background, or have them visit their aged Austrian grandmother who tells them they're descended from the Thonradels on the wrong side of the sheets, or have all the victims share a curious crescent-shaped birthmark.
>
> Another option, if you want to draw all the strands of the adventure together, is to change the description of Anna Shevlenko so that she matches Thonradel's prey fetish.

agent with the highest **Vampirology** if the players don't draw the connection themselves.)

POLICE RECORDS

Getting access to the *politzei*'s records requires using **Digital Intrusion** or **Disguise/Cover/Infiltration** to get in. These tests are at Difficulty 8, and remember to throw Heat at the agents if they fail. The agents still get to find the clues if they fail the test – the test is to check whether or not the spies are detected afterwards. Once they're in, using skills like **Data Recovery**, **Research, Criminology** and **Traffic Analysis** detects a pattern.

- Fourteen incidents in the last twenty years relate to kidnappings, missing persons and murders. All the victims are similar in age and appearance, and there's a suspiciously high proportion of actresses, models, drama students or prostitutes.
- Filtering human trafficking reports from Hungary turn up dozens of other possible victims.
- In 2003, a Lisky Bratva informant told police that the *mafiya* are sometimes ordered to be on the look-out for women matching that description.
  > That informant was found dead soon after contacting the police. He committed suicide by gassing himself with car exhaust.
- Cross-referencing all that with Simon Thonradel's movements is difficult, as he travels via private jet and has no police record – but there is a statistically significant correlation. Wherever Simon Thonradel goes, women matching the appearance of the woman in *The House of Ashes* die.

PROCUREMENT

The Lisky Bratva secure victims for Simon Thonradel's blood-thirst. When one of their recruiters finds a suitable woman, they either lure her into their clutches by promising her a better life in Western Europe, or else kidnap her and smuggle her via the Lisky Bratva's human-trafficking network.

HUMAN TRAFFICKING

If the prisoner camp in Hungary (see *The Zalozhniy Sanction*, p. 16) still exists, then Thonradel's victim is shipped from there. A Baldak Shipping truck brings her to Debrecen; she's then smuggled in the back of a car across the border into Austria, and brought to the Veronikagasse apartment block.

Investigating this link requires delving into the criminal underworld, and that's dangerous. **Criminology** or **Network** turns up the right guy to talk to – a former Russian mobster named **Peter Kozlov**, who fled to the neutral city of Vienna to avoid execution. Kozlov broke the code of *vorovskoe blago* and is now a *suki*, a traitor, a walking dead man. Kozlov's living on borrowed time and he knows it – the only reason his former comrades haven't killed him yet is because they don't consider him worth the breaking of the peace of Vienna. If he ever tries leaving the city, or if he talks to anyone, they'll kill him.

Kozlov's a nervous wretch who jumps at the slightest noise, convinced there's a Lisky Bratva assassin in every shadow. He still has his ear to the ground, and knows where the Lisky Bratva bring their "special deliveries." Getting him to talk requires a suitable bribe (a suitcase full of cash or a new identity and a way out of the city); **Intimidation** on its own won't work, but a 1-point spend and a very creative threat can also spur him into spilling what he knows. He can point the agents at the apartment block on Veronikagasse.

If the agents go through Kozlov, hit them (and him) with serious blowback (see p. 65).

LOCAL VICTIMS

If the agents destroyed the camp in Hungary, then they've disrupted the Lisky Bratva's human-trafficking ring, forcing the local *mafiya* to rely on local sources. Monitoring police channels with **Electronic Surveillance**, research with **Criminology** or gathering information with **CopTalk** or **Network** alerts the agents to the case of **Cecila Vida**, a Hungarian waitress who was reported missing by her flatmate three days ago. Interviewing her flatmate **Katrina** with **Interrogation** turns up the following clues:

- Cecila was a drama student and aspiring actress.
- She used to work in the red light district up until six months ago. She stopped after her pimp was shot by "Russian gangsters."
- Several times in the last few weeks, Cecila complained about being watched or followed. She even took photos with her cellphone of the men following her. Katrina tried to give those photos to the police, but they weren't interested.
  > **Cop Talk:** The case was investigated by **Kontrollinspekor Orban** (p. 59).
  > **Data Recovery:** The cellphone camera photos are poor quality, but a bit of digital wizardry gets a good headshot of a shaven-headed thug with a boxer's nose and – more importantly – a car's number plate. Running those clues through either **Streetwise** ('*know this guy?*') or the police computers with **Digital Intrusion** or more **CopTalk** traces the car to a **Georgiy Loganov**, with an address at the Veronikagasse apartment block, leading to *Rescue Mission* (p. 73).

DEALING WITH THE VAMPIRE

Armed with the knowledge of the vampire's preferred prey, the agents have a chance of dealing with Simon Thonradel before they extract Arkady Shevlenko. Let the players come up with their own method for doing so, but possibilities include:

- Trailing bait (in the form of the vampire's ideal victim) across the foyer of the State Opera, or on the streets near the Veronikagasse apartment block.
- Inserting suitable bait into the cast of the opera, or near Shevlenko's opera box.
- Waging a psych-ops attack on Thonradel by claiming to have the soul of his former lover
- Luring the vampire into a prepared trap, like a room wired with dozens of UV lamps or a few kilos of silver-impregnated C4.
- Cold-hearted agents could dose their victim with anti-vampire poison (possibility derived from the blood sample in Dr. Ingolf's lab) and stand well back.
- Ambitiously, the agents could get a spy into the Lisky Bratva's apartment block by disguising the spy as a perfect victim, letting her get kidnapped, and then finding Thonradel's resting place and staking him while he sleeps.

THE VAMPIRE'S PREY

If the agents don't intercede, then Thonradel feeds on his victim at some point on day three of the conference. The victim is brought to a derelict factory on the outskirts of the city. All the windows of the factory are blacked out, and all the exits are chained shut. The victim is "released" into the darkness of the factory. Thonradel then pursues her through the darkness, hunting her through the maze of rusted industrial machinery and damp concrete walls, until she can run no further and he drains her dry.

If the agents intercept Thonradel in the factory, then they need to deal with the Lisky Bratva thugs outside (2 per player character) and the vampire himself. The dark, cramped conditions of the derelict factory make for a potentially bloody firefight:

- Sharp spiky bits of metal, rusted saw-blades, hanging chains
- Crumbling concrete walls to be collapsed or smashed through
- Blacked-out broken glass in skylights
- Decaying floors and unstable walkways
- Pools of potentially flammable or toxic liquid
- Near-total darkness
- A damaged fire sprinkler system that can be filled with holy water, gasoline or some other accelerant

EFFECTS OF FEEDING

If Thonradel doesn't get to feed on a suitable victim, a kind Director might drop the vampire's Aberrance score down to 10 to reflect his weakened state. Alternatively, maybe denying Thonradel his preferred kink just makes him angry...

RESCUE MISSION

SCENE TYPE: Hazard
LEADS-IN: The Approach, Burned, Vampire Hunting, The Heart Doctor
LEADS-OUT: Vampire Hunting, Blood Opera

There are three possible rescue missions inherent in this operation. Firstly, there's Anna Shevlenko, Arkady's granddaughter, who arrives in Vienna on Day 2 and needs to be kept safe. Secondly, there's Thonradel's destined victim, a woman procured by the Lisky Bratva to feed the vampire's bloodthirst. Thirdly, it's possible that Lynne Feinberg ends up here.

AIRPORT PICK-UP

Anna Shevlenko arrives on a flight from Moscow on the afternoon of Day 2. She expects to be met by her grandfather Arkady, but instead she's met at the gate by **Zhenya Mihaylov** who she recognizes as her grandfather's assistant. Zhenya leads Anna out of the airport and into the car park to a waiting black van, where she's grabbed by three Lisky Bratva thugs and a thug boss. The van then drives to the Veronikagasse apartment building.

If the agents try to intercept Anna in the airport, before Zhenya picks her up, then there are another three thugs lurking in the airport concourse to deal with any troublemakers. The thugs are under orders to be subtle, so they'll block the agents' path, stall them with arguments about who owns a bag, or try to prevent their car from leaving. If that fails, there's always the tactic of pointing at an agent, shouting *"My God, he's got a bomb!"* and letting airport security tackle the player character.

Following the black van leads the agents to the Veronikagasse building. A **Driving** test at Difficulty 4 or a **Tradecraft** spend is needed to tail the van without being spotted; if this fails, the van tries to lose the agents, leading to a **Driving** contest against a thug with **Driving 6**. Zhenya Mihayov has her own car and drives to the Russian embassy, but the Lisky Bratva can call her in for support if necessary.

ACQUIRING ANNA

If the agents get to Anna first, then a 2-point **Reassurance** spend is needed to convince her to trust them (drop the spend down to 1-point if the agents have a really convincing story, or asked Arkady for some token or proof to show Anna that he sent them). If Anna doesn't trust the agents, she assumes they're enemies of her grandfather and tries to evade them, which may play right into Zhenya Mihayov's hands.

If the agents fail to grab Anna, then they'll need to locate the Lisky Bratva apartment block in some manner to get to *Rescue Mission* (p. 73).

Once Anna's secured and convinced that the agents are working with her grandfather, she can fill the agents in on any missing parts of the backstory. She knows her grandfather was Kim Philby's last handler, and he once told her that Philby gave him "insurance." She also knows that Arkady sometimes talked about defecting to the United States, although he always treated it as a joke. She knows that Arkady has enemies, and has heard of the Lisky Bratva. She'll urge the agents to proceed with the extraction – if Arkady's finally made the decision to escape, then something more important than his own life must be at stake.

The agents can then take Anna back to Vienna with them, or else put her on the next flight to Washington. The exception is if this is the last operation in the Quartet, and you want to use Anna for the Capstone (p. 78).

THE APARTMENT BLOCK

The Lisky Bratva own a large apartment building just off Veronikagasse. From the outside, it looks like a slightly run-down block of flats. It's close to the Gurtel ringroad, implying its part of Vienna's red light district, and several of the flats are used by prostitutes. In the basement of the apartment block is a concealed prison, used as a holding area for women imported via the Lisky Bratva human trafficking network. Both Anna Shevlenko and Thonradel's prey are kept here.

The agents can find the apartment block by interrogating or following thugs from other scenes, or with **Streetwise (Core Clue).**

ENEMY ASSETS

At any time, there's Px2 Thugs here. If they expect trouble, then bring it up to Px3 and add **Stefan Werner** to the mix. Normally, a *mafiya* boss wouldn't dare get so close to the criminal side of the business, but Werner needs to prove himself, so he'll be right in the front lines if there's a firefight with the agents.

The Lisky Bratva thugs are all armed with small arms (+0 damage), but there's a locker of heavier stuff in the apartment block – if they've got time to tool up, give them SMGs (+1 damage) and body armor. **Military Science** identifies the weapons as US-made; **Research** finds they're noted as stolen in Iraq. Following this lead brings the agents to Overwatch Security in *Treason in the Blood*.

BLOCK SECURITY

The Lisky Bratva fortified the apartment block.

- **Urban Survival:** This place is being watched. There are always people on the balconies on both sides of the street, and there are watchers loitering in cars outside. If the agents try spying on the apartment block, it requires a **Surveillance** test at **Difficulty 6**; failure draws Blowback of some sort.
- **Architecture:** The entrance to the basement from the street has been bricked up, and the windows on the lower floors are barred, as is the skylight on the roof.
- **Electronic Surveillance:** All entrances are alarmed. There are security cameras watching the doors, and there are small webcams attached to the streetlights at either end of the block.
- **Military Science:** The goons sitting on the doorstep are armed guards. There's also an apartment directly opposite the main entrance that would make a great firing position – and there are always two guys sitting out on the balcony there.
    - ▶ 1-point **Photography** spend: A telephoto lens shows that they've got rifles stashed in a canvas bag at their feet.
- **Traffic Analysis:** Literal traffic analysis pays dividends – a lot of cars come and go. Some are clearly customers – they arrive mostly in the late evening, stay for a few hours, then depart. Others must be deliveries – they arrive in either vans or Hungarian-registered cars, part in the small yard at the back of the building, and never stay long. The arrival of a customer always coincides with lights coming on in one of the upstairs apartments, but the "deliveries" never do. They're going somewhere else…
- A 1-point **Law** or **Accounting** spend traces ownership of the building through a shell company to **Stefan Werner**, via a very generous loan from the Black Sea Bank.

THE SECRET PRISON

The Lisky Bratva prison is concealed behind a false wall (**Architecture** or **Notice** spots it), and consists of a dozen small cells. Conditions are clinical and sterile – this is a factory farm, not a torture chamber. The *mafiya* use old KGB interrogation techniques like sleep deprivation and forced nudity to break the girls and ensure complete submission. The girls are kept locked in their cells until their jailer decides they are sufficiently terrified not to attempt an escape, whereupon they are transferred to one of the apartments run by the Lisky Bratva. Any woman who tries to escape or crosses her handlers is beaten and sent back to the prison until she is once again deemed compliant.

The jailer is **Georgiy Loganov**, a surprisingly charming, avuncular figure who is adept at making people trust him. He gives the impression that he truly regrets having to punish "his girls," and that he only wants the best for them. **Bullshit Detector** sees through him.

INTERROGATING PRISONERS

Grabbing a random thug and applying **Interrogation** can get **Stefan Werner**'s name; grabbing Stefan Werner and applying the same pressure can identify both **Sergei Rachov** and **Simon Thonradel**. Werner knows that the vampire is in town to pressure Arkady Shevlenko into spilling something, but doesn't know what Arkady's secret is. He does know that the vampire is protecting Shevlenko, and that Anna Shevlenko is part of the vampire's plot.

- If you haven't run *The Zalozhniy Sanction* yet, then Werner says that the real boss is in Odessa, and that the whole human trafficking operation is just cover for whatever the hell they're doing in Odessa. Only old Josef Lisky and Dr. Dorjiev know what's really going on – they don't tell him anything.

MOUNTING A RESCUE

Likely methods for extracting a target from the Veronikagasse house:

UNDERCOVER

Pretending to be a customer (**Streetwise**) gets the agent into the house. He'll be frisked for weapons (**Conceal** to hide a weapon) before being escorted upstairs to an apartment. From there, he can use **Reassurance** or **Intimidate** to get information out of the girl.

Getting back downstairs to the basement without being spotted means **Infiltration**, and opening the locked jail cell requires either **Mechanic** or **Filching** Loganov's keyring.

BREAK-IN

The doors are all reinforced and monitored by cameras. Taking out a camera is easy; using an **Electronic Surveillance** spend to loop the feed is a better bet. The door can be opened with **Mechanic** or **Explosive Devices**, both at Difficulty 4.

ASSAULT

The most satisfying, but also the loudest and most troublesome approach is to just go in guns blazing. Obviously enough, doing so draws plenty of Heat.

BLOOD OPERA

SCENE TYPE: Core
LEAD-IN: The Approach, Rescue Mission
LEADS-OUT: The Confession

Day 4 of the trade conference closes with a performance of Heinrich Marschner's Romantic Opera *Der Vampyre* (1828) based on John Polidori's classic vampire novel, *The Vampyre*, at the august Vienna State Opera. All the convention delegates are invited to this closing ceremony. Importantly for the agents, it's the only time after the Hotel Europa incident that Arkady Shevlenko is allowed out of the Russian embassy.

THE VIENNA STATE OPERA

The grand state opera house was built in the 1860s. The public hated it so much that one of the architects committed suicide, and the other architect died of a heart attack soon afterwards. (If your vampires date back to the 19th century, then this could be a cover-up for the construction of a vampiric crypt under the opera house). The opera house seats around 2,000 people between the stalls on the ground floor and three levels of boxes and balconies.

The building was rebuilt several times, and suffered considerable damage in the war. Beyond the stunning exterior and the grand lobby, it's a maze of small passageways, corridors, function rooms and staircases.

THE SET-UP

The performance starts at 9pm. Shevlenko's due to arrive at 8.15pm, along with his four handlers and the rest of the Russian contingent. Their first port of call is a drinks reception in the Gustav Mahler salon, before the bell sounds and everyone takes their seats for the opera. Shevlenko's seat is in a small opera box to the left of the stage, accompanied by three of his four handlers; Taras Kiminski is stationed outside the door to the box. There are two other seats in that opera box, both of which are assigned to members of the Russian delegation, but only one of whom – a narcoleptic diplomat called **Pasternak** – actually shows up. As the opera is overbooked, the agents can use **Digital Intrusion** or **High Society** to grab the empty seats, assuming Shevlenko's handlers aren't already aware of the agents' identities.

The opera house is crawling with Austrian police and security forces. There's a metal detector at the front door, although bodyguards of dignitaries are permitted to keep weapons. There are numerous security guards at the entrances to the building, as well as plainclothes officers mixing in the crowd. Assume there are around 250 Austrian police in or near the opera house, along with another 50 bodyguards and state security troops. The place is very, very secure.

Both Simon Thonradel and Sergei Rachov also show up on the guest list. Rachov's got a seat on the middle balcony, while Thonradel has a private box directly across from Shevlenko. Optionally, he's also got Anna Shevlenko or his prey as a hostage in the box with him.

Der Vampyre is a two-act opera. There's a 30-minute intermission at 10.30pm. After the opera, Shevlenko is supposed to return to the Russian Embassy – instead, he'll be brought to the Imperial Crypts near the Hofsburg Palace complex in the centre of Vienna for his final debriefing (see opposite).

THE EXTRACTION

All the agents have to do is get Arkady Shevlenko out of the opera without being stopped by his handlers, the security forces, or the vampire.

GETTING INTO THE OPERA

The agents can acquire tickets with a **High Society** or **Forgery** spend. Sneaking a weapon in requires **Conceal**. Alternative entrances include the stage doors at the rear, or the underground tunnels that connect to the national theatre next door.

Getting a copy of the seating chart and the associated names requires **Digital Intrusion** or breaking into the opera house beforehand.

GRABBING ARKADY

Let the players come up with their plan for this phase of the operation, but some possibilities include:

- Using **Architecture** to identify the closest bathroom to Arkady's box, then blowing a hole in the wall so he can escape through the gap during the intermission.
- Getting into Arkady's box, disabling his handlers, and then escorting him out.
- Eliminating Arkady's handlers one by one through poison, social manipulation, or other means.
- Causing an uproar with an explosion (**Explosive Devices**) or other distraction, then grabbing Arkady in the confusion.
- Alternatively, they could replicate the Hotel Europa extraction. Fake a heart attack, and grab Arkady via ambulance.
- **Art History** identifies several points in the opera that could provide cover for action – notably the final scene, where the vampire is struck by lightning for failing to sacrifice three women to his dark master within the allotted time period. The lightning strike is a big pyrotechnic effect on stage, and could mask a sniper shot or explosion.
- More prosaically, the agents could try intercepting Arkady on his way to or from the opera.
- Remind the players of Arkady's poor health. Any plan that involves running, climbing or any physical exertion on Arkady's part is likely to fail.

If the agents haven't already secured Anna Shevlenko, then they also need to get her to safety before the Lisky Bratva kill her in retribution.

GETTING TO SAFETY

Once Arkady is in the agents' hands, they need to bring him to a secure location like a safehouse (or, if they've made contact with Lynne Feinberg, the American embassy). They'll certainly be pursued by the Lisky Bratva and the vampire, as well as the Austrian police if they've drawn any Heat.

COUNTERMEASURES

The extract needs to overcome multiple obstacles:

- **The Handlers:** These four stick as close as they can to Shevlenko at all times. Volkov has a panic button that summons FSB security; Mihayov has one too, but her one alerts the vampire.
  - Remember, only Mihayov is working for the Lisky Bratva – the other three just want to protect Arkady and make sure he doesn't defect to the CIA. If it's clear that Arkady's being threatened by the Lisky Bratva or by supernatural monsters, they'll help protect him.
  - The three other handlers will be killed by Thonradel during the final debriefing.
- **The Vampire:** This is the really big obstacle. Thonradel follows Shevlenko from the Russian embassy to the opera house, and spends the whole opera watching him from across the auditorium. If he sees any threat to Shevlenko, he'll deal with it personally.
  - By "personally," we mean "inhumanly strong monster reduces troublesome player characters to a bloody pulp by smashing them off marble walls and gilded statues."
  - Thonradel doesn't mind drawing Heat or causing a scene if it gets him closer to Philby's secret. When he's the immortal god-king of Saudi Arabia and sinks his (metaphorical) fangs into the world's oil-rich jugular, a little diplomatic incident in Vienna won't matter.
  - Encourage the agents to come up with a countermeasure (see *Vampire Hunting*) for Thonradel before tackling the extraction. Feel free to hurt them if they don't.

OUT OF THE HOUSE OF ASHES ■ BLOOD OPERA / THE CONFESSION

THE FINAL DEBRIEFING

If everything goes wrong and the agents fail to extract Shevlenko, then there is still a brief window in which to recover the situation. After the opera, Shevlenko is driven a short distance to the imperial crypts on the grounds of the Hofberg Palace. There, he is met by Thonradel and Rachov. His three handlers are executed on the spot by Shevlenko; Mihayov drives the three corpses away.

Shevlenko is taken into the crypt via a secret entrance and interrogated.

The old man no longer has the strength to resist, so he gives in and tells the vampire everything he knows in exchange for Anna Shevlenko's safety. He tells Thonradel all the information in *The Confession*, below. (If Thonradel's dead or eliminated, use Rachov). If the agents follow Shevlenko's car, they can try rescuing him from the crypt, or just eavesdrop on the conversation with a microphone (**Electronic Surveillance**) and then race Thonradel to the dead drop.

- **The Security Forces:** Pulling guns in a building crammed with 1,500 diplomats, industrialists and dignitaries is… problematic.
  - Emphasise that resolving the extraction through firepower is a monumentally bad idea.
  - That said, a single sniper shot timed to go off at the same moment as the climax of the opera is a great way to incapacitate Thonradel.
- **The Lisky Bratva:** The only member of the Lisky Bratva at the opera is Sergei Rachov, who is little threat to the agents. However, once they're out on the streets of Vienna with Shevlenko, assume there are at least as many Lisky Bratva thugs as agents on their trail.

UNEXPECTED COMPLICATIONS

Throw in some of these if things are going too smoothly, or if the agents need a lucky break:

- Overzealous security guard spots an agent's firearm
- Performance is late starting due to a technical hitch
- Albert Carpenter shows up at the bar to keep an eye on things
- Heavy traffic delays a key individual
- Unexpected security presence watching a side door
- One of Shevlenko's handlers shows up unexpectedly
- Agent is mistaken for another conference delegate
- Pasternak falls asleep on an agent's shoulder
- Well-timed pyrotechnic or burst of applause
- Fat lady sings very loudly

THE CONFESSION

SCENE TYPE: Conclusion
LEAD-IN: Blood Opera

En route to the safehouse or wherever the agents intend to bring Arkady, he clutches his chest. The stress of the extraction was too much for him – **Diagnosis** confirms he's having another heart attack. He waves away any attempt to use **Medic** on him. He needs to tell his story first. In choking, pained gasps, he tells the agents about Kim Philby.

How much Shevlenko reveals at this point is up to the Director. If this is the first or second operation in *The Zalozhniy Quartet,* then Shevlenko doesn't know what the Albedo or Nigredo are, he doesn't know about the Rubedo, and has only a vague idea about vampires. If this is the final mission, though, then it's time for the big reveal where the agents learn all the secrets.

- Shevlenko was Kim Philby's handler back in Moscow in '88.
- On Philby's deathbed, the old spy entrusted Shevlenko with a secret. Philby's father, St. John, did something in 1931, something to do with vampires. He left Philby with "part of a key," and Philby left that part to him.
- Philby also gave him an amulet or talisman to protect; he's worn that talisman ever since.
- The vampires knew Philby revealed his secret to Shevlenko. The talisman protected Shevlenko from vampiric attack, and he took his own precautions to preclude physical interrogation.
- Shevlenko hid the item here in Vienna in 1993, when he first opened a dialogue with the CIA.
- Now, he's dying, and the vampires are moving. He wants the agents to take Philby's secret and put an end to it.
- In exchange, he wants them to protect Anna. Give her the talisman. He also hands over a USB stick containing secret FSB files – this data should be enough to buy Anna CIA protection. (It's also enough to reinstate Lynne Feinberg, if the agents give it to her, and she can arrange to shelter Anna from Lisky Bratva reprisals).
- Philby's secret is hidden in a cache outside Vienna. He gives the agents a set of GLONASS (the Russian equivalent of GPS) co-ordinates to find it. He's had his agents check on the cache several times in the last twenty years – it's still there, intact.

NIGHT'S BLACK AGENTS – THE ZALOZHNIY QUARTET

THE TALISMAN

Unscrupulous (or, as they'd put it, practical) agents may choose to keep Shevlenko's talisman instead of passing it onto Anna. The talisman is more than fifty years old, and most of its spiritual sanctity/occult power/alien power source/weird radiation is depleted. Still, it works as a Difficulty 5 Dread when worn, and can be used as a Difficulty 8 Dread *once* before completely burning out.

Once he's mouthed the co-ordinates, he blacks out. It's up to the Director if a successful **Medic** test can keep Shevlenko alive, or if it's time for the old spy to bow out.

FINAL CURTAIN

Following the GLONASS co-ordinates leads the agents to a copse of trees outside Vienna. Digging amid the roots of a tree (Rowan/Holly/Juniper/whatever vampires don't like in your game) turns up a small bundle buried three feet deep in the wormy soil. Unwrapping the bundle reveals an old metal strongbox with a broken lock. Inside is…

- If you're running this operation before *The Boxmen*, then the box contains the passbook to Box 1247 in the Beirut branch of the Swiss Koernersbank.
  > You'll need to eliminate the passbook later on – see p. 89 of *The Boxmen*.
- If you've already run *The Boxmen*, but not *Treason in the Blood*, then it consists of Shevlenko's old case files. He was working in the Middle East during the 60s and 70s. The files mention an agent of his named **Nikolai** who was based in Beirut. There are also photos taken with a portable camera of the catalog of the Iraqi National Museum – Shevlenko broke in there in '72, looking for documents related to St. John Philby. Following up that lead with **Research** brings the agents to Mohammed Al-Kirkuk.
- If this is the last operation in the quartet, then the strongbox contains the ritual needed to combine the Albedo and the Nigredo – and now run the Capstone below.

EXIT VECTORS

This operation uncovers leads pointing to the other operations in this book.

THE ZALOZHNIY SANCTION
- **Criminology:** The human trafficking trail points to Odessa.
- If **Interrogated**, Stefan Werner reveals that a major Lisky Bratva boss resides in Odessa, and handles the smuggling and shipping on that end.

THE BOXMEN
- **Research:** The passbook is a clear pointer to the Koernersbank in Zurich.
- **Bullshit Detector:** Shevlenko reacted with horror when the takeover of the Koernersbank was mentioned.
- **Accounting:** The Black Sea Bank funded Werner's purchase of the Veronikagasse house.

TREASON IN THE BLOOD
- **History:** Both the Philbys and Shevlenko were running around Beirut in the 1960s – what were they up to?
- **Research:** The box files may point the agents towards the old Mukhabarat archives.

CAPSTONE: RUBEDO RISING

The agents have the Nigredo, the Albedo, and the ritual to combine them into the Rubedo. They've got everything that St. John Philby died for, that Kim worked for, that the Conspiracy fears. They've got their hands wrapped around the throat of the world….

… and then a figure steps out of the copse of trees. It's someone the agents know – Anna Shevlenko, Albert Carpenter, or some other trusted friend. The traitor points a gun at the agents, and the moonlight gleams redly off blood-stained lips. In the shadows behind the traitor, the agents note the unmistakable time-skipping insect-shamble movements of zalozhniye.

THE LAST BETRAYAL: The Conspiracy's traitor explains that they've been watching the agents all along. They wanted the secret that Philby entrusted to Arkady Shevlenko, and now the agents have led them straight there. Out of a misguided sense of friendship and pity, the traitor gives the agents one last chance to switch sides and join the winning team. Join the traitor, become part of the Conspiracy, and there may be a place for them in the new world order. Everyone else… well, they've already started digging a grave here in the woods.

The traitor takes the Philby ritual, the Albedo and the Nigredo and leaves. Anyone who tries to resist or interfere gets killed. The zalozhniye move in as the traitor leaves.

There are P/2 zalozhniye, along with P Lisky Bratva thugs armed with SMGs (+1 damage) and equipped with night vision goggles. The zalozhniye are carrying guns, but they've also got grenades and tripwires, and would prefer to sadistically hunt the agents across the Austrian countryside rather than kill them outright. If the agents allow themselves to be chased, they can buy time to get clear of the wooded area, then turn and fight the monsters one at a time.

TRACKING THE TRAITOR: Either by capturing and **Interrogating** the last Lisky Bratva thug, or using technical skills like **Traffic Analysis**, the agents discover that the traitor has handed the three components of the Rubedo over to a vampire (Thonradel if he's still alive, or Albert Carpenter if he's a vampire, or some other horror of your creation). That vampire is now en route to Riyadh for the final apotheosis. See p. 133 of *Treason in the Blood*'s capstone for the Riyadh ritual.

THE BOX MEN

The worlds of the criminal and the spy intertwine more often than governments like to admit. Some of the best agents were criminals and con men before – or after, or even during – their service to the country. In this operation, the agents' target is a safe-deposit box inside a Swiss bank. A team of crooks also intend to break into the bank. The agents must either join forces with the criminals, or beat them at their own game.

This is the sexy, low-combat, *Ocean's 11* operation. Or it's the tense, sweaty, violent *Reservoir Dogs* operation. Or both.

EYES ONLY BRIEFING

The Koernersbank is a small Swiss private bank, catering to wealthy clients who value discretion and security above all else. The bank's heyday was in the middle of the 20th century, during the post-war reconstruction boom. In recent years, a series of poor investments resulted in the loss of several important clients, and the private-owned bank is in need of a white knight to save it. The bank found its savior in the form of the Black Sea Bank, bringing in new Russian oil and gas money to preserve old Swiss gold and Arabian petrodollars. In a few days' time, the final contracts will be signed and the Black Sea Bank – and through them, the Lisky Bratva – will own the Koernersbank.

They don't care about the bank. They just want one thing – the contents of Box 1274.

St. John Philby opened a private account with the Koernersbank in 1934, on the strength of a letter of introduction from his son's friend Lord Victor Rothschild. Kim Philby left the Albedo in a safe-deposit box in the Beirut branch of the bank in early January 1963, mere days before he defected to Moscow. He left it there as insurance, and intended to retrieve it in a few years. He never did.

The Beirut branch of the Koernersbank closed in the face of the Lebanese civil war in '75; its contents were shipped back to the mother bank in Zurich. Ever since then, Philby's security box has rested in the bank vault, waiting for someone to claim it.

Soon, the Lisky Bratva will have that box – unless someone steals it first.

THE THIEVES & THE WATCHERS

The agents aren't the only people preparing to rob the Koernersbank. A small team of experienced bank thieves led by Menena Chakroun is also plotting to break into the ultra-secure vault. When one of them is eliminated by the Lisky Bratva, they offer to join forces with the agents.

These thieves have their own agenda beyond profit, and finding out who to trust is a key challenge in the operation. Once the agents break into the vault and recover the Albedo along with the other treasures, they've got to escape Switzerland before the Lisky Bratva retaliate.

THE SPINE

There's every possibility that this operation goes all *Reservoir Dogs* when the team reaches the vault, but here's the likely chain of events.

The operation kicks off when the agents arrive in Zurich and learn that the Koernersbank is being taken over by the Black Sea Bank in **The Setup**. They run into Menena Chakroun for the first time when **Visiting the Koernersbank**. From there, they can do **Background Checks** on the Montavon family and the bank, and discover the upcoming **Shipment** of money from the Black Sea Bank.

Another of the rival thieves tries to steal from the agents, but gets blown up by a zalozhniy car bomb in **Death of a Chameleon**. That leads to a potential uneasy alliance with the rival thieves in **The Other Guys**.

By now, the agents know there something important in the Koernersbank vault, so it's time to start **Planning the Heist**. That leads on to **The Heist**. If they succeed, then they're **In The Vault** and can loot the place. At that point, the agents may be betrayed by one of the other thieves. If that happens, the thief makes off with the Albedo in **Stolen Albedo**.

At **The Safe House**, the agents are ambushed by the Lisky Bratva. If they make it out of there with the Albedo, then they can flee the country in **Bank Run**. If not, then they've got to **Recover The Albedo** before escaping.

ENTRY VECTORS

There are a number of ways into this adventure, from previous ops, from other operations in this collection, or from random chatter. The Director should salt as many leads as she feels necessary, or customize them to suit her campaign.

THE HEIST OF THE CENTURY

Elements of this operation were inspired by the infamous "heist of the century," in which a band of thieves broke into the ultra-secure vaults of the Antwerp Diamond Center and made off with millions of dollars worth of diamonds. It's worth reading descriptions of the crime to see how they pulled it off, where they went wrong (one of the criminals was convicted on the strength of a discarded sandwich) and how they might have been double-crossed (the ringleader, Leonardo Notarbartolo, claims that the whole thing was an insurance scam, and the vault was mostly empty).

OUTSIDE LEADS

These leads come from outside this book; from the corebook adventure *(S) Entries* or perhaps from other ops in the Director's previous campaign.

THE LENNART DOSSIER
- **Accounting** traces clear connections between the Conspiracy, the Lisky Bratva and the Black Sea Bank. The takeover of the Koernersbank is seen by most commentators as a bizarre misstep by the Black Sea Bank, with some speculating that the BSB is trying to buy respectability and a toe-hold in Switzerland. Certainly, the move makes little financial sense.

OTHER VECTORS
- **Criminology:** If the agents need cash to fund their shadow war, they could try robbing a bank — and bank security is always lower immediately before a takeover, as protocols are relaxed to cope with the influx of accountants, lawyers and other anonymous people in suits.
- **Network:** If your agents are or know criminal types, they could be tipped off about Chakroun's plan to break into the bank. She might even hire them.
- One of the Montavons might hire the agents, either to wreck the deal (Clarique) or tidy up a mess (Jean).

INSIDE LEADS

Intel gathered in other operations in this collection may lead the agents to Zurich and the Koernersbank. If the players don't quite stumble over the right leads in those scenarios, quite often the Director can plant this intel in the mouth (or dead fist, or laptop, or smartphone) of an NPC also on the trail of the Lisky Bratva or of the Philby Plot.

THE ZALOZHNIY SANCTION
- The Black Sea Bank is headquartered in Odessa, and is a key part of the money laundering chain that starts in Debrecen.
- The Serbian mafia know the Lisky Bratva own the Black Sea Bank, and want in.

OUT OF THE HOUSE OF ASHES
- Arkady Shevlenko gives the agents the passbook to Philby's safe-deposit box.
- The agents may have seen Shevlenko's reaction to the news of the Koernersbank sale.

TREASON IN THE BLOOD
- Nikolai's documents show that the Philbys had an account in the Koernersbank.
- Gold bullion looted from Iraq is part of the Black Sea Bank shipment to the Koernersbank.

ZURICH: QUICK AND DIRTY

The largest city in Switzerland, Zurich's one of the nicest – and most expensive – places to live. It's a linchpin of the world financial system, with the fourth largest stock exchange and lots of major corporation headquarters here. The city is built around and along the northern tip of Lake Zurich.

POPULATION
370,000 (roughly the same as Oakland or Minneapolis)

CONFLICT
The conflict in Zurich bubbles below the surface. With so much of the city dependent on the financial industry, Zurich's on the verge of being swallowed by the ongoing chaos in the world economy. That means that financiers and bankers are taking risks to hide huge losses or pulling their own money out of the system. Corruption and desperation drive the conflict in Zurich.

BACKDROPS
THE OLD TOWN: The medieval heart of the city, full of squares, narrow alleyways, bridges, and 18th-century guild houses.
TRAMS: Zurich's got an excellent public transport system, mixing buses, trams, trains and even a cable car. Car owners are a minority in the city, and hopping on and off trams is a great way to disappear.
GROSSMÜNSTER: A medieval Romanesque cathedral overlooking the river. The Grossmünster is the most recognizable landmark in Zurich.

THREE HOOKS
- Switzerland's famous neutrality even extends to electronic surveillance – it's got a home-grown, independent version of the ECHELON network called ONYX that eavesdrops on telecommunications. Getting access to ONYX would give the agents a way to track Conspiracy activity across Europe.
- Zurich is a city of choice for Russian crime syndicates to invest their money – especially the syndicates that evolved from state intelligence agencies in collapsed Soviet satellites. There's a thin line between financier, spy and crook – and the vampires' minions exist in that ambiguity.
- Kim Philby's not the only spy to use a Swiss bank as a stash – who knows what the conspiracy has locked away in a numbered account?

NIGHT'S BLACK AGENTS – THE ZALOZHNIY QUARTET

THE THIEVES

The agents' competitors – or partners – in the bank raid are four experienced criminals, each one an expert in their respective field. Ostensibly, they're doing this for the money, but they may have secret motivations. Several dirty secrets are listed for each of the thieves; pick the ones that suits your campaign best, or the one that will thrill or surprise your players the most. You don't have to decide on everyone's motivations immediately – you can leave some to be discovered in play.

One of the thieves is a traitor who'll betray the group to the Lisky Bratva, thus triggering the events in *The Safe House* (see p. 99). Pick *one* motivation with the ◉ symbol in the lists below. (Other motivations may prompt thieves to betray the group, but not to the Lisky Bratva). Optionally, you can make the traitor a Renfield.

When playing the thieves, look for ways to play them off against the agents. If an agent is very cautious and meticulous about planning, then play Kevin Lawson as headstrong and impetuous. An agent with a history in law enforcement should be needled by Florin's constant references to old crimes. Any would-be James Bonds should initially be rebuffed by Chakroun, but then have her slowly thaw and start flirting as the heist proceeds.

THE QUEEN OF THIEVES

A strikingly beautiful Moroccan, Menena Chakroun is the so-called "queen of thieves." She's responsible for planning the heist and assembling the team. Her particular specialties are safecracking and bypassing security systems. She started out as a penniless orphan on the streets of Marrakesh, and graduated from street thief to burglar to bank robber. She moved to Italy in the early 2000s and learned from some of the best thieves in the world before striking out on her own.

Criminology: Interpol tried to connect several high-profile robberies to her, but they couldn't make it stick.

Tradecraft: Every good spy learns when to walk away, and Chakroun has that down. If the job goes wrong, she'll walk away without hesitation. That doesn't mean you can't rely on her, it just means that she'll look out for her own safety ahead of everything else.

Negotiation: She's too professional and controlled for any other interpersonal approach to work. Threaten her, and she'll just walk away or shoot you. Trying to befriend her is useless – she doesn't have friends. Flirting only works on people who don't control their emotions, and Chakroun's got the heart of a black marble statue.

MENENA CHAKROUN

GENERAL ABILITIES: Athletics 10, Conceal 6, Cover 10, Filch 6, Hand-to-Hand 8, Health 8, Infiltration 8, Network 10, Preparedness 6, Sense Trouble 10, Shooting 4, Surveillance 10
Investigative Abilities: Criminology 3, Flattery 1, High Society 1, Streetwise 2, Tradecraft 1, Notice 2, Urban Survival 2
HIT THRESHOLD: 4
ALERTNESS MODIFIER: +2
STEALTH MODIFIER: +1
DAMAGE MODIFIER: -2 (fist)

PLAYING CHAKROUN

- Never raise your voice unless you're barking an order. Stay in control at all times.
- Be extremely professional.
- Sit up straight. Keep perfect poise. Look down at people – give the impression of high status.
- Try to take charge of any situation.

MOTIVATIONS & DIRTY SECRETS

Chakroun claims to have organized this bank job on her own initiative. She knows that security at the Koernersbank is weak right now, and that the vault contains a considerable haul. Secretly, though, she's doing because of…

- **No, really, it's just the money.** This is how she pays the bills.
- **THE PAYOFF:** Chakroun's working for Clarique Montavon (see p. 85), the black sheep of the family who own the Koernersbank. Montavon wants to scupper the deal between the family and the Black Sea Bank. Getting the haul isn't as important as disgracing the bank.
- **IMMORTALITY:** Chakroun's the illegitimate great-granddaughter of St. John Philby, via a woman of Ibn Saud's court. She learned of her great-grandfather's plot through her family, and intends to complete the Rubedo and become the vampire queen of Arabia.
- **THE BIDDING WAR:** She knows that the contents of Box 1274 are valuable not only to the Lisky Bratva, but to the FSB, the CIA, the player characters and several other parties. She intends to steal the box and sell it to the highest bidder.
- **REVENGE:** Chakroun's brother **Hassan** was taken by Lisky Bratva human traffickers. She doesn't know what happened to him, but she wants revenge.
- ◉ **RESCUE:** As above, only Hassan is a prisoner of the vampires. They hired Chakroun to retrieve the contents of Box 1274 before the bank is sold, to ensure that none of their human pawns tried to double-cross them and make off with the Albedo themselves.

THE WIZARD OF LOCKS

Massimo Florin looks like a middle-aged, sleepy clerk who should be mummified in a government office somewhere. He's so gentle as to almost seem serene; you'd expect him to be smoking a pipe or playing with his nephews or propping up a bar somewhere. Florin is a genius at making forgeries, cutting keys and dealing with physical security systems.

Forgery: Watching this guy at work makes it clear he's a master craftsmen.

Criminology: Florin's a legend in the underworld. He normally operates from a workshop in Turin — it would take a lot of money to get him out of his comfort zone.

MASSIMO FLORIN

GENERAL ABILITIES: Athletics 4, Conceal 8, Cover 6, Hand-to-Hand 2, Health 4, Mechanics 12, Network 6, Preparedness 18, Shooting 4
Investigative Abilities: Forgery 3
HIT THRESHOLD: 3
ALERTNESS MODIFIER: +1
STEALTH MODIFIER: +0
DAMAGE MODIFIER: -2 (fist)

PLAYING FLORIN

- Play up your age. Move slowly, grumble, and let other people do all the hard work.
- Observe people before speaking. Keep in the background.
- Test the people around you. Push them subtly. Ask them unsettling questions. For example, if an agent is cleaning a gun, ask them if they could shoot a child to complete a mission.
- Use a pen or some other handy prop as a pipe.

MOTIVATIONS & DIRTY SECRETS

Florin claims that Chakroun recruited him for one last job. While that may be true, Florin's real motivation is…

- Exactly what it seems. He's in this for the money.
- **MASTERMIND:** He recruited Chakroun to front the operation, and he's planning on taking all the cash. He's got another gang of thieves standing by to intercept the loot-laden player characters as they escape from the bank.
- **VATICAN ASSASSIN:** Florin's doing this for the Church's secret order of vampire-hunting monks. His aim is to recover the Albedo and bring it back to the vaults under Rome.
- **DUE DILIGENCE:** Florin's working with the Black Sea Bank, who hired him to test security at the Koernersbank. If the heist goes wrong, he turns the team over to the Black Sea Bank and walks away with a cheque for his services to the tune of €200,000. If they actually break in, then he retires on the proceeds and vanishes. He's playing both sides and will always back the winner.
- **SOMETHING TO PROVE:** Florin's an old, sick man. His hands have started to shake and his memory is no longer reliable. He wants to retire a legend by completing this last job. If the vampires were to offer him a cure, he might switch sides.
- ■ AGE AND TREACHERY: He knows the secrets of the underworld. He knows who's really running things behind the scenes. He'll rob from banks, he'll break into governments, he'll rob from the Cosa Nostra and he'll still sleep like a baby — but cross *them*!? Are you crazy? As soon as it becomes clear that the agents are after something related to the Conspiracy, then Florin calls his old friend in Odessa…

THE BEAST

Keith Lawson is an alarmingly gifted individual. He's monstrously fast and strong, with black belts in three martial arts. He's got brains to match, with degrees in electronic engineering and physics from Cambridge. He's worked as a mercenary and as an engineer (it's always handy to have the guy who can prospect for oil one week and organize ethnic cleansing to clear out inconvenient locals the next week). He served in the British Army for a few years, but left after crippling his SAS instructor when an argument turned physical. He's supremely confident and competent.

Military Science: He's clearly got extensive military training.

KEITH LAWSON

GENERAL ABILITIES: Athletics 10, Cover 4, Hand-to-Hand 12, Health 10, Infiltration 6, Shooting 8, Weapons 8
HIT THRESHOLD: 4
ALERTNESS MODIFIER: +2
STEALTH MODIFIER: +1
DAMAGE MODIFIER: -1 (brutal killer-elite fist)
Lawson gets one 4-point Hand-to-Hand or Shooting pool refresh once per session.

PLAYING LAWSON

- Move as if you're bigger and heavier than you are. Imagine you're a walking tank.
- You have to be the alpha male in any situation. Challenge any player characters who might be competition.
- You're a coiled spring of barely suppressed violence. Your first instinct when there's trouble is to lash out.

MOTIVATIONS & DIRTY SECRETS

Chakroun hired Lawson via a middleman — but what's the real story?

- It's the truth — Lawson's just hired muscle.
- **THE MI6 MAN:** His story about being kicked out of the SAS is a lie; Lawson's a deep cover MI6 agent, here to tie up a troublesome loose end. The Philby case has been on the books at the Circus for decades, and they've sent Lawson to retrieve the Albedo for Queen and Country.
- **THE MOSSAD CONNECTION:** Lawson's working for Mossad. Back during World War II, the Koernersbank accepted clients from Nazi Germany. A lot of stolen Jewish gold was stashed in the bank vaults. More importantly, the Koernersbank private clients list is in the vault, and on that list are the names and locations of several former Nazis and their families.
- **THE CLIENT:** Lawson's working for another client, who wants him to recover the box. This could be someone like **Arkady Shevlenko** (see p. 55) or **Dr. Dorjiev** (p. 7) or **Clarique Montavon** (p. 85). Lawson doesn't know who his employer is — he just knows that he's going to get box 1274 and deliver it.
- **THE ASSASSIN:** As above, only Lawson's target isn't the box — it's the player characters. He's under orders to either kill one of the player characters, kill *all* the players, or deliberately screw up the heist so that they're all arrested or discredited. In this scenario, his

employer is some enemy of the agents (probably not a vampire – go for a crime lord, ex-superior back at whatever TLA where the agent used to work, or some old rival).

- 🌙 **THE DEAD MAN:** Smart, fast, military training – sound familiar? Lawson's the exact sort of person that the Lisky Bratva make zalozhniye out of. He's literally a dead man walking. If you go for this option, then Lawson's face is scarred. He claims he was hit by a Molotov cocktail in Africa, but the truth is that he's a well-disguised dead man. (A 1-point **Disguise** spend can notice that his coloration comes from cosmetics.)

THE CHAMELEON

Arthur Smith is not his real name, of course. No one knows his real name. Smith's a Zelig-like human chameleon, adept at changing his appearance and demeanour to fit into any situation. He's a master of social engineering, a superlative con man and liar. Chakroun hired him to recon the bank.

ARTHUR SMITH

GENERAL ABILITIES: Athletics 6, Conceal 8, Cover 12, Disguise 12, Filch 12, Hand-to-Hand 4, Health 6, Infiltration 8, Sense Trouble 6
HIT THRESHOLD: 3
ALERTNESS MODIFIER: +2
STEALTH MODIFIER: +1
DAMAGE MODIFIER: -2 (fist)

PLAYING SMITH

Smith doesn't have any traits or quirks of his own. He changes his entire personality to match the role he's playing.

MOTIVATIONS & DIRTY SECRETS

Smith dies in *Death of a Chameleon* (p. 89). Optionally, you can bring him back as the traitor in the group later in the operation. There are two options for this:

- 🌙 **HE FAKED IT:** He was working for the Lisky Bratva all along, and his role was to get the agents involved in the heist so they could be corralled and eliminated. His "death" was just another act – he slipped out of the car an instant before it exploded, and vanished in the confusion.
- 🌙 **NECROMANCY:** One of the vampires (or Dr. Dorjiev) brought Smith back to life to betray the agents. He'll show up as a grotesquely burned walking corpse later on in the operation.

THE MONTAVONS

The Montavon family have been the primary shareholders of the Koernersbank ever since it was founded, and presided over the bank's rise and subsequent decline. Five members of the family play potential roles in this operation. (All have basic civilian statistics.)

ANDREAS MONTAVON — THE PATRIARCH: Andreas presided over the slow decline of the Koernersbank. He's old, bitter and increasingly senile, raging impotently against imagined threats; he regularly attends a private psychiatric clinic to treat incipient dementia. These days, he's mostly a figurehead for Julie and Johan. His declining mental faculties make him a prime target for con artists using **Reassurance** and **Disguise**.

JULIE MONTAVON — THE HEIR APPARENT: Andreas' eldest child and the effective head of the board, she oversees the bank's investment portfolio. She's determined to preserve the bank's reputation through the takeover. She knows about the Black Sea Bank's connections to the Lisky Bratva, but **High Society** gives the agents leverage over her.

JOHAN GALLION — THE MASTERMIND: Julie's lover, and the bank's best investment analyst. He's also the architect of the deal with the Black Sea Bank. He wants Andreas out of the way, and has even contemplated murdering the old man. Gallion believes he's untouchable – if the agents can get past his security to hit him with **Intimidation**, he'll fold.

JEAN MONTAVON — THE GAMBLER: Andreas' second child, Jean gladhandles the clients and runs the day-to-day operations of the head office. He's got a moderately serious gambling problem, and Julie's resorted to having him watched by private detectives to ensure he doesn't dip into the bank's own funds; Johan Gallion loathes him. **Flattery, Flirting** or **Gambling** are excellent approaches.

CLARIQUE MONTAVON — THE BLACK SHEEP: Clarique is Andreas' sister and perennial thorn in his side. She sees herself as the guardian of the bank's reputation and heritage, and voted against the deal with the Black Sea Bank. She and Julie used to be close, but quarrelled over the Black Sea Bank and Julie's closeness with Johan Gallion. **Negotiation** is the best way to deal with her – she's willing to deal with the agents.

THE BLACK SEA BANK

Buying the Koernersbank is necessary overkill. The Lisky Bratva know that Kim Philby left something – possibly the Albedo itself – in a safe-deposit box in the Koernersbank. They just don't know *which* box. Therefore, they're going to buy all of them. Once they buy the Koernersbank, they'll be able to identify which box belonged to the Philbys, and then steal the Albedo from their own bank.

VIKTOR KOZEL: The representative of the Black Sea Bank. Kozel knows the bank is rotten, and that he's really working for Josef Lisky, but the money is more than enough to suppress any stirrings of his conscience. He doesn't know why the Black Sea Bank's masters are interested in the Koernersbank, and he doesn't intend to find out. Asking the wrong questions is never good for one's health. If the agents can prove a connection between the Lisky Bratva and the Black Sea Bank, they can combine **Law** and **Intimidation** or **Interrogation** to threaten Kozel. He's not a combatant.

MARKO SHWETZ: Officially, he's here as a "security consultant" to the Black Sea Bank. Shwetz is one of Josef Lisky's lieutenants. He knows about the Lisky Bratva's secret masters in the Conspiracy, and worships them as gods. Shwetz is a fanatic; killing the zalozhniy or a vampire in front of him breaks his faith in the immortality of his monstrous overlords. Use the Mafioso stats for Schwetz.

- **Electronic Surveillance:** If you haven't run *Out of the House of Ashes,* then at some point over the course of the operation, Schwetz gets a call from Stefan Werner in Vienna, telling him that "Shevlenko is in hand" and urging him to complete the bank deal as quickly as possible. The agents can eavesdrop on this call by tapping Schwetz's phone (or checking his voicemail after they kill him).
- Alternatively, Schwetz can report back to Dr. Dorjiev in Odessa if *The Zalozhniy Sanction* is up next.
- **Negotiation:** If Schwetz's faith is broken by the destruction of a zalozhniy, then the agents can talk him into giving up what he knows about the Conspiracy before he eats a bullet.

THE ZALOZHNIY: The Lisky Bratva sent a single zalozhniy to Zurich to deal with any trouble. This particular zalozhniy was created from the corpse of a French spy, **Lili Blaise**, who stumbled across the Lisky Bratva's human-trafficking ring in Odessa and was captured and executed with a single shot to the heart. If the agents get a shot of the zalozhniy with **Photography**, then **Research, Tradecraft** or **Network** can dig up information about Blaise's disappearance.

NIGHT'S BLACK AGENTS – THE ZALOZHNIY QUARTET

THE SET-UP

SCENE TYPE: Introduction
LEADS-OUT: Visiting the Koernersbank, The Shipment, Background Checks

The first step is gathering information. If the agents have open **Network** spots, they can take **Olli Rast** as a contact; Olli's a financial analyst who specializes in the impact of war and terrorism on national economies, so he's got a working knowledge of espionage and covert actions, and owes the player characters a few favours. If they need equipment or weapons, then their fixer is a young Armenian called **Jivan**, who sells black-market gear out of the back of his car.

All the Core Clues point towards investigating the Koernersbank.

Accounting (Core Clue): The Koernersbank is in negotiations with the Black Sea Bank. The takeover should be complete within a few days.

- **1-point spend:** The Black Sea Bank is cash-rich, but they're still bleeding themselves white to buy the Koernersbank. In fact, they're paying well over the odds according to rumors. In fact, they're going to transfer a lot of cash and gold to the bank as part of the deal. Robbing *that* could bankroll the agents for years.

Cop Talk (Core Clue): The Zurich police are concerned about the Black Sea Bank's private security. They're uncooperative and heavily armed.

- **1-point spend:** There's a shipment coming in on a plane from Russia in the next few days that's going to be escorted under armed guard to the bank.

Criminology (Core Clue): *Proving* ties between the Lisky Bratva and the Koernersbank is hard, but it's easy enough to dig up rumors and allegations that the Black Sea Bank is owned by the mob.

- Banks often drop their security before takeovers.

High Society (Core Clue): The Montavon family are the primary shareholders in the Koernersbank – the Black Sea Bank is buying them out. Not all the family are happy about this. If the agents follow up on this, see *Background Checks*, opposite, p. 87.

History or **Research:** The agent knows the history of the bank, especially its strong connections to oil money in the '40s, '50s and '60s, and its decline in the '70s – and its somewhat shady dealings with the Nazis during the war.

- A **1-point spend** turns up the interesting fact that St. John Philby was rumored to be a client. (Only mention this if the agents are already aware of the Philby connection).

Traffic Analysis: Monitoring on Lisky Bratva traffic confirms that they're involved with the upcoming takeover. They're moving considerable assets into position.

- **1-point spend:** There's a shipment of gold and cash coming into the bank soon, protected by the Lisky Bratva. They're also talking about "the handover" – apparently, someone big is coming in a few days. Maybe even Josef Lisky himself.

VISITING THE KOERNERSBANK

SCENE TYPE: Core
LEADS-OUT: The Shipment, Background Checks, The Monaco Operation, Death of a Chameleon

The Koernersbank's head office is located in the heart of Zurich, in a 17th century building. The outer walls of the building are preserved, but it was hollowed out and rebuilt in the 1960s. Walking through the heavy iron-bound doors of the Koernersbank is like stepping back to the gilded age of the 1930s; everything's oak-panelled, leather-bound or made of polished brass. The only concession to modernity are the discrete computer systems and concealed security camera.

The Koernersbank is not open to the public. The agents can arrange an appointment with a suitable **Cover**, or bluff their way in with **Disguise**. **Accounting** or **Law** can also work – there are plenty of Black Sea Bank staff coming and going, so a well-dressed agent can bypass security by following them and enter the foyer. Getting past the ground floor is much harder, though – access to either the underground vault or the offices upstairs requires a keycard, and there are guards posted to ensure no-one sneaks past with a group.

THE MEETING

If the agents are here on plausible business, they're met by the unctuous **Jean Montavon.** He ushers them into a side room and provides them with refreshments. They're kept waiting for more than twenty minutes before Montavon returns. He apologizes for the delay, and explains that the bank is in the middle of a merger with the Black Sea Bank. He assures them that the Koernersbank customers will be wholly unaffected by this change – how can he help them?

THE PASSBOOK

Each private customer of the Koernersbank is issued with a passbook, a document used to identify the bearer as being authorized to access a safe-deposit box in the bank. The passbook consists of a six folded pages of legal documentation, signed by the bank manager. Each sheet of paper bears several cunningly concealed watermarks and other authentication symbols. Creating a forgery of a passbook is virtually impossible without access to an existing passbook, and even then is very difficult (a 3-point **Forgery** spend).

If the agents played through *Out of the House of Ashes*, they may have Philby's original passbook, which simplifies matters immensely. The agents won't be able to take the contents of the box, but they can use it as an excuse to get into the vault. That passbook also plays a part in *Death of a Chameleon*, p. 89.

---

again. Due to the merger, the contents of the vault have been frozen. Of course the contents of the safe-deposit box will be kept completely private, but nothing can be removed from the vault until the merger is complete. He is desperately sorry about this delay.

Intimidation/Negotiation: If the agents push Montavon, he digs out the contract signed when St. John Philby opened the account. He points to a clause that states that the bank may temporarily restrict access to the vaults in exceptional circumstances.

- One of the files in the folder notes the times the box was opened. It hasn't been opened since 1963.
- **Law:** Montavon's on shaky grounds; those "exceptional circumstances" are intended to be wars, natural disasters, or other acts of God.
- **Bullshit Detector:** Montavon's being pressured by someone – presumably the Lisky Bratva – to keep the contents of the vault intact.
- Using **Intimidation, Negotiation** or **Law** convinces Montavon to show *one* agent into the vault for the express purpose of confirming that Box 1274 is intact.

INTO THE VAULT

Montavon asks the designated agent to wait obtains the vault key and the safe-deposit box key from the manager's office. The pair are then escorted by Russian-accented guards into the vault (see p. 96). On the way, the agent can spot the other security systems (the security camera, the heat and motion sensors, and the combination lock).

- **Notice (Core Clue)** spots a discarded credit card receipt in the waste-paper bin – it's a bill for several thousand Swiss francs worth of drinks at a private casino in Monaco.

Montavon won't discuss the contents of the vault unless the agents have the correct passbook. If they have Philby's passbook (or a proper forgery – see sidebar), then Montavon hides his surprise and closely examines the book before apologizing

Inside, Montavon unlocks Box 1274 and withdraws the metal drawer from the wall. He carries the box over to a small private booth for the agent to examine.

Notice or **Electronic Surveillance** spots a recently installed concealed camera inside the booth. There are also guards waiting outside. Tell the player that taking anything from the box without being detected is impossible. (If the agent tries, the guards intercept him before he leaves the vault, escort him to a private room, and recover the stolen item. If the agent cooperates, he might get to walk out of the bank alive.)

THE STRANGER

At some point when the agents are in or near the Koernersbank (for example, when meeting Jean Montavon), one of them spots a striking figure – Menena Chakroun. She seems to be ignoring the agents, but **Tradecraft (core clue)** shows she's keeping them under surveillance. Whoever she is, she's good – she watches the agents until they notice her, then disappears (vanishing into a crowd, stepping into a taxi, losing her tail by ducking into a shop and exiting via a hidden back route). Chakroun won't make contact with the agents yet – just establish her existence in this encounter.

If the agents manage to keep up with her when she tries to vanish, then she'll first try ducking into a mosque and hide out or escape in the crowd (refresh her Surveillance pool, and add +1 to non-North African agents' Difficulties). If that fails, she'll call in backup from Lawson and Smith. You may be able to segue neatly into *Death of a Chameleon* or *The Other Guys* from here.

BACKGROUND CHECKS

SCENE TYPE: Alternate
LEADS-IN: The Setup, Visiting the Koernersbank, Planning the Heist
LEADS-OUT: Planning the Heist, The Other Guys

If the agents know they're after Box 1274, they may already be planning a heist or want to learn more about the bank. If they don't yet know how important the Koernersbank is, it's time to raise the stakes by revealing more of the Lisky Bratva presence.

The Montavons are the best source of information about the internal workings of the Koernersbank. **High Society** or **Research** gets the agents a list of the Montavon family. From there, there are multiple possible avenues of investigation, any of which can get the agents the inside scoop on the state of the bank.

All the Montavons have passcards and keys to get into the basement, and have access to the bank's paperwork like blank passbooks, employee ID cards or the computer system. All the Montavons except Clarique know the combination for the vault's magnetic lock. If the agents are planning their heist, then **Filch** or social engineering can grab what they need.

THE PARTY

High Society can get the agents a invitation to a black-tie party hosted by Julie Montavon to mark the end of the family's control of the bank. Other guests at the party include her lover **Johan Gallion,** her brother **Jean** and **Victor Kozel** from the Black Sea Bank. The party gives the agents a chance to get close to the Montavons, learn about Jean's gambling habit, or sneak off and **Filch** a swipe card. Clarique deliberately snubs the party.

- **Military Science:** The agents overhear Kozel and Johan Gallion arguing about the bank. Kozel wants to hire a private security firm, **Overwatch Security**, for added protection. Gallion retorts that the bank's current contractors, **SBS Security**, are specialists in protecting financial institutions, and that Overwatch are a bunch of trigger-happy mercenaries. If the agents dig into Overwatch's background, then **Criminology** suggests the Lisky Bratva are secretly running the company. Overwatch are currently stationed in Baghdad (see *Treason in the Blood*, p. 106).

THE CLINIC

Examining footage of Andreas Montavon (obtained with **Electronic Surveillance**) with **Diagnosis (Core Clue)** suggests he's suffering from the early stages of dementia; following his car with **Driving** or hacking his records with **Digital Intrusion** can get the address of the Adlersruhe private psychiatric clinic in the mountains outside Zurich. The clinic looks like a ski resort with unusually high security – the patients here are all paying for private and discretion. Andreas has an agreement with his daughter Julie that he can stay on as head of the board on condition that he visits the clinic whenever he is stressed or upset. If the agents break into the clinic (**Infiltration, Disguise**), they can pose as doctors (with **Diagnosis** or **Shrink**) or drug Andreas (**Pharmacy**) into telling them about the upcoming shipment or the bank's security systems. When vulnerable, Andreas also complains about Jean's gambling and his arguments with his sister Clarique.

Montavon's memory loss forced him to write down his pass codes for both the basement access door and the bank vault. The latter is an unforgivable breach of security. He keeps the bank vault passcode on a piece of paper in his wallet. (**Diagnosis** suggests he's suffering from memory loss and is probably taking precautions.) He hasn't written down the combination to the safe in the manager's office; instead, he asks Julie to open it for him.

CLARIQUE MONTAVON

If the agents discover (either via gossip, via Andreas' ramblings, or with a 1-point **High Society** spend) that Clarique Montavon is quarrelling with her family, they can visit her in her rambling townhouse. She's an eccentric collector, with an extensive library of books on occult and spiritualist topics and several cabinets of waxen death masks, but unlike her brother, she is still in full command of her faculties.

She mistrusts the Black Sea Bank; if the agents show her that there is a connection between the Black Sea Bank and the Lisky Bratva with **Criminology** coupled with their own experiences, then she decides that sabotaging the deal is in the best interest of the Koernersbank. If the agents remove whatever the Black Sea Bank is after *before* the deal is signed, then the Lisky Bratva will pull out. She can't get the agents into the vault, and can't endanger her own position, but can help them in other ways. She can:

- Get them a blank passbook
- Get them the passcodes for the basement
- Tell them about Jean's gambling trouble
- Tell them about the shipment
- Advise them about the bank security. Clarique doesn't know the technical details, but she can give an overview.

If Menena Chakroun is working for Clarique, then Clarique may order her to recruit the agents.

THE MONACO OPERATION

Spotting the receipt in the waste-paper bin in the bank (or a **1-point Streetwise spend**, or gossip at the party, or via Clarique) uncovers Jean's gambling habit. He makes regular trips to Monaco to gamble. Sometimes, he goes with friends, or with bank clients. Jean is a sub-par gambler, but whenever he loses big, his sister bails him out. An agent in Monaco could use **Gambling** to break Jean (Jean's got Gambling 2, but his preferred game is poker, and the other players at the table have Gambling 5).

If the agents force Jean into losing a lot of money, then **Intimidation** can be used to threaten him. The agents need to be circumspect – if they push Jean too much, he won't co-operate. He won't hand over the contents of the vault just because he owes a few hundred thousand Euros. If the agents admit that they only want one safe-deposit box, then Jean is more likely to co-operate. With the right pressure, they can force him to:

- Give information about the Black Sea Bank, and the shipment
- Give information about the Montavon family
- Give them the combination to the vault
- Help the agents unwittingly – Jean won't knowingly help them rob the bank, but they could force him to, say, bring the agents to his office in the bank so they can filch his swipe card or shoulder-surf his password.

VICTOR KOZEL

Spying on Kozel with **Electronic Surveillance** gets the following information when he reports to Josef Lisky via phone. He checks in with his boss once per day.

THE BOXMEN ■ **BACKGROUND CHECKS / THE SHIPMENT / DEATH OF A CHAMELEON**

- The Black Sea Bank is sending in a shipment of cash and diamonds under heavy armed guard. It's flying into Zurich airport, and escorted through the city in an armored van by both "specialist security" and the Swiss police. (See *The Shipment,* below).
- The "specialist security," the armored van and the plane are to remain in Zurich until "the Philby Box" is located.
  > **Military Science:** Obviously, whatever's in the Philby box must be extremely valuable. If the deal goes through and the Lisky Bratva collect the box from the Koernersbank, getting it back will be almost impossible.
- If this is the final operation in the **Quartet,** then Josef Lisky himself is flying in once the deal is done. (See *Killing Uncle Joe* on p. 103).

THE SHIPMENT

SCENE TYPE: Core
LEADS-IN: The Setup, Visiting the Koernersbank, Background Checks

The Black Sea Bank shipment arrives a day or two after the start of the operation. The shipment, consisting of ten million dollars in cash, gold and diamonds, flies into Zurich airport in a privately owned Tupolev Tu-154MLux, and is then escorted into the city centre in an armored van, accompanied by two police vehicles and two 4x4s full of armed private security troopers. Marko Schwetz oversees the shipment.

- **Military Science** recognizes the guards as Lisky Bratva thugs
- There are P+8 thugs escorting the shipment, along with 8 armed police.

On arrival at the Koernersbank, the van is driven into the secure garage, unloaded, and the contents are carried down into the vault. There are plenty of staff milling around during this transfer; if the agents have an employee ID, they can use the distraction of the shipment transfer to get a look at the vault's security systems.

- **Electronic Surveillance** spots the cameras and heat sensors in the corridor, and the motion detectors in the vault.
- **Architecture** notices the pressure plate under the vault.
- Opening the vault requires both a combination and a special key. The key is brought down by **Julie Montavon**; **Notice** lets the character spot her returning it to the manager's office safe.

Once the shipment arrive, the van remains in the garage. The Lisky Bratva security team leaves the immediate area, but stay in Zurich until the deal is complete.

BLOWBACK

Before the Lisky Bratva shipment shows up, then any blowback should be in the form of added Heat or police sweeps. The zalozhniy might also harass the agents by breaking into their hotel room, stalking them through the streets or eliminating contacts.

Once the Lisky Bratva have armed assets in place, they can risk hitting back at the agents with assassination attempts, beatings or increased surveillance. They want to keep things low-key to avoid imperilling the Koernersbank deal, so there won't be any explosives.

DEATH OF A CHAMELEON

SCENE TYPE: Core
LEAD-IN: Visiting the Koernersbank
LEAD-OUT: The Other Guys

Run this scene at any point after the agents first visit the Koernersbank. Ever since she spotted them at the bank, **Menena Chakroun** suspected the agents were more than they seemed. She initially assumed they were a Lisky Bratva security team of professional assassins, but now she suspects (correctly) they are a rival band of thieves. In this scene, she tries to hamstring them.

If the agents have Philby's passbook, then that's the target of Chakroun's operation. Otherwise, she's after something else of interest – plans of the bank, security system schematics, or maybe she's just interested in finding out who the agents are. We'll refer to whatever item Chakroun wants as the target. The operation is simple – **Arthur Smith**, the chameleon, will brush past the agent and lift the target. (If the agents are keeping the target in a hotel room or other sanctuary, then Smith breaks in there while they're out.) The beast, **Keith Lawson**, is in place to provide support if Smith gets into trouble.

What none of the thieves know is that Smith is being stalked by a zalozhniy.

CONTACT

It starts seemingly innocently. An American tourist wearing sunglasses and a loud shirt accidentally jostles against one of the agents (or passes them in the corridor outside their hotel room). Call for **Sense Trouble** tests at this point at Difficulty 7. If successful, the agent realizes that the "tourist" just pickpocketed the target (or else just came out of the agent's hotel room). Smith's already out of reach, but his Lead in the foot chase starts at 3.

If the Sense Trouble test is failed, then the agents don't realize that Smith stole from them for several seconds, which gives Smith time to get clear. He ditches his sunglasses and strips off the Hawaiian shirt; the American accent and the clumsy tourist act get dumped too. A **Surveillance** test (Difficulty 5) lets the agents spot him despite his change of appearance, and his Lead starts at 4. Otherwise, picking Smith out of the crowd takes another few precious seconds, and his Lead starts at 5.

THE CHASE

It's **Athletics** vs **Athletics** through the streets of Zurich. Smith's very good at blending in and hiding in crowds, and he'll switch appearance several times if given the opportunity. His potential disguises are, in order:

- *American tourist* (sunglasses, loud shirt)
- Ditching the previous disguise, he's an *unemployed local* (t-shirt, slumped shoulders, strong Swiss accent)
- After doglegging through a department store, he's a *family man* (sweater, baseball cap, bags of shopping, sticks close to a woman and two kids to give the impression he's with them).
- Pulling a shirt and a fake beard out of the bags, he becomes an *aggrieved banker* who'll sic the police on the agents.

Whenever Smith switches appearance, call for **Disguise** or **Surveillance** tests (Difficulty 6) or a 1-point **Notice** spend to spot him in the crowds; otherwise, he gains a point of Lead before the agents spot him again.

Possible hazards:

- Rain-slick cobblestones
- Crowded department store
- Flock of pigeons in a square flying up and blocking the agent's view
- Path blocked by a really big guy (Keith Lawson) who does the irritating *"you're going left? I'll also go left"* apologetic dance when "trying" to get out of the way.
  - **Urban Survival** or **Tradecraft** confirm that Lawson's deliberately stalling the agents.

BLAST

If Smith's Lead reaches 7, he gets clear of the agents for long enough to reach his parked car. They'll be able to home in on his location by the sound of the upcoming explosion.

If it hits 0, they're on the verge of catching up with him when he arrives at his car. He pulls open the door and throws himself into the driver's seat. He turns the key...

... and there's a puff of thick oily smoke from the engine, followed by an explosion. As car bombs go, it's positively restrained, with a blast radius that encompasses Smith's Citroen and leaves the neighboring cars mostly undamaged. The explosion is enough to kill Smith instantly. The target is incinerated instantly.

Hearts skip a beat. Clocks stop ticking for an instant. There's a timeless moment as the zalozhniy feasts on Smith's premature death.

If the agents were right on Smith's heels, then **Notice (Core Clue)** spots Menena Chakroun and Keith Lawson in the crowd of horrified onlookers. Lawson stares at the burning wreck with fury in his eyes; Chakroun grabs his arm and drags him away. She never looks back, but its clear that the pair were in league with the thief. **Urban Survival** lets the agents follow them back to their safe house and *The Other Guys*.

Vampirology (Core Clue): The agents also see a dark figure on a nearby rooftop, looking down at the explosion. The figure's face is hidden by a scarf. It's the zalozhniy.

THE ASSASSIN (OPTIONAL)

If the agents are known to the Lisky Bratva, then the zalozhniy isn't just doing a Batman impression on the rooftop — it's up there with a sniper rifle. **Sense Trouble** (Difficulty 5) gives the agents a chance to dive for cover before the monster snaps off a few shots, using the chaos of the explosion as cover for this opportunistic attack.

THE OTHER GUYS

SCENE TYPE: Core
LEAD-IN: Death of a Chameleon
LEADS-OUT: The Mark, Planning the Heist

Once the agents work out that someone else is trying to break into the Koernersbank vaults, they need to decide what to do about them – spy on them, eliminate them, team up with them, or warn them off?

If the agents don't make contact with Menena Chakroun's team, then there are other ways to get everyone together:

- Menena contacts the agents and sets up a meeting. She needs their help after the death of Arthur Smith. (Alternatively, she's told to set up a meeting by her patron).
- One of the agent's **Network** contacts like **Olli Rast** or **Jamil** can put them in touch – Chakroun already called on that contact with a similar request.
- For that matter, if the agents use **Network** to find an expert safecracker, they're put in touch with Massimo Florin.
- The agents run into the opposition when doing groundwork for the bank job – they might spot Keith Lawson staking out the bank, or meet Menena Chakroun at the Montavon party.
- Whatever you do, *don't* have both teams break into the bank at the same time without realizing it – it'll just turn into a farcical comedy.

If the agents ignore or rebuff Chakroun, then she'll call off her plan and instead rob the agents once they escape from the bank.

SPYING ON THE COMPETITION

Chakroun's team are based out of a run-down flat. They've taken precautions: all the windows are blocked, they've got webcams watching the front door and the stairwell, and they keep track of any cars that spend too long parked nearby. They communicate with mobile phones, but change SIMs frequently to avoid anyone eavesdropping or triangulating their positions. They've got moderately solid **Covers** as tourists. Chakroun and Lawson take their tradecraft seriously, but Florin heads down to the corner cafe, The Hunter's Rest, for a few beers every evening.

THE APPROACH

If Chakroun makes an approach to the team, she does so covertly. She phones them and offers to meet with them somewhere neutral and public to discuss a business proposition. She brings Florin with her to the meeting; Lawson lurks nearby as backup. (**Tradecraft** spots the hulking bodyguard – he's there to show she's a pro who takes precautions.)

Chakroun's already done her homework on the agents. She knows they are not part of the Lisky Bratva, and that they are very dangerous. She guesses that they're taking advantage of the bank's weakened security, just like she is. She points out that both sides need each other – she's already done the groundwork, but Smith's death blew a hole in her plan.

If the agents had the passbook from *Out of the House of Ashes*, then Chakroun apologizes for the attempted theft. It was Smith's idea, and he's dead.

She offers a deal – an equal split of the proceeds from the vault.

- **Bullshit Detector:** Chakroun's a pro. If she's lying, the agent can't tell.

CHAKROUN'S PLAN

The original plan – before Arthur Smith got killed – was as follows:

- Arthur Smith convinces **Lucille Primeau** (see *The Mark*) to remove her possessions from the bank vault. He accompanies her into the vault. While there, he photographs the vault's security systems using a hidden camera.
- The team already know that they'll need a key to the vault and individual keys to the safe-deposit boxes; these are stored in a safe in the manager's office.
- The team gain access to the roof using a zipline from a building across the street.
- They break into the bank and make their way down to the vault.
- There are two night watchman – disabling them is Lawson's job.
- They use the watchman's card to get into the basement.
- Florin opens the vault, based on Smith's photographs.
- They grab what they can and leave via the side door.
- If the alarm sounds and they're unable to escape in time, they have police uniforms stashed in a bag. They hide upstairs, disguise themselves as police, and try to slip away in the confusion.
- The team rendezvouses at a safe house after the heist. Chakroun has several candidates – a derelict apartment, a farmhouse in the mountains, an airport hotel – but hasn't picked one yet.

Now that Smith's dead, there's a big hole in their plan – they need information about the vault's security systems.

NIGHT'S BLACK AGENTS – THE ZALOZHNIY QUARTET

THE MARK

SCENE TYPE: Alternate
LEAD-IN: The Other Guys
LEAD-OUT: Planning the Heist

Lucille Primeau is an elderly widow who inherited her husband's art collection, valued at several million euro. She has an account with the Koernersbank, and stores several paintings in a safe-deposit box there. Arthur Smith posed as an art dealer and won Primeau's trust over the course of several months. He intended to convince her to take one of the paintings, *The Dancer*, out of the vault so it could be properly valued.

The agents can try to pick up where Smith left off. Primeau is paranoid and believes that everyone is trying to cheat her out of her money, but a good **Cover** and lots of **Reassurance** can convince her to trust the agents, as long as they pose as Smith's business partners or offspring. Once they've hoodwinked Primeau, it's off to the bank to bluff past Jean Montavon.

Visiting the bank with Primeau's passbook lets the agents get a look at the inside of the vault and the bank's security protocols. (See *Into The Vault*, p. 96, for a similar visit.) The agents have to set up a fake art dealer to value the painting after the bank visit in order to maintain the deception.

PLANNING THE HEIST

SCENE TYPE: Core
LEADS-IN: The Other Guys, The Mark, Background Checks
LEADS-OUT: The Heist

With or without Chakroun's team, all clues point towards the vault of the Koernersbank.

Don't linger too long on planning the heist. Let the players case the target and plan out a rough plan of attack, but don't let the game stall into an endless discussion of approaches and fallback plans. Once they have a plan, run with it.

BANK LAYOUT

The Koernersbank building is three stories tall. The upper two stories contain offices and storerooms, as well as the computer server room. The lobby and meeting rooms are the ground floor.

The vault is in the basement. Stairs descend from the ground floor to the basement; the garage door opens onto a steep ramp that also goes down to the basement.

There are three ground-floor entrances to the bank – the front door, the garage door (for deliveries and armored trucks) and a fire exit at the rear. All the windows are narrow and barred, but there is a roof access door.

There's no easy access via the sewers, unless the agents want to lay their hands on a lot of explosives and take down half the building from below.

RECONNAISSANCE

EXTERIOR: Scoping out the outside of the building with **Architecture** or **Electronic Surveillance** spots the location of the external security systems, but getting close enough to examine the wiring requires either a **Photography** spend (for long-range high-quality shots) or using **Disguise** or **Urban Survival**.

INTERIOR: The internal layout of the building is best obtained by visiting the bank in **Disguise** or with a **Cover**. Most visitors to the bank only see the lobby and one or two of the offices, but not the two upper floors and the vault. To scout out the whole building, the agents need a pretext for wandering around and getting measurements. **Architecture** or **Notice** spots hiding places and security systems. Alternatively, the agents can dig up the old plans of the building with **Research** – the bank renovated the structure in the 1960s, but the original shell is still there.

BASEMENT: Getting to the vault requires the agents to have a passbook or otherwise bluff their way in. Access to the basement is controlled via swipe cards coupled with a four-digit pin to open the door to the stairs. All the staff have these cards.

The corridor leading to the vault is watched by security cameras and heat-sensitive sensors, coupled with a pressure plate in the floor just in front of the vault door.

The vault door has a mechanical and a magnetic lock. Opening the mechanical lock requires a special key which is kept in a safe, along with the keys to all the safe-deposit boxes. This safe is in the manager's office on the middle floor. Taking more than one safe-deposit box key at a time triggers an alert.

The magnetic lock requires another passcode. Unlike the basement door, the passcode for the vault is known only to a handful of bank employees – all the Montavons have the code, as does Gallion. The door also has internal trembler switchers that are tripped if the door is damaged.

Inside the vault, there's another security camera and a motion detector. Each individual safe-deposit box has its own key and combination lock.

SECURITY STAFF

During the day, there are four security guards in the bank. There are two night watchman who patrol the entire building. In addition, the bank's security cameras are monitored at night by a private security firm, **SBS Security** – if they spot anything unusual, they'll either alert the watchmen or contact the police.

There's a police station nearby, and they'll respond within five minutes to any external alarms.

Military Science lets the agents work out patrol patterns and likely police response times and movements.

As an added headache, once **The Shipment** (p. 89) has arrived, there's also a Lisky Bratva security team in town who are monitoring the bank. They'll arrive soon after the police, and pursue the agents with considerably more lethal intent.

Criminology or **Electronic Surveillance** can trace the bank's connection to SBS Security through various channels. Ambitious agents can break into SBS Security's offices (**Infiltration** and eliminate the guys watching the camera feed from the bank).

ALARMS

The bank operates on an escalating series of alarms.

- **ALERT:** Something's up. An alert shows up on the screens at SBS Security and in the security office in the bank. The night watchmen check it out. If an alert isn't cancelled within fifteen minutes, it triggers an internal alarm. Alerts can be triggered by:

BANK STAFF

Random bank staff to have their lives ruined by the agents:

- **MANFRED AMIEL:** Middle manager, drinks too much.
- **HANNA ZUBRIGGEN:** Client liaison, just out of college, overly trusting.
- **FARIDA IKRAAM:** Cleaner, refugee from Iraq.
- **ADOLF NEF:** Middle-aged night watchmen, lazy.
- **RUDI KOLLER:** Young night watchman, frustrated novelist.

> Typing the wrong PIN code into the basement access door
> Activating the pressure plate in the basement corridor
> Activating the motion detector in the basement corridor or vault
> Entering the wrong combination into a safe
> Being spotted by a security camera

- **INTERNAL ALARM:** Something's gone wrong. An internal alarm can be heard throughout the bank, and immediately draws the attention of the night watchmen and SBS security. If they don't cancel the alarm, it triggers an external alarm after two minutes.
> Forcing open a window or door
> Forcing open a safe
> Forcing open a safe-deposit box
> Entering the wrong combination into the vault door

- **EXTERNAL ALARM:** The bank's being robbed. The police are alerted, either by SBS security or by an automated alarm call. This automated alarm is hardwired, and triggers an alert if the line is cut.

THE ROUTINE

Bank staff begin arriving at 7am, and the bank opens its doors at 10am. It officially closes at 4pm, and the staff are mostly gone by 7pm. Cleaners visit from 6pm to 8pm, and the night watchman is in place from 7pm to 7am.

During the night, the night watchmen stay in the security office on the middle floor, and take it in turns to patrol the whole building once per hour. They have to check in with SBS security once every thirty minutes; if they fail to do so, that triggers an **alert**.

Deliveries arrive in the early hours of the morning and come in through the garage. **Urban Survival** notes that both the cleaners and delivery trucks don't have keys – they're buzzed into the building by the night watchmen.

VINCENT DAROUD

A **1-point Streetwise spend** puts the agents in touch with **Vincent Daroud**, an architect and security consultant who helped design the Koernersbank's security systems. Daroud was disgraced and ruined when he was convicted of

THE INELEGANT APPROACH

Or, "Why don't we just shoot our way in?" If the agents think of eschewing the clockwork intricacy of a heist in favor of an all-guns-blazing bank holdup, point out that the Koernersbank is right in the middle of Zurich. They might be able to get the safe-deposit box, but they'd be surrounded by police and draw more Heat than they can reasonably handle. If they're dead set on it, run with it, but the challenge then becomes getting *out* instead of getting *in*.

Similarly, the agents might try kidnapping a Montavon and demanding the box in exchange. The family's personal security is handled by SBS Security, but as soon as the Philby box comes into play, the Lisky Bratva take over, and they don't care about hostages.

raping a teenage schoolgirl; he now lives alone in a small village in the Alps. If the agents hunt him down (**Research** or **Cop Talk**) and **Intimidate** him, then he can give them insider information about the bank vault. He's a 3-point pool that can be spent on any investigative ability during the heist. (Optionally, if the agents are competing against Chakroun's team, then they run into Keith Lawson here, and he decides to eliminate Daroud rather than let the agents use him.)

PREPARATIONS

Preparedness or **Network** can get the agents whatever basic tools they need, like wirecutters, drills, explosives, costumes or other items that don't need to be custom-made. Unusual items, like swipe cards, passbooks or safe keys need to be stolen or built with **Forgery**.

NIGHT'S BLACK AGENTS – THE ZALOZHNIY QUARTET

THE HEIST

SCENE TYPE: Core
LEAD-IN: Planning the Heist
LEADS-OUT: In The Vault, Recovering the Albedo

Time to move. If you're feeling ambitious, run this scene in something close to real-time – have a ticking clock on the table and make the players sweat. This scene is presented as a series of problems for the agents to overcome.

A generous Director might let agents spend Investigative Ability points *retroactively*, just like the *In the Nick of Time* Preparedness cherry (see p. 33 of *Night's Black Agents*).

PROBLEM: GETTING IN

How do the agents get into the bank?

- **THROUGH THE FRONT DOOR? Infiltration** or **Mechanics** (Difficulty 6) picks the lock, but there's a security camera watching it, and the door also needs a swipe card to disable the automatic **internal alarm**. **Forgery** can produce swipe cards and keys.
- **IN DISGUISE? Disguise** gets the characters past the door (either as bank staff during the day, or cleaners at night). It won't get them down to the vault, though.
- **THROUGH THE GARAGE?** Same as the front door. Alternatively, the guards can buzz the agents in if they steal a cleaner's van.
- **THROUGH THE ROOF?** Getting onto the roof with a zipline is easy, but can draw attention – either the agents wait until the street is clear, or they use **Infiltration** (Difficulty 4). The roof door can be opened with **Infiltration** or **Mechanics** (Difficulty 6); if the test fails, it triggers an **alert**. The downside is that the agents arrive right on top of the building, and have to make their way down all three floors.
- **THROUGH A WALL?** Getting access to a neighboring building is trivially easy, but the walls are thick concrete. Drilling through would take hours and make a lot of noise. Blowing a hole with **Explosive Devices** is easy, but abandons subtlety from the outset.

PROBLEM: DISABLING THE ALARMS

If the agents want to try isolating the bank, they can try, but it's tricky.

- **INDIVIDUAL ALARMS** can be disabled with **Infiltration** (Difficulty 3 for the ones on doors or windows, Difficulty 5 for the vault)
- Cutting the bank's phone lines and internet connection requires **Architecture** and **Digital Intrusion** (Difficulty 3) to do so without alerting neighboring offices. Taking down the mobile phone network requires **Digital Intrusion** (Difficulty 5) or blowing up several key phone masts simultaneously. Doing so alerts SBS Security.
- Disabling the bank's hardwired connection to the police requires a specially built circuit to mimic a "connection active" signal while blocking alarms. Building a circuit in advance requires **Cryptography** or **Forgery** or **Preparedness**; doing so on the fly requires **Infiltration** (Difficulty 5).

PROBLEM: SECURITY CAMERAS

- Putting an individual security camera on a loop requires **Electronic Surveillance** (possibly with a spend, if the agent has to do so while the camera feed is being actively monitored).
- Putting *all* the security cameras out of action requires access to the secure server on the middle floor of the building and using **Digital Intrusion**.
- Alternatively, an agent could hack into the SBS systems computers with **Digital Intrusion** and spoof their system.
- Sneaking past a security camera requires **Infiltration** (Difficulty 3).
- Being spotted by a security camera means an **alert** (or an **exterior alarm**, if the agent was caught right out in the open).

PROBLEM: THE GUARDS

Those two night watchmen patrol the bank and investigate any suspicious activity.

- Sneaking past the guards is a Difficulty 5 **Infiltration** test if they're in the same room, or Difficulty 3 if they're nearby but don't have line of sight to the agents.
- Working out their patrol patterns requires **Military Science**.
- Removing the guards (either drugging them with **Pharmacy**, or taking them out) means the agents don't need to worry about being discovered by a wandering night watchman, but it means that any alert will **escalate** into a **interior** or **exterior alarm**.
- Both the guards have swipe cards.

PROBLEM: GETTING THE KEYS

The safe in the manager's office has both the keys to the vault and to the individual safe-deposit boxes.

- Opening the safe requires a **Mechanics** or **Infiltration** test (Difficulty 5) or **Explosive Devices** (Difficulty 4). Alternatively, the agents can disable the alarm with an **Infiltration** test (Difficulty 3) and then spend several minutes drilling into the safe.
- Inside, they can obtain the key to the vault, and they find the keys to all the safe-deposit boxes hanging from

the roof of the safe on a motorized carousel. **Notice** spots that there's another alarm system attached to the safe-deposit keys — if they take more than one key, it'll sound an **alert**. Disabling this alarm is a Difficulty 5 **Infiltration** test.
- Being able to open only one safe-deposit box may not matter to the agents, if they only want the contents of Box 1274. The bank thieves, however, may not be satisfied with only a single box.

PROBLEM: IDENTIFYING THE BOX

If the agents don't know which safe-deposit box they're looking for, they can check the old files on the second floor. **Research** shows that the Black Sea Bank were especially interested an account opened by "Harold Philby." According to the bank's private records, which the Black Sea Bank have yet to get their hands on, Philby owned Box 1274, the contents of which were transferred from the Beirut branch in 1975.

PROBLEM: GETTING INTO THE BASEMENT

The basement can be accessed either via the stairs from the ground floor, or via the garage ramp, but both doors need a swipe card and a PIN number to open.

- If the agents haven't already used **Filch** or **Forgery** to obtain a swipe card, then **Infiltration** (Difficulty 5) and a swipe card spoofer can be used to bypass the card reader.
- **Digital Intrusion** (Difficulty 4) or **Infiltration** (Difficulty 4) lets the agents bypass the PIN code. If they've got a swipe card, then **Digital Intrusion** (Difficulty 3) pulls the matching pin off it.
- If the agents are using the garage door, then **Cryptography** or **Notice** shows that there is a greasy residue on the PIN keypad. Only one or two employees use this door, and the buttons that make up their PINs are marked by fingerprints. The agents have had a lucky break — one of the PINs has three repeated digits (it's 1112) so they can get through that door with only a few tries.
- Repeated failures to enter a PIN trigger an **alert**; breaking down the door is an **internal alarm**.

PROBLEM: THE VAULT CORRIDOR

The vault corridor is watched by a security camera and heat-sensitive sensors.

- The security camera can be spoofed with **Electronic Surveillance**, as above, or dodged with **Infiltration** tests (Difficulty 3).
- If the agents know the heat sensors are there, they can obtain thermal suits that hide their body heat beforehand, or whip them out with **Preparedness** (or spray hairspray on the sensors, temporarily blinding them).
- Alternatively, if the agents wait until a guard patrols the corridor, they've then got a short window during which any alerts from the heat sensors are ignored, as the security team assumes that the sensors are picking up on the guard's body heat.
- If the heat sensors are triggered, it causes an alert.

PROBLEM: THE VAULT DOOR

The vault door requires a unique key to open the mechanical lock, and a combination to disable the magnetic lock. There's also a pressure plate under the door.

- The pressure plate can be spotted by **Architecture** and disabled with **Infiltration** (Difficulty 4). Standing on the plate triggers an **alert.**
- The unique key can be replicated with **Forgery,** but only if the agents have photographs of it. Otherwise, the agents can steal the key from the manager's office upstairs, or use **Explosive Devices** to blow open the lock (triggering an **External Alarm**).
- The combination controls the magnetic lock. If the agents obtained the combination, either

NIGHT'S BLACK AGENTS – THE ZALOZHNIY QUARTET

ADDED COMPLICATIONS

If the heist's going too smoothly, throw in one of these optional hazards:

- **LISKY BRATVA GUARDS:** Someone's tipped off the enemy, and they've put added security in place. There are now P+2 guards in the building, and they're armed. The difficulty for all **Infiltration** tests to sneak past increases by one, and any **alert** will be investigated immediately.
- **CHANGED SECURITY SYSTEM:** There's an unexpected new security system that stymies the break-in. Maybe the roof door has been replaced with a steel security door that can't be opened, or the Lisky Bratva have added more security cameras.
- **MISUNDERSTANDING:** One of the thieves (probably Kevin Lawson) jumps to the conclusion that the agents are planning to betray the group, and pulls a gun. This works best if it happens just after the agents screw up ('*you set off that alarm deliberately, you bastard!*')
- **SLIP-UP:** One of the team makes a mistake. They drop a tool, they leave a door open, they sneeze at just the wrong time. The guards come to investigate.
- The Conspiracy has added an occult security system to the vault – a sigil drawn in blood on the vault door, visible only under UV light. Breaking the magical seal alerts the Conspiracy.
- A psychic vampire has conditioned the bank guards to be its slaves. It can hop into their bodies at will and see through their eyes. If the guards are alerted, then one of them gets glowing eyes, supernatural strength and a telepathic hotline to the Conspiracy.
- Their unnatural attention is focussed on the Koernersbank tonight, causing unnatural effects like radio static, time skips, weird magnetic fields and other reality glitches.
- COMMENTARY Hijacking a cleaning van, an easy **Disguise** test. Building a false wall and hiding behind it until the staff go home, a cheap **Architecture** spend and a little patience. Finding out that you're now locked in a bank with a hungry vampire? Priceless.

from Jean or Andreas Montavon, they can enter the code and disable the magnetic lock. Otherwise, it's an **Infiltration** test (Difficulty 8, but **Cryptography** can be spend to reduce the difficulty by 2 points per spend). If this test is failed, it triggers an **alert.**

PROBLEM: INSIDE THE VAULT

They're nearly there – just one more security camera and a motion detector to deal with.

- The motion detector can be defeated by moving extremely slowly. That's fine normally, but if there are stressful conditions in the vault, call for **Stability** tests to stay cool and move slowly enough to avoid triggering the **interior alarm.**
- The security camera can be spoofed or dodged like the rest.
- There are more than 2,000 boxes in the vault, all of which are individually locked. The keys from the safe can open them, but only one at a time. If the agents don't have the keys, then they've got to drill open each box, which takes two minutes per box. Spending a point of **Mechanics** drops the time to drill open a box to one minute.

IN THE VAULT

SCENE TYPE: Core
LEADS-IN: The Heist
LEADS-OUT: Stolen Albedo, The Safe House

Once the team get into the vault, review the motivations of the thieves and slam them up against the agent's plans.

If one or more of the thieves wants the box for themselves, then look for opportunities for the thief to make off with the box, like:

- Grabbing the box and slamming the vault door on the agents, trapping them inside. **Preparedness** coupled with **Explosive Devices** lets the agents blow up the door from inside (it's easier to break out of a vault than to break in).
- Switching the box for another identical container, then feigning injury. **Diagnosis** or **Bullshit Detector** spots the act, while a **Notice** spend spots the switch.
- Triggering an alarm during the escape, forcing the agents to deal with guards. In the confusion, the thief grabs the box contents.
- Sabotaging the getaway car (or planting a bomb in it). **Sense Trouble** gives advance warning of the bomb.
- Pulling a gun on the agents at the right moment and walking out with the case.

One of the thieves may also be working for the Lisky Bratva; if that thief knows where the safe house is, they'll be on the lookout for a way to escape the group. If the thief doesn't know where the safe house is, then they've got a cellphone or a tracking bug to lead the enemy to the agents.

THE PHILBY BOX

Box 1274 contains:

- The Albedo, in whatever form fits your campaign. Whatever it is, it's held inside a battered leather briefcase that's unusually heavy. A close examination of the case shows that it's got thin lead sheets inside the lining to block x-rays. Optionally, the case is also protected by a Block of some sort, like withered black roses wound around the handle, the Host smeared on the lock, or a thin silver wire wrapped around the case.
- If this is the last operation in the campaign and you haven't introduced it yet, the case also contains a single sheet of typed paper, describing the ritual needed to combine the Albedo and Nigredo into the Rubedo.
- A battered copy of Kipling's *Kim*.
- A few thousand dollars worth of cash, in a mix of dollars, English pounds, gold coins and Saudi riyals.
- If you haven't run *Out of the House of Ashes*, then there's a sheaf of black-and-white photos of various people. They're photos taken by St. John and Kim Philby over the years (possibly for some occult purpose, if your campaign leans that way.) Combining **Photography** and **Research** (or **History**) identifies most of them as British spies and handlers like Nicholas Elliot and Gertrude Bell. One photo shows a young, nervous-looking Russian glancing sidelong at the camera; the background is a smoky cafe in Beirut. The agents can identify this man as **Arkady Shevlenko**. He is the only one of the subjects of the photos who is still alive.
- If you haven't run *Treason in the Blood*, then the box also contains various personal effects belonging to Kim Philby. There's a passport, some money, and several unsent letters. One's for his editor at the *Observer*, another to his wife Eleanor, and the third is to the curator of the National Museum of Iraq, asking for a list of documents written by Gertrude Bell in the museum's collection. All the letters are dated a day before Philby vanished in Beirut to defect to Moscow.

THE OTHER BOXES

Most of the other boxes contain documents of marginal use to the agents – corporate contracts, wills, deeds and other legal papers. Others contain jewellery, precious metals, gemstones and cash. If the thieves loot the entire bank vault, the total haul is approximately twenty million dollars. If the agents are pressed for time, then they can grab two million without risk, and another million for every five minutes they spend looting (every ten minutes if they've got to drill through each box individually).

If the Black Sea Bank shipment has arrived, then add in the following:

- Another ten million in easily portable diamonds and cash.
- Black Sea Bank internal documents that point at the bank's other questionable activity – following up on these leads with **Research, Accounting** or **Traffic Analysis** brings the agents to some other node in the conspiracy or operation in the **Quartet**.
  - **Odessa:** The Black Sea Bank is headquartered there, and the management are uncomfortable having "the procedure" carried out so close to home. They're also concerned that the Turkish shipments are attracting attention.
  - **Baghdad:** The "flow of product" may dry up soon unless steps are taken.
  - **Vienna:** Black Sea Bank agents are attending the trade conference in Vienna, and they're smuggling in a vampire.
- If your vampires have a specialized requirement, then there's something suitably vampiric in the vault (bags of purified blood, a human brain kept alive by a weird life support device and locked into an emotional loop, torn fragments of the Koran soaked in wine, syringes of something glowing – or even a staked, quiescent vampire in a coffin, stored in the vault for safe keeping until it can be revived with the correct sacrifice/punished for turning on its elders/resurrected with the Rubedo/devoured by its blood-siblings).

Other items of note in the boxes:

- A briefcase full of gold Krugerrands.
- A collection of antique (but still functional) 18th and 19th century firearms, including one with six silver bullets.
- Several pieces of art; **Art History** lets the agents spot the two small pieces by Rembrandt that will sell for another million dollars each on the black market.
- Passports and ID documents for senior bank staff, worth 20 points of **Cover** after using **Forgery** on them to switch the photos.
- The Koernersbank's own internal documentation, including a damning report suppressed by Julie Montavon about the Black Sea Bank. If Andreas or the other shareholders saw this, they'd call off the deal.
- Optionally, a lead unrelated to the current operation that opens a new front against the Conspiracy, such as:
  - ⊕ The Montavon's family history is in the vault. Looking through it with **History**, the agents discover that the Montavons have connections to the Knights Templar, and there are accounts that the Templars were involved with (or opposed to) vampires. The Black Sea Bank is buying the Koernersbank to eliminate a dormant asset of their enemies. Are there other Templar-descended groups out there who could be allies of the agents?
  - ⊛ The archives of an auction house in Zurich. **Vampirology** or **Art History** spot a photo of an artefact called the Shadox Reliquary, a silver-inlaid skull that was found in England in the 1950s. That skull has unusually vampiric fangs. It was auctioned off to a private collector in Boston in 1995.
  - ⊛ ⊕ A collection of 16th century books on alchemy and the occult; there could be vital information about the Enemy in here.

- ▸ ☠ A multinational biotech firm with an office in Zurich keeps important documents in the vault, including copies of patent applications. Right now, they're working on a genetic therapy for various blood diseases. **Vampirology** or **Forensic Pathology** draws a connection between this new therapy and vampirism. Has the company stumbled across a cure? Are they trying to reverse-engineer the mutation? Or are they pawns of the Conspiracy?
- ▸ 👽 One of the relics in the vault is extra-terrestrial in origin (**Astronomy**). It belongs to a New-Age religion/cult that's best known for extracting money from celebrities – but do they hide a deeper secret?

GETTING OUT

If the agents haven't set off any alarms yet, then they've got to get out of the vault without being spotted. They've got to retrace their steps, sneaking past the guards and the security systems once again before finally escaping the bank and fleeing to the safe house. If any of the thieves are going to try betraying the group, now's an excellent time to pull a gun or kick an agent out of the car. (Another option is for the thief to have a few goons – say, P high-quality thugs in a black van - lurking outside the bank to ambush the agents and steal the loot.)

Escaping the bank without setting off any alarms means the agents escape with only +1 Heat (reflecting the heightened state of alert in the Swiss police after a bank robbery). The robbery is not discovered until the following morning.

If the agents set off alarms, then they're got to evade the police. If they just set off an **alert** or an **internal alarm** (i.e. the guards realize the bank has been robbed just after the agents escape), then the streets are crawling with police cars within a few minutes. The agents now have +2 Heat, and they'll need to evade police checkpoints with a **Drive** roll (Difficulty 6, but an **Urban Survival** spend brings it down to Difficulty 4). If the test fails, then it's chase scene time, with the agents starting at Lead 3.

If the **external alarm** goes off, then the agents blast their way out of the bank just in time to see the strobing blue lights zoom around the corner. They've now got +3 Heat and a Lead of 2 over Zurich's finest on their heels.

To escape the cops, the agents need to get a Lead of 10. As all this is part of the heist, the agents may have made preparations to throw off pursuers and boost their lead (spike strips across key intersections, nitro booster built into the getaway car, hacking into the police computers to monitor and disrupt communications, car changes in dark multilevel car parks). Chase encounters:

- Police helicopter swoops low overhead, trying to blind the driver with a spotlight
- Traffic jam as late-night revellers spill out of pubs and nightclubs
- Racing police cars down narrow alleyways
- Hairpin turns on treacherous mountain roads

The agents can get one bonus point of Lead by dropping some of the loot, and another point of bonus Lead by kicking one of the thieves out of the car to lighten the load (or, to put it another way, the thieves can get a bonus point of Lead by kicking an agent out of the car).

Once the agents hit Lead 7 or more, add in a car full of Lisky Bratva thugs with submachine guns to spice things up. If the agents run out of lead, then they run into a police road block; smashing through it successful requires a **Drive** test at Difficulty 6; failure means everyone in the car takes damage *and* the car's wrecked – they get through the roadblock, but they've got to ditch the car and escape on foot. Move onto *The Safe House*, opposite, or *Stolen Albedo*, below, depending on circumstances.

THEY SCREWED UP

It's possible that the agents fail to break into the vault (they set off an alarm and flee before the police arrive, there's a *Reservoir Dogs*-style falling out and one of the agents gets crippled, they decide that the vault's impregnable and switch to a backup plan). If this happens, then the bank buyout goes through, the Lisky Bratva get into the vault, and they find the Albedo. Monitoring them with **Traffic Analysis**/grabbing a thug and **Interrogating** him/noticing that they've still got plenty of security in place with **Military Science** reveals that the Lisky Bratva are going to move the Albedo to Zurich airport and fly it out of Switzerland. The agents can try intercepting it in *Recovering the Albedo,* p. 100.

STOLEN ALBEDO

SCENE TYPE: Subplot
LEADS-IN: In The Vault
LEADS-OUT: The Safe House, Recovering the Albedo, Bank Run

If a treacherous thief gets away with the Philby box, the agents have to recover it. This might take the form of a foot or car chase if the thief doesn't make a clean getaway (in which case, you might be in for a three-way chase between agents, thieves and cops/Lisky Bratva security). However, if the thief does melt away into the night, they've got to hit the streets and find him. Each of the potential Albedo thieves has his or her own escape plan – see the individual write-ups below for Chakroun, Lawson, and Florin.

The identity of the thief's handlers/clients varies – they may be Lisky Bratva operatives, they might be working for the Third Party (see *Treason in the Blood*, p. 106), vampire-hunting monks, MI6 officers or something weirder. Whoever they are, there are P/2 of them, and they're good (use Bodyguard statistics from *Night's Black Agents*, p. 69).

BUYING THE ALBEDO

The agents may be able to buy off the thief, at the price of any profit from the heist. The thief wants it all – or, at least, all the portable loot. If the agents won't deal, he can go to the Lisky Bratva instead.

CHAKROUN

She's had all this planned well in advance. She walks into her reserved suite at a five-star hotel, where she's stashed the gear she needs to set up a new identity. If she's selling the case to the Lisky Bratva, or handing it over to some other client, then she sets up a meeting at a point in the middle of Lake Zurich, identified by GPS co-ordinates. She'll meet them there in a speedboat, make the handover, then escape to a waiting car parked on a back road down by the south-western shore of the lake.

- **Streetwise** lets the agents track Chakroun by her distinctive appearance to her hotel. They get there too late, but breaking into her room with **Infiltration** or **Disguise** lets them use **Electronic Surveillance** to find that she made a call from the room phone to a boat hire place.
- Heading to the boat hire place and using **Outdoor Survival** spots Chakroun's boat, and then you're either into a chase scene on the water or a sniper shot followed by some SCUBA diving.

FLORIN

Massimo Florin heads back to The Hunter's Rest, the same bar he frequented before the heist. The bartender, **Paulo**, there is actually an old colleague of his, and they planned the whole double-cross together. He hides the Albedo in the friend's flat until it's time to make the trade.

Florin's preferred meeting place is in Zurich airport. He'll have his friend Paulo stash the case in a parked car in the car park, then meet his buyer in a coffee shop next to the departure gates. He'll make the trade, hand over the keys to the car, then stroll onto a plane and vanish.

- **Human Terrain** remembers that the old bartender and Florin seemed unusually close. He knew Florin's food and drink orders without the thief having to ask.
- Heading back to the bar and questioning a waitress with **Flirting** sends the agents to the airport just in time to interrupt the handover.

LAWSON

Lawson doesn't plan, he improvises. If he ends up with the Albedo, he'll stick to the back alleyways, thinking on his feet. He doesn't have any friends or contacts in Zurich that he can trust. He contacts the Lisky Bratva or his handlers by phone, and sets up a handover on the Adliswil-Felsenegg cable-car. He'll be on one car, the handler on the other, and they'll hand over the case at the half-way point.

- **Electronic Surveillance** let the agents triangulate his cellphone and track him through the streets to the base of the cable-car.
- After that, you've got a fist-fight/gunfight on the cable car, with Lawson's handlers turning up half-way through.

THE SAFE HOUSE

SCENE TYPE: Antagonist Action
LEADS-IN: In The Vault, Stolen Albedo
LEADS-OUT: Recovering the Albedo, Bank Run

The agents decamp to their safe house, with or without the Albedo. If the agents haven't picked a safe house, then go with Chakroun's suggestion of an isolated farmhouse in the mountains. Chakroun's already prepared the safe house with necessary supplies. There's a full medical kit, three clean cars with full gas tanks, a cache of ammo and guns, and power tools for opening safe-deposit boxes. She's also got a folder of fake passports that should be enough **Cover** to get through security checks (they're only 1-point **Covers**).

Chakroun proposes that they split the loot here and vanish (or, if the Albedo's gone, that they hunt down the treacherous thief first and then split).

Preparing the Ground: For added nastiness – if the Lisky Bratva know about the safe house in advance, then they may have already booby-trapped the place. They won't use explosives to avoid damaging the Albedo, but there could be man-traps (+1 damage and lose that many point of **Athletics**), trip-wires (triggers a concealed gun) or poisoned food waiting for the agents.

THE TRAITOR

One of the thieves is a traitor, and has betrayed the location of the safe house to the Lisky Bratva. A 1-point **Bullshit Detector** spend might pick up on nervousness, a 1-point **Notice** spend spots the traitor sending a cellphone text message, a 1-point **Vampirology** spend spots that the traitor has deliberately cut open a finger and left a trail of blood right to their door (the blood splatters are too small and widely spaced to be tracked by conventional methods, but a vampire could follow the trail like a supernatural bloodhound).

That 1-point spend gives the agents a minute's advance warning before the Lisky Bratva arrive. If they don't have that advance warning, the first sign of the enemy is when a sniper-scope laser dot appears on someone's chest.

As soon as the attack starts, the traitor tries to escape or hide, grabbing the Albedo in the process. Ideally, the enemy gets hold of the Albedo in this scene, but if the players make a heroic effort and manage to hold onto it, you can skip *Recovering the Albedo* and jump straight to *Bank Run*.

ENEMY FORCES

Outside the safe house, the Lisky Bratva have:

- Px2 armed thugs, with gas grenades and masks
- 2 thugs with sniper rifles (+2 damage, +4 Shooting) and night-vision goggles, if necessary.
- P/2 thug bosses (+4 Athletics, Hand-to-Hand, Health and Shooting)
- The zalozhniy (if the zalozhniy isn't already inside the safe house)
- Marko Schwetz, leading from the rear.

Their tactics vary depend on the location of the safe house.

- **ISOLATED:** Full-on assault. The snipers open up first, then the thugs move in with gas grenades to flush the agents out into the open.
- Time to break out **Mechanics** to improvise weapons out of farm tools and equipment
- If the hideout is a ski lodge, then there are skis and poles for a high-speed chase on the piste.
- The Lisky Bratva's primary goal is to recover the Albedo. The player characters are secondary, and if they get the Albedo, the Lisky Bratva will withdraw leaving only a few thugs to clean up.
- **SUBURBAN:** Sniper attacks to start, and then hit the safe house from all sides. They'll try to capture or eliminate the agents as quickly as possible.
  - P/2 thugs kick in the door, another P/2 thugs enter through windows or back entrances. The rest wait outside as backup or to grab any agents who run.
  - Zurich doesn't have any skyscrapers or tower blocks; a suburban hideout is going to be a small house or a house converted into a few flats.
  - Here, the Lisky Bratva are under a time limit – they don't want to draw Heat any more than the agents do. The Lisky Bratva have low-level infiltrators in the Swiss police, but don't have not enough pull to make a massive gun battle disappear.
- **CITY CENTRE:** Too many witnesses for a direct assault, so the Lisky Bratva start with silenced sniper shots from nearby rooftops. P thugs and a thug boss then kick in the door of the safe house, while the rest of the thugs are held in reserve on the streets outside.
  - This approach forces the Lisky Bratva to rely on fisticuffs instead of guns for the most part. They'll try to take the agents without anyone noticing.

MOVING ON

If the agents manage to keep the Albedo, then have a dying thug gasp *"they're coming for you..."* and make a strange sign with his blood-stained fingers. **Occult Studies** identifies it as a curse. The Lisky Bratva know the agents have the Albedo, and they'll tip the police off. **Criminology (Core Clue)** suggests that it'll be easy for the Conspiracy to retrieve the Albedo from an Interpol evidence locker. The agents need to get out of Switzerland and disappear. Move onto *Bank Run,* p. 102.

If the agents lose the Albedo to the Lisky Bratva, then they've got to get it back. **Interrogating (Core Clue)** a dying thug reveals that they'll bring the Albedo back to Zurich, then ship it to the airport where it'll be loaded onto their private plane and flown off. If you don't have a dying thug to hand, a dropped cellphone and **Traffic Analysis** (or a quick hit of redial and a Difficulty 4 **Disguise** test) can intercept enemy communications and give the same information. Run *Recovering the Albedo*.

RECOVERING THE ALBEDO

SCENE TYPE: Subplot
LEAD-IN: The Safe house
LEAD-OUT: Bank Run

So, the bad guys have the Albedo. Time to steal it again.

SECURITY ARRANGEMENTS

The convoy to the airport is identical to the one in *The Shipment* (p. 89) – one armored bank truck containing the Albedo, guarded by several vans of Lisky Bratva thugs. Remove any thugs that the agents eliminated at *The Safe House;* if the agents eliminated more than a handful of thugs, then the Lisky Bratva will recruit more from either the Koernersbank's own private security contacts or local criminal elements – either way is an opening for agents to use **Disguise** to infiltrate the enemy force.

All the goons are armed and twitchy.

- **Traffic Analysis** gets the agents rough numbers of the opposition.

If the agents have a Heat of 1, add on two cops in a police car; if they've got Heat 2, then it's two cop cars. If the agent's Heat is 3 or more, then the cops get upgraded to full-on special forces.

- **Cop Talk** or **Traffic Analysis** confirms the police presence.

The Albedo's carried in a bulletproof briefcase that's handcuffed to **Victor Kozel**.

THE ROUTE

The most direct route to the airport is along the A1 — it's a relatively short drive of around 12 kilometres. Staging a car crash or road works can divert the convoy onto back roads.

The convoy departs from the Koernersbank in the early evening, and arrives at the airport at twilight.

RUNNING THE HIJACK

Where do the agents hit the convoy?

AT THE BANK

If the agents can break back into the bank (or convince one of the Montavons or other bank staff to smuggle them in), they can grab the Albedo after it's removed from the vault, either by attacking the armored car in the basement loading bay or by grabbing Victor Kozel.

- If they can pull this off, then they only need to deal with a handful of security guards inside the bank.
- Of course, they've just robbed a bank *again*, this time in broad daylight. That's +3 Heat right there, more if they go in shooting.
- Getting out will be tricky. The best option is to grab that armored truck…

ON THE ROAD

This gives the agents the most scope for dirty tricks, like sniper attacks, improvised explosive devices, ram-raiding or hijacking police communications to order the convoy diverted to a prepared ambush.

- The truck's got Armor 5, and has narrow armoured windows (Armour 2, and the Hit Threshold for putting a bullet through the window is 4.
- The truck driver's got **Driving** 8, and the truck's got a Speed of 0 and a Manoeuvre of -1.
- Knocking the truck off the road requires a heavy vehicle and a **Driving** contest against the truck driver.

- **Military Science** or **Outdoor Survival** identifies ambush locations on the roads. Spending points from either skill sets up Tactical Factfinding Benefits, forcing **Driving** tests on the bad guys or giving a pool for **Shooting** or **Explosive Devices** tests. Possible nasty tricks:
- Lining up sniper shots on nice straight roads
- Concealed tire spikes or claymore mines
- Separating the armored car from its escorts with oil slicks or smoke pots
- Fake police checkpoints

AT THE AIRPORT

The cops peel off as soon as the convoy passes the security checkpoint outside the airport. The Lisky Bratva's Tu-154 is waiting in a private hangar in a quiet part of the airfield. There are at least another two thugs guarding the plane; add on extra security if you want stiffer opposition.

- The plane gets ready to leave as soon as the convoy arrives. Kozel's flying out tonight.
- He takes P thugs with him on the plane, plus the zalozhniy if it's still around.

- Sneaking onto the plane, hijacking it, and flying out of Switzerland kills this scene and the next in one swift move, assuming the agents can **Infiltrate** the plane, eliminate the crew, and then use **Piloting** to fly it somewhere safe to disappear.
- **Data Recovery** on the plane's flight computer gets its ultimate destination — the Lisky Bratva intend to deliver the Albedo to the Conspiracy. Where's the next rung up in your Conspyramid located?
- If this is the last operation in the **Quartet,** then you can run *Killing Uncle Joe* on top of the fight to recover the Albedo.
- My, look at those drums of airplane fuel. Won't they make a lovely (Class 3, 4 if you hit a really big tank) explosion?

NO ALBEDO?

If the agents fail to recover the Albedo from the bank, and then fail again to steal it from the secure convoy, then the Conspiracy gets their cold dead hands on that half of the Rubedo. The agents haven't lost yet, though — their failure here just makes recovering the Nigredo all the more important.

NIGHT'S BLACK AGENTS – THE ZALOZHNIY QUARTET

BANK RUN

SCENE TYPE: Conclusion
LEAD-IN: The Safe house, Recoving the Albedo

By this point in the operation, the agents should have the Albedo, as the Lisky Bratva either failed to recover it or failed to hold it. The Conspiracy doesn't have the assets in place in Zurich to recapture the Albedo.

The police do. The Lisky Bratva therefore use their contacts in the police to dump all the Heat they can on the agents. They tip off the police about who carried out the crime (optionally, they produce the traitor or a captured thief to give evidence fingering the agents). The agents' known Cover identities and descriptions are given to the Swiss police and Interpol. The Conspiracy intends to retrieve the Albedo from the police once the agents are arrested.

In game terms, the Heat on the agents is increased by +3 (+4 if they've killed police). Their current Covers are burned – using them will alert the cops. Flashing money or other ill-gotten proceeds of the bank heist also draws unwanted attention.

Just getting out of Switzerland won't be enough – every police force in Europe is on the look-out for the notorious gang of bank robbers. The agents need to disappear.

ESCAPING THE NET

Use the Extended Chase rules (*Night's Black Agents,* p. 90). The agents' Hot Lead starts at 7-their current Heat. To escape the cops, they need to get their Hot Lead up to 7 (escaping Interpol's jurisdiction or just lying low) or come up with rock-solid **Covers** (at least 5 points) coupled with **Disguise**.

GETTING OUT OF SWITZERLAND

The Swiss take their security seriously. The agents run into police checkpoints on all the major roads leading out of Zurich, checking for people matching the agents' description. The airports also have security stepped up.

- Moving on the streets of any town becomes a nerve-wracking experience, as every passing officer scrutinises the agents' faces.
- If you haven't had one already, you're pretty much obliged to have a high-speed Alpine car chase along narrow mountain roads with sharp bends, treacherous conditions and big dramatic cliffs.
- **Electronic Surveillance** suggests that mentioning the agents' names on the telephone would be unwise – the authorities are monitoring voice and data traffic for clues.

INCREASING HOT LEAD

As the agents don't have a set destination to reach in this chase, there are other ways to dodge their pursuers.

- **LYING LOW:** If the agents hide out in a quiet country village in Tuscany or an anonymous suburb in Poland for a few weeks, the Heat subsides and their Hot Lead rises. Of course, laying low like this means the agents aren't fighting the good fight against the vampires. (**Disguise, Streetwise, Human Terrain** to blend in).
- **RUNNING TO A SAFETY:** Going to a place of Safety (see *Night's Black Agents,* p. 36) gives the agents two points of Hot Lead immediately. (No skills required, but make a Hot Lead test when the agents arrive at the Safety. If the test fails, burn it.)
- **FAKING THEIR DEATHS:** Pushing a car over a cliff into a deep lake, staging an explosion (with some convenient Lisky Bratva-goon corpses to be burned beyond recognition) or putting on a show for anyone watching can convince the authorities that the agents are dead. (**Criminology, Forensic Pathology, Chemistry**).
- **THROWING SOMEONE TO THE WOLVES:** The agents can either frame some other poor patsy for the Koernersbank job, or else give false information to a disposable asset (like one of the thieves) about their plans, then arrange for the police to capture that asset. While the police are following up on a fake lead to Bermuda, the agents escape into the night. (**Bullshit Detector** to make sure the asset's fooled, **Criminology, Cop Talk**).
- **MAKING A DEAL:** If the agents have worthwhile intel about the Lisky Bratva's criminal dealings, they could find a trustworthy and open-minded Interpol agent and make a deal – they give him a dossier on the Lisky Bratva, she pulls some of the Heat off them. (This approach works best if the agents (a) don't have innocent blood on their hands and (b) only robbed the Philby box and didn't steal millions of dollars.) Any of the following information is worth a Hot Lead boost of one or two points, depending on how much proof the agents can provide:
    - The Koernersbank's own internal report on the Black Sea Bank.
    - The Lisky Bratva human-trafficking ring in Austria and Romania
    - Their dealings with the Serbian mafia
    - Their weapons-smuggling ring in Baghdad and Odessa

NETWORK CONNECTIONS

The agents can still use their Network, but they're very, very hot. At the very least, a **Reassurance** or **Intimidate** spend is needed to convince a contact to help such wanted criminals.

- 🩸 A contact is very likely to betray the agents to the cops or the Lisky Bratva.

FENCING THE LOOT

If the agents intend to convert any stolen diamonds or gold into cash, they'll need to fence it. Doing so requires a **Network** contact or a **Streetwise/Criminology** spend to put them in touch with a quiet, bespectacled man who calls himself **Hans Schmidt**. Make a Hot Lead test (Difficulty 5) at this point. If the test fails, he offers then a sickening small percentage of the loot's actual value (5%), or else alerts the Lisky Bratva. If successful, he offers 10%. **Accounting/Negotiation** spends can bump the pay up to a maximum of 20%. Alternatively, the agents can stash their share of the loot for a few years in a cache and retire on it after the campaign's done.

FINAL CURTAIN

The final curtain on this mission falls when the agents have the Albedo and are clear of any pursuit. Play this as a low-key triumph, the first step towards striking a significant blow against the Conspiracy — unless this is the last operation in the **Quartet,** in which case run *Killing Uncle Joe.*

EXIT VECTORS

This operation uncovers leads pointing to the other operations in this book.

THE ZALOZHNIY SANCTION

- **Accounting:** The Black Sea Bank is headquartered in Odessa, and there's plenty of evidence that the Lisky Bratva are laundering money from illegal activity through the bank.
- **Research:** Lil Blaise, the French spy used to create the zalozhniy encountered in this operation, vanished in Odessa.

- **Electronic Surveillance:** Schwetz may report back to Dorjiev in Odessa.

OUT OF THE HOUSE OF ASHES

- **Photography:** Arkady Shevlenko's photo was in the Philby box, and he's in Vienna.
- **Electronic Surveillance:** Schwetz was told to complete the bank buyout as quickly as possible, as the Lisky Bratva's operatives in Vienna were on the verge of "acquiring Shevlenko."

TREASON IN THE BLOOD

- **Military Science:** Victor Kozel wanted to hire Overwatch Security to protect the bank; they're based in Baghdad.
- Kim Philby's unsent letter to Iraqi National Museum asked about Gertrude Bell's documents. If the agents visit the national museum (or do online **Research**), they'll soon find Mohammed al-Kirkuk.

CAPSTONE: KILLING UNCLE JOE

The *vor of vors*, Josef Lisky — old Uncle Joe himself — is coming to Zurich to oversee the final buyout of the Koernersbank. He intends to take possession of the Albedo himself, so he can personally deliver it to his vampiric masters.

Now, though, the agents have taken both the Albedo and the Nigredo, and are on the verge of achieving the Rubedo. They've got leverage over Josef Lisky himself. Point out (**Tradecraft** or **Criminology** or **Vampirology**) that they can use the Albedo and Rubedo to cut a deal with Lisky if the players don't think of this option themselves. The agents can get in touch with Josef Lisky through the Montavons.

Alternatively, Lisky can contact the agents through an intermediary — which means finding a Solace, beating the unfortunate Solace half to death, and then jamming a cellphone with a single number jammed into the victim's mouth).

THE DEAL

Lisky's sick of the agents' interference. They've ruined his operations from Baghdad to Zurich, they've cost him dozens of lives and millions of dollars. They've killed the dead — and enough is enough. It is time to talk business. What will it cost Lisky to make this problem go away?

He wants the Albedo, the Nigredo, and a blood oath that the agents will retire off to some Caribbean island and never interfere in the shadow world again. In exchange, he offers a truce, a promise that the Lisky Bratva and the Conspiracy will not strike back at the agents, and whatever else the agents want. Money? Immortality? Appeal to the agents' Drives. If someone wants Restoration, then Josef can arrange it. If they want revenge on a particular vampire, then the Conspiracy will sacrifice one of their own in exchange for the Rubedo. If they want to know all the secrets of the world, then they can step into the shadows and become part of the Conspiracy themselves.

Lisky's preconditions for the meeting are:

- All the agents must be present. Anyone who isn't present will be hunted down and killed.

- The meeting must take place in either Odessa, Vienna, Zurich or Baghdad – all cities where the Lisky Bratva have assets in place already, but outside the heart of the Conspiracy, wherever that is.
- The agents can pick where the meeting takes place, but it must be somewhere public, somewhere central. No tricks, or the deal is off.
- They have the word of a *vor*.

Josef's offer is partially genuine – by this point in the *Quartet,* the agents have inflicted catastrophic damage on his organization and are in possession of the elements of the Rubedo. Lisky needs to salvage the situation, and if buying the agents off will work, he'll do that. However, given the choice, he'd much prefer to capture the agents, take the stolen items back, and then torture them to death.

For the agents, this is their chase to get to the next rung of the Conspiracy. Josef Lisky knows where the vampires are. He reports directly to some sinister undead master – and if they can't extract that information from him, then killing Josef Lisky will decapitate the Lisky Bratva.

SETTING UP THE DEAL

The ball's in the agents' court. Where do they make their stand? Where do they hold the meeting? Now's the time to set up the biggest Tactical Fact-Finding Benefit of the whole game. They need to pick a place that isn't an obvious trap, but which gives them the edge they need to kill or capture Josef Lisky. Potential tactics:

- **Art History:** Both Vienna and Zurich have clock museums that can be weaponized and used against zalozhniy bodyguards (see p. 50).
- **Military Science** plus **Network** plus a Baghdad meet could equal fire support from a Blackhawk gunship.
- **Human Terrain:** Josef Lisky's reputation among the *mafiya* has taken a pounding. If the agents make contact with some of his more ambitious lieutenants, they could arrange for some inside help if the agents meet in Odessa. *You give us Josef, we give you his organization…*

- **Architecture** lets the agents set up secret passages, false walls, lines-of-fire – or maybe just identify the exact spot in that Viennese square where the setting sun casts the shadow of a really huge crucifix at just the right moment.
- **Criminology** plus all the evidence assembled by the agents could bring in Interpol, the CIA, the Vatican Vampire Hunters or whatever other shadowy groups the agents have connections to.
- **Criminology** also points out that Vienna's neutral territory, which limits Josef's ability to bring in bodyguards.
- **Urban Survival** or **Network** lets the agents blend into whatever city they choose, keeping their preparations under the Lisky Bratva's radar.
- By this point in the campaign, an agent with **Vampirology** should know enough to set up Blocks or Banes for use against the vampires.

THE OPPOSITION

As the agents know where Lisky is for once, they can use **Traffic Analysis** (or surveillance **Photography**) to spy on him and identify his bodyguards and entourage. He travels with three bodyguards, six aides/accountants/lawyers, and his direct connection to the Conspiracy. If there are any Operatives or zalozhniye unaccounted for, add them to Lisky's assets, to a maximum of P agent-equivalent bad guys.

Lisky travels in a private jet, and gets from place to place in an armored saloon car (nothing so showy and obvious as a limo). Once the agents pick the location for the meeting, he leaves for that city immediately. While his plane's in the air, he activates any Lisky Bratva assets in the city to investigate the meeting site. If the agents have eliminated all these assets, he's forced to go in blind. If they haven't eliminated all the assets, then the agents need to either make **Conceal** and **Surveillance** rolls or spend points to keep any preparations hidden from the Lisky Bratva investigators.

If the agents keep track of Lisky's jet (and for that, they'll need access to a military-grade radar network via **Data Intrusion** or military contacts), then it makes an unscheduled stop at a rural airfield somewhere en route. This is to pick up **The Double** – a poor Russian farmer surgically altered to resemble Josef Lisky. The Double is Lisky's insurance policy to ensure the agents don't screw him over. The Double has been altered by the conspiracy in some fashion.

- He might be a Renfield, or some other supernatural horror like a vorthr. **Vampirology** spots the telltale signs (blood on the lips, a musty stench, inability to step on cracks).
- ✠ The Double is a corrupt priest, a worshipper of the vampires. **Occult Studies** or **Vampirology** picks up on his mumbled prayers during the meeting.
- ⊗ The Double is a literal double, a *doppleganger* created by the Conspiracy's occult powers. They conjured it from Lisky's shadow. **Notice** spots the lack of a shadow beneath the Doppleganger.
- 👽 The Double is mind-controlled using alien super-science; effectively, his body is a puppet that Lisky operates remotely. **Bullshit Detector** notes the slight delay in Lisky's reactions and body language; **Diagnosis** spots the white line of a implantation scar.
- ☣ The Double's a carrier for some vampiric pathogen or engineered virus. Only those in close proximity risk infection. Lisky has a cure; his plan is to have the double infect the agents by touching them, then use the cure as leverage if the agents don't sell him the Rubedo. **Diagnosis** spots the Double's symptoms, while **Bullshit Detector** picks up on the overly familiar body language.
- If nothing else fits, then his abdominal cavity's packed with plastic explosive, wired to a detonator in Lisky's pocket. **Notice** spots the Double's discomfort; **Electronic Surveillance** detects a carrier wave.
- **Criminology** notes that the Double's prison tattoos aren't right – there are subtle tell-tale clues like the number of spires

This is the big finale for your campaign. It's either a high-stakes deal, or an epic action scene, or else the first turns into the second when the Double is revealed or when the agents launch their ambush. Go for broke here – let all those Tag-Team spends pay off big time, but also don't pull any punches. Enemy reactions are:

- **THE DOUBLE:** Depending on the Conspiracy's modifications, the Double either attacks the agents or explodes (Class 3 explosion).
- **JOSEF LISKY:** Fights to get to the Rubedo. He knows that the Conspiracy will kill him if he doesn't walk out of here with the Rubedo components.
- **THE CONSPIRACY HANDLER:** Tries to walk out of here immediately.
- **BODYGUARDS/ZALOZHNIY/ OPERATIVES:** Attacks the agents. The agents' preparations should be enough to deal with most of these guys.
- **REST OF THE ENTOURAGE:** They're mooks to be eliminated with casual ease.

GOING DEEP, GOING DARK

Once Lisky (or the Conspiracy Handler) is captured, **Interrogation** reveals who the Lisky Bratva's secret masters are… and where they are. Lisky's testimony gets the agents to the next rung of the Conspyramid, and maybe gives them a glimpse of their ultimate foe…

on the cathedral on Lisky's arm not matching the number of times he's been in prison.

When he arrives at the city, Lisky's entourage splits in two. The Double, Lisky's contact with the Conspiracy, one of the bodyguards and the other non-combatants drive straight to the meeting site via the most direct and obvious route. Meanwhile, the real Lisky and the other two bodyguards head to the meeting undercover. They'll take public transport if the option's available; otherwise, they drive in an unremarkable car and then lurk in the crowds/backstreets/catacombs/ruins/ delete as appropriate near the meeting site.

THE HANDOVER

"Josef Lisky" – the Double – arrives at the meeting place. Most of his entourage hangs back, while the Double, one bodyguard and a lawyer come forward to make the handover. The lawyer has a suitcase full of cash, plus whatever else the agents asked for.

When the agents spot whatever telltale gives the Double away, they can use **Negotiation** to force Lisky to reveal himself. If the agents still seem to be acting in good faith, then Lisky emerges from the shadows to make the final handover personally. If they're trying to capture or kill Lisky, then they'll have to alter their plans to take the Double into account.

TREASON IN THE BLOOD

This operation pits the agents against more supernatural horrors than any other. They've got to deal with the legacy of St. John Philby, the Conspiracy's machinations, and the interference of other, even more mysterious factions who have an interest in the Rubedo…

The name of this operation is taken from Anthony Cave Brown's superb dual biography of the Philbys, pere et fils. That book, and Tim Powers' novel *Declare*, about a different occult Philby plot, are heartily recommended reading for Directors seeking powerful inspiration for running this operation.

EYES ONLY BRIEFING

Recent upheavals in the Middle East put the Conspiracy on the trail of the Nigredo, the mysterious second part of Philby's secret. While rolling up the Lisky Bratva's weapons-smuggling ring, the agents learn that the political diary of Gertrude Bell contains the location of the Nigredo's hiding place. The search for the diary brings the agents into the crossfire between the Conspiracy and a mysterious third faction.

From Baghdad, the trail leads to Beirut, where the agents race another group to recover the Nigredo from St. John Philby's grave. That turns out to be a trap – Arab spies working for Philby removed the Nigredo in 1975. Through unlikely sources, the agents identify these spies, and head to Riyadh.

In Riyadh, they meet with Haroun al-Murrah, a Saudi sheikh whose grandfather worked with Philby. He leads the agents to a cave in the deep desert, where they find a misbegotten vampiric horror that may once have been St. John Philby. They recover the Nigredo from the cave – only to be betrayed. The Conspiracy steals the Nigredo and attempts to smuggle it out of Iraq, leaving the agents for dead. The agents must escape the death-trap and chase the Nigredo before it reaches Istanbul.

THE SPINE

There are two possible starting points to this operation. The most likely starting point is **Overwatch Security**, a private military company that's part of the Lisky Bratva weapons-smuggling ring. Breaking into the Overwatch base leads the agents to **The Museum Researcher**, an academic in the Iraqi National Museum. (Alternately, the Researcher leads the agents to Overwatch). From there, the agents go in search of the diary of Gertrude Bell, a British spy and one of the architects of the old Kingdom of Iraq. They end up in the **Mukhabarat Archive**, where they're attacked by a zalozhniy assassin.

A multitude of leads bring them **to Beirut**, where the Nigredo is rumored to rest. They dig up Harry St. John Philby's grave in **The Exhumation,** but the Nigredo's not there. What is there is a trap that nearly kills them. The Nigredo was taken by Arab spies in '74, as they discover thanks to an old Russian in **KGB Beirut.**

Optionally, there's a brief detour at this point to talk to some **Old Ghosts** in Cyprus.

Tracing the Arabs leads the agents to Sheikh Haroun al-Murrah in **King Saud's City.** He remembers an old cave in the desert that he visited as a child. The agents go into the Empty Quarter in **Hajj Shaitan**, where they recover the Nigredo from a feral vampire-thing in a dark well. They possess it only briefly before **Treason in the Blood** takes the Nigredo from them and leaves them for dead. After escaping the death trap, the agents follow the Nigredo and discover it's on **The Last Train To Istanbul**. They've got one final chance to snatch the prize out from under the fangs of the vampires…

ENTRY VECTORS

There are a number of ways into this adventure, from previous ops, from other operations in this collection, or from random chatter. The Director should salt as many leads as she feels necessary, or customize them to suit her campaign.

OUTSIDE LEADS

These leads come from outside this book; from the corebook adventure *(S) Entries* or perhaps from other ops in the Director's previous campaign.

THE LENNART DOSSIER

- **Military Science:** Lennart mentions Overwatch Security as a suspect organization.
- There are scanned copies of books by Gertrude Bell, Harry Philby and T.E. Lawrence (of Arabia) in the dossier. **Research** suggests that Lennart tried to get access to the archives of the National Museum of Iraq during reconstruction after the Iraq war.

OTHER VECTORS

- While breaking into a Conspiracy stronghold (vampire crypt, Lisky Bratva brothel, corporate headquarters), the agents spot (**Art History** or **Archaeology**) a relic stolen from the Iraqi National Museum. Investigating the museum leads the agents to Mohammed al-Kirkuk.
- A **Network** contact points the agents towards Overwatch Security. That contact then dies mysteriously – they're eliminated by the Third Party.
- The agents run into a Conspiracy kill team armed with cutting-edge weapons like M27 Infantry Automatic Rifles. Tracing the weapons with **Military Science** points the agents to Iraq and the Overwatch Security smuggling.

INSIDE LEADS

Intel gathered in other operations in this collection may lead the agents to Baghdad and Gertrude Bell's missing journal. If the players don't quite stumble over the right leads in those scenarios, quite often the Director can plant this intel in the mouth (or dead fist, or laptop, or smartphone) of an NPC also on the trail of the Lisky Bratva or of the Philby Plot.

THE ZALOZHNIY SANCTION

- **Interrogation:** Beating up a string of Turkish smugglers and Ukranian gangsters lets the agents follow the trail of weapons from the Odessan warehouse to the Baghdad mercenary compound.
- **Research:** The Philby dossier in the Dragovir museum mentions Mohammed al-Kirkuk.

OUT OF THE HOUSE OF ASHES

- **Research:** Arkady Shevlenko's old case notes point the agents towards Mohammed al-Kirkuk and the Iraqi National Museum.
- **Military Science** or **Accounting:** Serial numbers on guns carried by Lisky Bratva thugs can be traced to US arsenals in Baghdad.

BAGHDAD: QUICK AND DIRTY

Capital of Iraq and one of the most important cities in the Middle East since its founding in the 8th century A.D. The city suffered considerable damage during the Iraq War, and the streets are still extremely dangerous. You've got gunfire, bombings and kidnappings in the shadow of medieval walls.

POPULATION
7.2 million (a bit smaller than New York City)

CONFLICT
Take your pick – you've got Sunni/Shia divides in the Iraqi population (the Sunnis are a minority, but held the majority of government positions under Saddam), you've got a weak national government trying to extricate itself from western influences, you've got western agents trying to ensure that Iran doesn't grab control over Iraq and its oil fields, and you've got crime and corruption and larcenous corporations with private military contractors.

BACKDROPS
THE HANDS OF VICTORY, a monument built by Saddam Hussein to commemorate victory in the Iran/Iraq war. The hands form arches leading to a parade ground.

THE NATIONAL MUSEUM OF IRAQ: Founded by the British archaeologist Gertrude Bell during the early reign of King Faisal, the museum formerly housed the largest collection of antiquities in the Middle East.

THE GREEN ZONE: Officially, it's the International Zone, and officially, it doesn't exist any more – the occupying forces handed control of the Green Zone back to the Iraqi government in 2011. Still, the area around the Republican Palace is safer and more secure than the rest of the city.

THREE HOOKS
- In 2011, a canal in Sadr City, one of Baghdad's suburbs, turned blood red. Authorities blamed the alarming color on pollution or waste from a nearby slaughterhouse. Who'd dump thousands of gallons of blood into the waters of the canal?
- Before his execution in 2006, several bizarre occult rumours circulated around Saddam Hussein. One claimed that he had a magic stone implanted in his upper arm that made him unkillable; another insisted that he controlled an army of "cow-sized scorpions" (made, obviously, using alien technology retrieved from a UFO shot down by the United States during Operation Desert Storm.
- The ruins of Babylon are only a few dozen kilometers outside Baghdad, and Babylonian mythology spoke of vampiric *ekimmu*, the ghosts of the unquiet dead, who could possess evil men and taboo-breakers and give them supernatural powers. Who knows what horrors the war unleashed?

THE BOXMEN
- **Military Science:** Victor Kozel wanted to hire Overwatch Security for the bank.
- **Languages:** Kim Philby's unsent letter to the curator of the Iraqi National Museum leads the agents to Baghdad.

THE THIRD PARTY

This operation introduces another faction with an interest in the Rubedo. This faction is opposed to the vampiric Conspiracy – but that doesn't necessarily make them the good guys. This "Third Party" proves to be ruthless and dangerous, but they can be allies of convenience for the agents during *Treason in the Blood*. The true nature of the Third Party is up to the Director, but the following facts are always true:

- The Third Party knows that they're up against supernatural opposition.
- They know that Kim Philby knew about the Conspiracy, and that he was in possession of something that the Conspiracy desperately want.
- They've got extensive backing, possibly from a western government.
- They're *not* KGB/FSB (but might be a different Russian/ex-Soviet group, like the military GRU intelligence section).
- The Third Party's agents on the ground communicate with their mysterious patrons through secure channels only – they don't know who they're really working for.
- The Third Party prefer to keep things quiet, but are willing to use lethal force to remove obstacles.
- ⊚ The Third Party's goals should be clearly opposed to the ideals of one or more agents.

With those restrictions in mind, some likely candidates for Third Party status include:

- A splinter faction within the Conspiracy, who are opposed to the Lisky Bratva's masters. If you're using the Linea Dracula, then they're the Hungarian line. If you've got mutant vampires, then the Third Party are an offshoot who retained more of their humanity.
- A shadowy faction within the CIA, founded by James Jesus Angleton after Philby defected. They sent the extraction team in *Out of the House of Ashes*.
- A long-running MI6 operation. British Intelligence never forgot the injury and humiliation caused by the Cambridge Five, and they intend to finally resolve the Philby situation. Albert Carpenter in *Out of the House of Ashes* might be part of this operation.
- Vampire-hunting Catholic priests, run by the Vatican (the same group that Florin may have been working for in *The Boxmen*). Rome's been watching the vampires for more than a century.
- A Mossad-backed strike force, dedicated to protecting Israel against supernatural threats. They're less concerned with vampires, and more worried about Iran or another hostile government getting their hands on occult weapons or vampires.
- They're part of the VEVAK, the Iranian foreign-intel section. Their backers intend to sell the Nigredo back to the vampires in exchange for things that only the Conspiracy can provide. The VEVAK's field agents don't know about their masters' intentions.

WHY NOW?

The Conspiracy's been looking for the Nigredo for years. Recently, a document came into their possession which suggests that Philby shared some of his vampiric secrets with the other members of the Intrusives, a cell of British spies operating out of Cairo in the early 20th century. (How'd they get this document? Pick from "they found it in a government archive opened during the upheavals of the Arab Spring," "they looted it from Mukhabarat archives in post-war Iraq," or "they've got a mole in MI6.") They already had Overwatch Security as their asset in Iraq. The private military company isn't an ideal tool for the job, but they'll work with what they have.

Ideally, pick one of the players, and have that agent's old mentor/best friend be part of the conspiracy. The mentor shows up under the pseudonym **Mr. Red** in Beirut (see p. 118). This works especially well if you seed references and flashbacks to Mr. Red long before the agents actually meet him. Work him into the backstory of your campaign, and then bring him onstage. If you've already got such a figure in your campaign backstory, use him if at all possible.

The Third Party are *not* the good guys. They may be opposed to the Conspiracy, and they may be temporary allies for the agents, but their ultimate goals don't match with those of the agents. They might want to capture vampires and use them as living weapons, or maybe the secret head of the Third Party is a vampire, and they're unwitting pawns of an old monster. They treat the agents as interlopers or amateurs who are in over their heads.

OVERWATCH SECURITY

SCENE TYPE: Introductory (or Alternate)
LEAD-IN: The Museum Researcher
LEAD-OUTS: The Museum Researcher

Overwatch Security is a PMC (Private Military Company) operating in Baghdad, providing protection for western businessmen and corporate interests. Most of Overwatch's soldiers are from Latin America, but in the last few years, the company began recruiting aggressively in the Ukraine and the Russian Federation, which left it open to infiltration by the Lisky Bratva. The company has offices in Texas and Washington, but its official head office is in Bolivia. In Iraq, Overwatch operates out of a military base north of Baghdad.

The Lisky Bratva effectively runs Overwatch; most of the soldiers work for the *mafiya*, and the base commander works for the Conspiracy.

- **Military Science:** Overwatch is a small PMC with a questionable reputation.
- **Criminology:** Looking at photos of Overwatch personnel shows a high percentage of them have Russian prison tattoos.

WEAPONS SMUGGLING

The Lisky Bratva's trade in American-made weapons starts here. Overwatch has a contract to protect several warehouses where weapons intended for the Iraqi army are stored. The security forces take a portion of each shipment that passes through the warehouse, and then pay corrupt clerks in the Iraqi army to report the weapons as "destroyed." The weapons are then brought to the Overwatch base, and from there they are smuggled across the border into Turkey and then on to Odessa.

- **Interrogation:** Turkish smugglers point the agents to the Overwatch base.
- **Research** or **Law:** Digging through US government records shows several reports about missing weapons. The one common factor is that the weapons were stored in facilities guarded by Overwatch.
- **Streetwise:** Local criminals know about Overwatch's corruption. The PMC has a terrible reputation for shooting without provocation. On the streets, their nickname is "the Russians," and it's an open secret that they're smuggling weapons out of Iraq.
- **Electronic Surveillance:** The US army crates have RFID tags (see *The Zalozhniy Sanction*) and can be traced to the Overwatch base.

THE COMMANDER

The commander of the Overwatch forces in Iraq is Lieutenant Colonel **Benjamin Weddle**, formerly of the US Army. He retired in 2004 to escape the shadow of bribery allegations during his last tour in Iraq, and signed on with Overwatch three months later. He discovered the Lisky Bratva's influence over the Baghdad operation, and tried to remove it – and that attracted the Conspiracy's attention. One of the vampires visited Weddle to ensure his eternal loyalty. At the Director's discretion, he's a Renfield, or is under the psychic control/domination/blood magic of a vampire, or maybe they just showed him pictures of his kids and made it clear how tasty they'd be.

Weddle's in his mid-50s with iron-grey hair and a military bearing; he's tougher than most men half his age. He feels betrayed by the US government for not appreciating how tough it was to keep the peace in Iraq after the invasion; he wasn't taking bribes, he was working within the local system.

- **Research:** He left the army after allegations of bribery. Prior to that, his reputation was that he was a man who could get the job done, but who never considered all the consequences of his actions. Winning hearts and minds was always a problem for him.
- **Bullshit Detector:** Talking to Weddle picks up on the fact that he's controlled or coerced.
- **Traffic Analysis** or **Human Terrain:** Watching Weddle, or monitoring his communications, shows that he's got a direct line to the Conspiracy. He's on the same tier of the Conspiramid as Dr. Dorjiev (although he's much less important to the vampires).

BREAKING INTO THE BASE

The Overwatch compound is a former Iraqi military base. The site was bombed during both Gulf Wars, and the southern approach is still mostly rubble. The base is protected by land mines and barbed-wire fences on all sides. At any time, there are up to 200 staff on the base, half of whom are armed combatants.

- Sneaking onto the base with **Infiltration** is tricky (Difficulty 6), but doable. A 1-point **Military Science spend** lets the agents identify an easy way into the base – the guards don't check familiar vehicles, so a Difficulty 3 **Conceal** test lets the agents paint a stolen vehicle to look just like an Overwatch car and drive right onto the base.
- A good **Disguise** or **Cover** test (Difficulty 4) coupled with **Military Science** or **Law** lets an agent bluff his way onto the base as a new recruit or a client.
- **Electronic Surveillance** lets the agents identify that the company uses an encrypted intranet for communication and co-ordination. To get in, they need to get access to the network (either by sneaking onto the base, stealing an Overwatch vehicle with **Infiltration** (Difficulty 4) or Grand Theft Auto or laptop with **Filch** (Difficulty 5), or climbing up to a communications relay tower with **Athletics** at

Difficulty 5), then use **Digital Intrusion** to get in (Difficulty 5).
- **Traffic Analysis** coupled with observation of the base lets the agents spot a convoy of two trucks and two Humvees heading north. The convoy's carrying both weapons and items looted from the National Museum. Intercepting the convoy (requiring **Driving** and **Shooting** contests against the 4 drivers and 8 guards; use the Soldier stats from p. 69 of *Night's Black Agents*) lets the agents find the clues without having to break into the base.
  > If you haven't run *The Zalozhniy Sanction* yet, then **Interrogation** or **Streetwise** lets the agents discover that the convoy's ultimate destination is the Turkish port of Samsun. From there, the crates are bound for Odessa. If the agents pick up on that trail instead of investigating the Iraqi National Museum, run with it – you can always bring them back to Baghdad later.
  > If you've run *The Zalozhniy Sanction* already and the agents have brought down the Lisky Bratva's smuggling ring in Odessa, then the convoy's ultimate destination is somewhere close to the heartland of your vampiric conspiracy. If the first vampire was Dracula, then it's heading for Transylvania via the port of Constanta in Romania. If the vampires were made in a US laboratory, then the weapons are sold on the black market in Turkey and **Accounting** traces the money to the States. In any event, the agents discover the general geographical heartland of the Conspiracy.

If the agents fail the listed skill tests, they still get onto the base and find the information they need – but they're spotted by Overwatch, and have to fight or escape under fire. Assume there are two Overwatch guards per player character (use the Soldier statistics from p. 69 of *Night's Black Agents*), with reinforcements showing up soon after the fight kicks off. If the agents don't get out quickly, they'll be taken down by weight of numbers. Getting into a fight also brings Heat.

THE MUSEUM CONNECTION

Mixed in with the stolen weapons are several crates that were stolen from the vaults of the National Museum of Iraq. Some of the crates contain artifacts like carvings and pottery fragments, but most are old documents dating back to the 1920s and '30s, to the days of the British Mandate of Mesopotamia.

- **Languages (Core Clue):** There's a cover letter in one of the crates. It's a Russian-language report written by **Mohammed al-Kirkuk**, a researcher in the museum who's obviously working for the Lisky Bratva. In the report, he apologizes for the delay in locating "*The Bell Journal,*" (1-point **Languages** spend: he uses the transliteration for "Bell" rather than the translation, implying a personal name) and complains about increased security and interference. Tracing al-Kirkuk leads the agents to *The Museum Researcher*. (If the agents go in electronically via the Overwatch intranet, then this core clue is obtained with **Traffic Analysis**, which notices an unlikely number of emails to the base from malkirkuk@natmuseum.iq.)

> **OVERWATCH BLOWBACK**
>
> The agents might not expect to pick up much Heat in Baghdad. The city is still wracked with violence, so gunshots, fist-fights and the occasional spot of bloody murder shouldn't draw much attention (attacks on Westerners excepted). However, the Director should still track Heat normally, but in this case it represents the likelihood of interference from Overwatch Security as well as the local police. As soon as Overwatch are aware of the agents' presence, they'll help the local police track them down.
>
> However, if the agents get out of Baghdad without raising their Heat by more than 1, lower their Heat by 3. Baghdad is a terrible place to try and pick up a dropped trail.

THE MUSEUM RESEARCHER

SCENE TYPE: Core or Introduction
LEAD-IN: Overwatch Security
LEAD-OUTS: The Mukhabarat Archive, Overwatch Security

The National Museum of Iraq is one of the greatest collections of antiquities in the world. The museum was founded in 1926 by Gertrude Bell (a name that will quickly become of great significance to the agents), and boasts a vast archive of artifacts and treasures dating back more than 5,000 years, from the dawn of civilization in the fertile crescent of Mesopotamia to the glory days of Baghdad under the Caliphs to the modern era. Many of the museum's treasures were stolen during the chaos of the Iraq War in 2003.

Research lets the agents identify Mohammed al-Kirkuk as a researcher and translator working in the museum. He lives in an apartment close to the museum.

Similarly, checking the museum with **Archaeology** points the agents at al-Kirkuk; his co-workers gossip about his ready cash, his secretive ways, and his unusual interest in the Philby clan and certain occult topics.

GERTRUDE BELL

Gertrude Bell (1868-1926) was an English archaeologist and explorer. Born to a wealthy family, she traveled widely in the Middle East. She was once of the first western women to explore the interior of Arabia. During World War I, she worked with the Red Cross as an administrator before joining British Military Intelligence in Cairo.

The infamous "Intrusives" – a group of spies and political officers that included Lawrence of Arabia and Harry St. John Philby – were based in Cairo. During the post-war negotiations in Versailles, she argued for self-governed Arab states that would be a partner to British interests in the Middle East. She was an architect of the Kingdom of Iraq that was created in 1921 under her close friend King Feisal I. She remained in Iraq as an advisor to the king, and founded the country's National Museum and library.

She died in 1926, in Baghdad, of an overdose of sleeping pills.

MOHAMMED AL-KIRKUK

Al-Kirkuk's an Iraqi-born, English-educated academic. His parents fled Iraq at the start of the Iran-Iraq war, and he ended up studying the history of his native land at Oxford. He speaks with an upper-class British accent. The Conspiracy recruited him six months ago, offering him a payoff if he helped them extract certain valuable documents from the museum's archives. They caught him at just the right time, when he was always already disillusioned with work in the museum due to pressure from pro-Islamic elements to ignore certain parts of Iraq's history.

The agents can easily track al Kirkuk down at the museum. The researcher is obviously nervous – he shoots frightened glances at every stranger, and never takes the same route home twice. **Tradecraft** confirms that he's using basic escape-and-evasion tactics. A 1-point spend tells the agent that whoever trained him learned from the KGB.

Urban Survival lets the agents spot the people watching al Kirkuk. He is under observation from two separate groups – thugs working for the Third Party, and a small army of street urchins and beggars who take an unusual interest in al Kirkuk's movements. **Urban Survival** lets the agents spot the urchins. A test of Surveillance (Difficulty 4+whatever Stealth bonus the Third Party guys have) spots the Third Party without letting them spot the agents. A failed test of Surveillance still spots the Third Party, but makes them aware of their own watchers.

If the agents confront al-Kirkuk, he tries to run, starting with a Lead of 2. He's got **Athletics 4**; the agents can easy use **Urban Survival** or **Preparedness** to have an ambush set up in advance. The point is to show how jumpy he is, not to have a challenging chase scene. If he gets to a Lead of 5, then he has time to phone Overwatch Security. The agents can still question al-Kirkuk, but they'll need to escape the Overwatch thugs who arrive shortly afterwards.

THE CONFESSION

Applying **Intimidation** to al Kirkuk makes him talk. He asks the agents to accompany him back to his apartment so they can speak privately; if they refuse, he becomes agitated and begs the agents to get him off the streets before *they* see him talking.

Once he's safe in his cramped, book-strewn apartment, al Kirkuk confesses to the agents.

- **Electronic Surveillance (Core Clue):** Tapping or checking his phone reveals he's in regular contact with Overwatch Security, a Private Military Contractor operating in Baghdad. They are his primary channel to the Conspiracy – he's never heard of the Lisky Bratva or vampires. He thinks he's working for some shadowy group within the CIA.
- **Interrogation (Core Clue):** The Conspiracy hired him to look for specific references in the museum's archives – anything related to Harry St. John Philby or the other British agents, anything connected to the supernatural.
  - A few weeks ago, he found a reference in an old document index to a book that was supposed to be part of the museum's collection. The book in question was the diary of Gertrude Bell.
  - **History:** Gertrude Bell (1868-1926) was a British explorer, archaeologist and administrator who was intimately involved in setting up the Kingdom of Iraq in the 1920s.
  - Bell kept diaries all her life, but this one was something special. It was the diary she kept to share with Major Doughty-Wylie, who was the great (unconsummated) love of her life. This other diary was a repository of her hopes and fears and secrets that she chose not to share with her family. After Wylie's death in 1915, she continued to write in this second diary. It contains her recollections and observations about the early days of Iraq, her work in Arabian archaeology, and her work with the Intrusives – a group of British army spies attached to the Arab Bureau.
  - St. John Philby was also part of the Arab Bureau, and her public diaries contain her oddly truncated impressions of him. Al-Kirkuk believes that the secret diary contained more about Philby.
- He was unable to find the diary in the museum archives, despite the reference to it in the document index. The last reference to it was in 1967. **Tradecraft (Core Clue)** suggests that it was seized by the Iraqi Mukhabarat (Iraqi Intelligence Service) after the coup in '68. If that's true, it may be buried in the archives of the Studies and Research Directorate. Following that clue brings the agents to the *Mukhabarat Archive*.

If the agents sweep the room for bugs first, a one-point **Notice** or **Electronic Devices** spend finds a small listening device hidden in a lamp. Al-Kirkuk's laptop is also infected with a trojan virus – someone's spying on him. The Third Party found out about the Bell diary through this channel.

AT YOUR DOOR

As the agents interrogate al-Kirkuk, they hear a knock at the door of his apartment. Lurking outside are two assassins sent by the Third Party to eliminate the researcher. If the agents don't intercede, then al-Kirkuk goes to the door to look through the spyhole, and they shoot him dead through the thin wooden door. If the agents do intercede, you've got a fight scene as the assassins smash into the apartment to kill the researcher and the agents.

There are two assassins outside the door. If you've more than 4 players, then there's another assassin or two (up to a maximum of P/2 bad guys) lurking outside or training a sniper rifle on the window of the apartment. Use the upgraded "gym rat" thug stats (*Night's Black Agents,* p. 70) for these guys; they're local muscle. They're carrying SIG-Sauer 9mms (+1 damage) and big nasty knives, and are wearing body armor (-2 armor against bullets, -1 armor against knives and punches), making this a potentially tough fight in the cramped confines of the apartment (and don't forget that Overwatch Security may show up soon too, if al-Kirkuk called them). The assassins try to escape after they've eliminated al-Kirkuk.

If the agents take one of the assassins alive, **Interrogation (Core Clue)** reveals he was hired by a "Western spy" to eliminate al-Kirkuk and the agents; he gives the name of a hotel, the Al Sadeer, used by many western businessmen. If they visit the hotel, see *Al Sadeer*, p. 115. (If the agents don't take anyone alive, then a considerate Director might let them dig up the same information with **Streetwise** and a lot of shoe leather. Alternatively, one of the street urchins can slip the agents a note with the name of the hotel – the urchins are Katun's eyes in Baghdad. For more on Katun, see *Old Ghosts*, p. 123.)

THE MUKHABARAT ARCHIVE

SCENE TYPE: Core
LEAD-IN: The Museum Researcher
LEAD-OUTS: To Beirut

The old Mukhabarat building was demolished by cruise missiles back in 1993; the archives were split up and moved to half-a-dozen secure locations scattered across Baghdad. Al-Kirkuk found the archive where the Bell diary is kept, and can tell the agents where it is if he's still alive. Otherwise, finding the right building requires a little legwork. The agents can either use **Network** to whistle up an ex-IIS torturer who knows where the books are buried (or a UN War Crimes Commission analyst who knows about the old IIS). Alternatively, they can use **Streetwise** and a lot of bribery to find the archive, or bluff their way into a government office with Bureaucracy and dig up the location with **Research**. The files in question date back to before the 14th July Revolution of 1958, so they're not considered sensitive.

THE ARCHIVE

The old archive is housed in what was once a warehouse. The sprawling building is a crumbling maze of shelves and crates of seemingly random documents made yellowed and brittle by exposure. The Mukhabarat archive is shared with other government departments, so there are old police records and tax returns dating back to the British Mandate here too, nestled next to torture transcripts and secret police surveillance files. Other crates contain the personal items confiscated from political prisoners; there are rows of glass jars containing severed hands and other organs, boxes of clothes, faded photographs and maps, an endless warren of nightmare bureaucracy. The archive went untended for years, and the warehouse was home to vagrants and rats. In recent months, the Iraqi government paid for a watchman to drive the beggars out, but the rats still live here. There are no working lights, other than the sunlight filtering down through the grimy plastic panels in the roof.

Getting in is easy. The door is padlocked, but there's a broken window next to it that can be forced easily. The watchman can be bypassed by a failsafe **Infiltration** test.

FINDING THE DIARY

While the archive is poorly organized, the agents can start searching for the diary by looking for other documents that were taken from the National Museum. The trail leads off into the darker reaches of the warehouse. **Research** lets a character navigate the ramshackle filing system; someone with **Languages** is also needed, as most of the documents are in Arabic.

WE'RE NOT ALONE

If one of the agents has the building under surveillance, then call for a Surveillance test (Difficulty 4) to spot a shadowy figure sneaking into the archive through a hole in the roof. The figure is humanoid, but moves with inhuman speed. If the agents have run into them before, they recognize it: it's a zalozhniy. (If the agents have an NPC watching their backs, then the zalozhniy murders their ally before entering the building.)

If the agents don't have the archives under surveillance, then call for **Sense Trouble** tests (Difficulty 6) as they search the stacks. If successful, the agents hear muffled thumps off in the distance, and can get ready for danger. If unsuccessful, then the agents get taken by surprise in *Fire in the Stacks*, below.

THE OTHER INTRUDERS

Two other factions got to the archive ahead of the agents.

The first were two men from the Third Party. They learned about the Bell diary by spying on al-Kirkuk, and found it just as the agents arrived.

The second intruder is a zalozhniy sent by the Conspiracy to capture the diary. The zalozhniy arrives several minutes after the agents, but it moves through the warehouse with terrible swiftness and eliminates the two Third Party men. It also contacted the Iraqi police to warn them of intruders in the government archive.

THE BELL BOX

Turning a corner in the archive, the agents find one stack of shelves that contains a half-dozen large, heavy boxes marked "National Museum." Ask for a **Notice** spend at this point — a 1-point spend lets the agents spot that one of the boxes was recently opened, and that there are blood splatters on the floor nearby. If anyone moves the box roughly, they trigger the zalozhniy-planted incendiary grenade attached to the underside of the shelf. Alternatively, the blast can be timed to go off a minute or two after the agents find the box. Conceal (Difficulty 5) finds the grenade ahead of time; **Sense Trouble** (Difficulty 6) gives the agents a split-second warning of the danger; disabling the booby trap requires **Explosive Devices** (Difficulty 3). If the blast kills an agent, remember to describe the sudden bubble of slow-time as the zalozhniy feeds on the death (remember to boost the zalozhniy's Athletics or Health too).

If the grenade goes off, it hits the agents as a Class 1 explosion, and also sets the surrounding documents and boxes on fire. You know what burns really, really well? A giant secret police archive full of fifty-year-old paper.

Inside the box (assuming it's not on fire) are two bodies, both white Westerners in dark clothing. **Diagnosis** shows that their necks were broken. A quick search turns up cellphones and pistols, but no wallets, passports or other identity cards. **Tradecraft** or **Notice (Core Clue)** suggests they're spooks, and that one of them is wearing a shoe with a hollow heel. Inside is a phone SIM. See *The SIM Card*, p. 116. (If the grenade does go off and the zalozhniy attacks, then the agents can find the SIM in the confusion with **Notice**).

FIRE IN THE STACKS

Lurking in the rafters above the agents is the zalozhniy. It's got Gertude Bell's diary clutched in its hands. Its mission was to kill the Third Party men and recover the diary, but the agents are tempting targets of opportunity.

If the agents failed the earlier Sense Trouble test, the zalozhniy gets the drop on them. If they succeeded, then determine order of action normally. (The zalozhniy may still go first, but at least the agents have a chance to Jump In.)

If the agents are the ones to trigger the incendiary device, then the zalozhniy just jumps down and topples one heavy stack of documents on top of them, to trap them in the burning building. Dodging the falling shelves requires an **Athletics** test at Difficulty 5; failure means being hit for +1 damage. If an agent fails by a margin of 3 or more, they're trapped under the shelves and stuck until freed (requiring a continuing Athletics Difficulty of 8).

If the incendiary device hasn't yet been triggered, then the zalozhniy drops down and uses Throw to fling some unfortunate agent into the booby-trapped box. The incendiary goes boom (and adding insult to injury, the zalozhniy is shielded from the explosion by the body of the guy it just threw into the bomb). The creature will try the shelf-toppling move next round if it can before fleeing.

Notice spots the Bell diary, which the zalozhniy has tucked into a webbed pocket on its jacket.

THE CHASE

After one or two rounds of combat, the zalozhniy flees, and you're into a chase scene through the library and then through the streets of Baghdad. The zalozhniy's lead starts at 3 (or if the agents stopped to rescue one of their own.

In the library, you've got:

- Stacks of boxes to be toppled, vaulted over, or smashed through
- Narrow corridors lined with papers and documents
- Rafters to climb on and jump between
- Fire. Lots of fire.
- Panicked (or vampire-controlled) rats, swarming over the agents
- Panicked (or vampire-controlled) police officers, who showed up to investigate the break-in

Once the chase moves out of the archive, you've got:

- A police cordon (cars, helicopters)
- Construction sites and half-rebuilt buildings
- Narrow alleyways
- Traffic jams

The zalozhniy may steal a car or a motorcycle and use that to switch the chase to **Driving** if its **Athletics** pool runs low. The police keep trying to stop the agents, but don't interfere with the zalozhniy's escape.

IF THE AGENTS WIN

Then they catch up with the zalozhniy. Well done, you've caught the nightmarish undead killing machine. Clever agents may just use **Filch** (Difficulty 6) to grab the diary and then flee. Otherwise, they'll need to incapacitate the monster before recovering the diary.

IF THE ZALOZHNIY ESCAPES

If the creature's Lead reaches 10, then the zalozhniy escapes from the agents.

However, they weren't the only ones chasing it. The agents see the zalozhniy sprinting across a square, much too far away for them to catch up—and then a truck comes out of nowhere, smashing into the monster and sending it sprawling. Two more spies, dressed like the dead guys in the archive, emerge from the truck. One of them temporarily incapacitates the zalozhniy with a suitable Block (or with a long burst of machine-pistol fire to its face) and grabs the diary; the other sprays suppressive fire to keep the player characters from getting too close (he's got **Shooting 8**, and he'll spend it all to create a nigh-impassable field of fire).

Photography or **Notice** lets the agents get the truck's license number as it drives off with the diary. **Streetwise** can also follow the truck by questioning local informants. Running that number through police records with **Cop Talk** or **Digital Intrusion** (Difficulty 6) discovers that the truck was rented by **Bridger Investments**.

Also, note that getting run over by a truck won't kill a zalozhniy. The agents may still need to put it down after the Third Party steal the diary.

THE AL SADEER

SCENE TYPE: Alternate
LEAD-IN: The Museum Researcher
LEAD-OUT: To Beirut

The Al Sadeer hotel (***) is popular with western businessmen. It's right in the middle of the Green Zone. If the agents describe or show a photo of the assassins to the receptionist, together with **Cop Talk (Core Clue)** or **Flattery**, they learn that those men visited the hotel yesterday for a meeting with representatives from a firm called *Bridger Investments*.

If the agents get access to the hotel's computers (**Digital Intrusion**, Difficulty 4 or a suitable **Disguise**), then they can dig up the following information:

- The hotel scans the passports of the guests. The names on the passports are probably fake, but the agents now have photos of Mr. Black and Mr. White.
- They can get the phone records for the hotel and the number of the room rented by Bridger Investments. **Traffic Analysis** shows one unusual phone number – the same one as the SIM card in *To Beirut* (p. 116).

If you've already run *The Mukhabarat Archive*, then either hotel records (**Data Recovery**) or the receptionist (**Flattery**) reveal that the Bridger Investment people checked out and took a taxi to the airport. They're on a plane heading for Beirut.

Accounting lets the agents dig into the background of Bridger Investments. It has the hallmarks of a cut-out company – it's a murky financial services firm whose employees travel a lot, especially in politically unstable or significant parts of the world, and which has access to a lot of cash when needed.

THE HOTEL SHOOTOUT

As an optional complication, have a team of Overwatch Security goons show up at the hotel soon after the agents arrive. The Conspiracy's spies followed the same clues that led the agents here. There's one soldier per agent, led by an ex-special ops tough guy (see p. 70 of *Night's Black Agents* for statistics for both). If they spot the agents (**Disguise** or **Surveillance**, Difficulty 5 to avoid), they'll attempt to arrest them, claiming they were responsible for an attack on their base. The Overwatch team won't start a shooting war in the middle of the hotel, but they'll follow the agents until they have a clear shot.

TO BEIRUT

SCENE TYPE: Core
LEAD-IN: The Mukhabarat Archive
LEAD-OUT: Beirut Streets

The next part of this operation is in Beirut. Three potential leads point the agents there – Gertrude Bell's diary, the SIM card from the dead spy, and investigating *The Al Sadeer* (above).

THE DIARY

Bell's diary covers the last four years of her life (1922 to mid-1926). Most of the entries are interesting, but irrelevant to the investigation – she talks about the birth pangs of the Kingdom of Iraq, her relationship with King Faisal and the British government, the decline of her family's finances, the death of her sibling Hugo, and her work in establishing the National Museum and National Library in Iraq.

Occult Studies or **Vampirology:** If vampires were around in the 1920s in your campaign, then the diary contains hints that Bell knew something about them. She might describe putting Blocks on windows, or include a throwaway reference about *ghuls*.

History: One section of the diary is directly relevant to the agents' investigation. In 1922, Bell describes how she was awoken one night by the approach of riders. Going out to meet them, she was surprised to see that they were Bedouin from the deep desert – and then one of them took off his *keffiya* (headdress) to reveal the bearded features of Harry St. John Philby. By 1922, Bell's initial positive assessment to St. John had given way to distaste after Philby's support of Ibn Saud became known. She regarded him as a troublemaker and an opportunist, and suspected him of disloyalty to the crown. Nonetheless, she was eager to hear news from Amman where Philby was stationed, and invited him in. He rapidly became drunk.

Their conversation turned to politics and religion, as the two were so interconnected. She spoke of the difficulties in balancing Sunni and Shi'ite factions in Iraq, he complained about Zionist interference. He then abruptly confessed that he was considering converting to Islam "for political reasons." Bell, a lifelong atheist, make some passing remark about all religions being equally foolish. Philby then produced a "talisman" from under his shirt, and declared that this was all the faith he needed.

This talisman is the Nigredo, so Bell's diary describes it in an appropriate way. It might be a vial of blood, a fragment of alien metal, a locket, a radio tube, or whatever else fits your conception of the Nigredo element. (If you've dated

BEIRUT: QUICK AND DIRTY

The capital of Lebanon suffered hugely during the civil war in (1975-1990), but has bounced back to become a high-end tourist destination. Hezbollah forces and refugees occupied parts of the city after the Lebanon-Israel conflict of 2008.

POPULATION
750,000 in the city itself, with as many again close by (similar in size to Austin, Texas)

CONFLICT
Beirut's practically a byword for conflict. The civil war divided the city along religious and cultural lines, and it became a proxy war for neighboring countries like Palestine, Israel and Syria. While the war's over, Beirut still crawls with spies and terrorists. Tensions between Israel and the Palestinian territories boil over into Beirut.

BACKDROPS
MARTYR'S SQUARE: A large public square in downtown Beirut; demonstrations and rallies often take place here. Nearby souks offer cover for a quick getaway.

BEIRUT WATERFRONT: The waterfront district – skyscrapers, yacht marinas, shopping and foreign money. It's the best place for western agents to blend in.

ROMAN BATHS: Located just east of the Grand Serail, the residence of the Lebanese Prime Minister, the ruins of the baths were discovered in 1960. They're surrounded by gardens and are a popular venue for concerts and performances.

THREE HOOKS
- Two brothers, George and Michel Tanalian, were arrested in November 2011 on suspicion of murdering eleven people, mostly taxi drivers. After shooting and robbing the victims, they drove the taxis to remote locations outside Beirut and then burned them to destroy any evidence – like exsanguination.
- The CIA station in Beirut was shut down in 2011 after the identities of many of the agents there were compromised. (Allegations that the CIA repeatedly used a nearby Pizza Hut as a meeting place are strongly denied by Langley.) Beirut's a major crossing point for intelligence in the Middle East, so the closure of the station there is a big setback for US interests there.
- The Beirut river turned red in February of 2012. The authorities claimed that a factory dumped red dye into the sewers. Far be it from us to imply that the river turned to blood as part of the same occult ritual that affected Baghdad (see p. 107), or that high concentrations of alien microorganisms can stain a river red.

---

the Nigredo immovably to after Bell's death in 1926, the talisman matches the description of Shevlenko's talisman from p. 53, and Philby talked about how the talisman will protect him as he storms the gates of heaven.) Philby waved the talisman, calling it "his gateway to Heaven." He gestured to the Bedouin outside the door, calling them his "spiritual brothers" and saying that they knew to bury the talisman with him.

- **History (Core Clue):** Philby died in Beirut in 1960. He's buried in the Muslim cemetery in the Basta quarter of Beirut. If Bell's diary is correct, the Nigredo must be there too.

THE SIM CARD

The spies' cell phones are disposable burners, used only for a single operation. The SIM card, though, is more important – it's clearly the communications channel used by the spies to contact their employers. Putting the card into a cellphone doesn't work, as it is protected by encryption. A few hours' work with **Cryptography (Core Clue)** lets the agents break the protection and use the card.

The card has a single number on it. Call it, and you hear the distinctive clicks and whispers of a call being re-routed from relay to relay, bounced around the world a half-dozen times before a voice answers. "*Red*," says the voice. "*Who is this?*"

One of the agents recognizes the voice – it's their old friend/partner/mentor/superior/contact/whatever (see p. 108).

If the agent introduces himself, then Red hesitates before answering. "*This is awkward,*" he says, "*we need to talk. Meet me in the Kit Kat club in Beirut, tomorrow night at 10pm.*"

If the agent doesn't make himself known to Red, then Red realizes who the agents are. "*I don't know how you got this number, but we need to talk. Meet me in the Kit Kat club in Beirut, tomorrow night at 10pm. If you don't, we'll know you're working for them and deal with you accordingly.*"

BEIRUT STREETS

SCENE TYPE: Alternate
LEAD-IN: To Beirut
LEAD-OUTS: The Kit Kat Club Meeting, The Exhumation, The Records Office

If the agents already know about *The Kit Kat Club Meeting* or *The Exhumation*, then they can move on to those scenes after arriving in Beirut. However, if they've ended up in Beirut by tracking Bridger Investments or following up some other tip, they'll need to do some legwork first.

Criminology: The Lisky Bratva have little or no presence here. Beirut's gangs are mostly tied to Hezbullah splinter groups.

History: Both Kim and St. John Philby spent time in Beirut in the 1960s; it was a low point for both of them. St. John was in effective exile from Saudi Arabia, after quarrelling with Ibn Saud's heir, King Saud. Kim was working as a journalist after leaving MI6 under suspicion of being the "Third Man" in the Burgess/Maclean spy ring.

In September of 1960, St. John visited Beirut for the last time. He suffered a heart attack at a party (where a panicked waitress exclaimed "God! I've poisoned him!") and died in a hospital several days later. He's buried in the Muslim cemetery attached to the Bashoura mosque. The cemetery was the site of a battle between Muslim and Christian forces during the Lebanese civil war, so finding his grave (if it still exists) means a few hours' research. See *The Records Office*, below.

Some accounts claim that Philby was disinterred and his grave used for a member of the Palestinian Liberation Organization during the civil war. If that's true, there may be nothing left of the Nigredo or Philby.

Urban Survival or **High Society (Core Clue):** The Bridger Investments team in Baghdad stayed in a high-end hotel, so checking similar hotels in Beirut for the names they used in Baghdad puts the agents on their trail. They spot Mr. Red and Mr. Black getting into a cab outside the Four Seasons hotel; following the cab leads the agents to *The Kit Kat Club Meeting*.

Alternatively, if you've got Mr. Red as an old friend of one of the agents, then Red can contact that agent directly and set up the meeting.

THE RECORDS OFFICE

SCENE TYPE: Alternate
LEAD-IN: Beirut Streets
LEAD-OUT: The Exhumation

After the Mukhabarat archive, the Beirut records office seems airy and well-organized. Digging through old records with **Research** to find the exact plot where Philby was buried will take several hours — offer the agents a chance to make a **Research** spend to speed things along.

While the agents search, an old man approaches them. He looks shrivelled by long years of too much sunshine, but his eyes are bright and alert. He's carrying a sheaf of newspapers — there's a public reading room attached to the records office where you can read the day's newspapers for free. **Languages** notices that he's got a mix of newspapers there, in Arabic, Russian, English and French. He introduces himself as **Nicky**; he retired here many years ago, and he spends a lot of time reading and researching here to occupy his mind. Can he help the player characters?

If they accept, then Nicky digs up the burial records for the Bashoura Mosque with ease. He asks the agents why they are interested in the burial records for Hajji Abdullah — that was St. John Philby's Muslim name, and the name he's buried under. He also asks if they are part of the same group as "the other gentleman" — one of the Third Party agents visited the Records Office ahead of the agents.

"Nicky" is actually **Nikolai**, an ex-KGB agent. Arkady Shevlenko (see p. 55) sent Nikolai to Beirut in 1974, and he's been here ever since, watching over the graveyard. He'll show up again later — for now, just establish him as a potential player.

Research (Core Clue) eventually identifies the right plot in the Bashoura cemetery. See *The Exhumation* (p. 119).

NIGHT'S BLACK AGENTS – THE ZALOZHNIY QUARTET

THE KIT KAT CLUB MEETING

SCENE TYPE: Antagonist Reaction
LEAD-IN: Beirut Streets, To Beirut
LEAD-OUT: The Exhumation (in unlikely circumstances: The Arab Boy)

The original Kit Kat Club where the Philbys drank is long gone; the new Kit Kat is a neon monstrosity aimed at western tourists, blasting techno music out into the Mediterranean night. Towards the back of the club, there's a quieter area, and it is there that the agents find Mr. Red. He's sitting with anther man, who introduces himself as Mr. Black. **Military Science** doesn't pick up on any suspiciously burly club patrons or guys wearing bulky, concealing clothes nearby – Mr. Red is here without any obvious backup or protection, which could be a gesture of trust.

PLAYING MR. RED

Ideally, Red is an old contact or mentor of one of the agents, so play him in an avuncular, friendly fashion. Play up his connection to the agent – reminisce about old times, ask about the agent's Solace, laugh at old jokes.

- Make physical contact with the agent, to establish trust.
- Direct most of your conversation to the agent; be polite to the others, but focus on your old friend.
- Glance at your watch – you're up against a deadline.

The other man, Black, is nervous at this display of familiarity, but lets Red take the lead. A few minutes after the conversation starts, Mr. White arrives at the club and sits down. **Archaeology** spots a folded map under his arm that looks like a map of a graveyard.

While Black and White participate only minimally in the conversation, try to portray them as cynical, uncaring or paranoid. They obviously don't want to be here, and would prefer to eliminate the agents instead of warning them off.

THE BLACK AND THE WHITE

As their pseudonyms suggest, the Third Party knows about the Albedo, the Nigredo, the Rubedo and the Philby plot. How much they actually reveal to the agents depends on when the Director runs this operation.

- If this is the first operation in the *Quartet,* then Red just calls the Nigredo "the Philby artifact," and never mentions the Albedo or the Rubedo. He tells the agents that they won't hear from the Third Party again after tonight.
- If this is the second or third operation, then he's slightly more forthcoming. He admits they're opposed to the Lisky Bratva and the mafiya's vampire masters, and outlines the connection between the Philbys, the Saudi royal family, and vampirism. He acknowledges the agents' efforts against the vampires, but now it's time for the professionals to step in and handle things.
- If this is the final operation in the *Quartet,* then it's cards-on-the-table time. Red knows the agents have the Albedo. He offers the agents a way out of the shadow world - or a place in the Third Party organization if they prefer. If they want to retire, he can arrange that, but if they want to really take the fight to the vampires, then they should join him. However, as long as they have the Albedo, they're in danger. He suggests that the agents join him at the graveyard to retrieve the Nigredo, then they'll both go and get the Albedo from wherever the agents have stashed it, and finally they'll take both parts to a place of safety.

Red explains the situation:

- His backers know about the Philby plot, and he believes the Nigredo element is right here in Beirut. He won't say where if the agents don't know already.
  - **Human Terrain (Core Clue):** Red and Black are both wearing slip-on shoes, and there's a faint smell of incense clinging to their clothing. They must have visited a mosque earlier. One mosque in particular has a connection with Harry Philby – the mosque overlooking the Muslim cemetery where he was buried. They can follow the Third Party men to the Bashoura cemetery (see *The Exhumation,* below).
- He apologizes for the "misunderstanding" at al-Kirkuk's place. Black sent the thugs to kill the researcher, not the agents.
  - Mr. Black shrugs apologetically at this. He doesn't seem overly nonplussed at nearly murdering a player character.
- He's here to warn the agents not to interfere. His backers have ordered him to recover the Philby artifact. If the agents refuse to stay away from the Third Party's operation in Beirut, then… well, they know the stakes of this game. They won't be the first spies to die here in Beirut. Red doesn't want to have to kill them, but his backers don't have the same compunctions.
- If the agents point out that Philby's grave is unlikely to be intact after more than fifty years, Red assures them that the Third Party has confirmed that there is something supernatural in the graveyard, and it must be the Nigredo.

If your players are wimpish enough to back down and take Red's deal, then they'll miss out on the fun and games in *The Exhumation*. They can investigate the aftermath of the exhumation the next day, and then be contacted by Bell's agent in *The Arab Boy,* p. 122. Otherwise, they can follow the agents to the graveyard (or plant a tracking device with **Electronic Surveillance**

TREASON IN THE BLOOD ■ THE KIT KAT CLUB MEETING / THE EXHUMATION

GOING ALONG WITH RED

If the agents are currently working with the Third Party, then this plays out slightly differently. They're escorted by Red to the grave site and allowed to watch as his men start digging up Hajji Abdullah. They see Black get a radio message from White, alerting him to Nikolai's presence. The agents may intervene at this point, saving Nikolai from being shot, but the excavation continues regardless.

and probably **Preparedness**) and *The Exhumation*.

Mr. Red pays for all the drinks with a Bridger Investments corporate credit card.

STARTING TROUBLE

These guys are threatening us? I kill them!
If your players go lethally proactive on the Third Party, then you've got a fight on your hands. Red tries to escape out through the back of the club; Black and White provide covering fire. Use the Bodyguard statistics for the pair, adding on +2 Heath, +2 Shooting and let them use Thriller Combat rules – they're *good*. Fill out the opposition at the graveyard with extra thugs if the agents eliminate Black or White here.

Red heads straight for the graveyard if attacked in the club.

THE EXHUMATION

SCENE TYPE: Core
LEAD-INS: To Beirut, Beirut Streets, The Kit-Kat Club, The Records Office
LEAD-OUTS: KGB Beirut, The Arab Boy (if everyone's knocked out: Old Ghosts)

An unseasonal fog rolls off the sea and clouds the northern part of the city, including the Bashoura cemetery. The minaret of the nearby mosque rises out of the mists like an accusing finger, and the headlights of cars passing on the General Food Chehab turn the fog-shrouded buildings into looming ghosts. There's an otherworldly feel to the city tonight as the agents approach.

THE THIRD PARTY

The Third Party team in the cemetery consists of Mr. Red and Mr. Black (if he's still alive), plus Px2 thugs hired as muscle and protection. Mr. White's perched in the minaret of a nearby building with a sniper rifle, just in case the Lisky Bratva or the player characters show up. (In fact, his sniper perch is atop the old Beirut branch of the Koernersbank; the building was converted to offices in the 1990s, but the name of the bank is still visible in a frieze on the second story. If you've already run *The Boxmen*, the agent with the highest **Notice** spots the frieze on the way into the cemetery; if not, drop it in as an **Architecture** clue sometime during this scene's aftermath.)

They know the rough location of the grave; they're going to dig it up, recover the Nigredo, then exfiltrate the city.

THE SOVIET SPY

Also lurking in the graveyard is Nikolai, an ex-KGB spy assigned to watch over Philby's grave. He's here to find out who the Third Party are. He knows the graveyard very well indeed, and has bypassed the outer security cordon of goons.

THE GRAVE

What the Third Party don't know is that St. John Philby's body and the Nigredo were both removed in 1963, shortly before Kim Philby defected to Moscow. Both items were taken by Bedouin agents working with him. They left a trap for any KGB or other agencies who went looking for the Nigredo. That trap is about to be triggered.

HOW IT ALL GOES DOWN

If the agents heed the Third Party warning and stay away from the graveyard, here's how events unfold without their presence:

- The Third Party arrive and find Philby's grave. Half the thugs are sent to watch the entrances to the cemetery; the others start digging.
- Nikolai sneaks past the outer ring of thugs.
- Mr. White spots movement through the night-vision scope of his rifle; he radios Black to check it out.
- Black finds Nikolai and shoots him in the stomach, leaving him to die.
- The diggers find the box in the grave. Red opens it. Bad things happen.

Events will play out differently if the agents show up at the graveyard, or if Red invites them to accompany him.

GETTING INTO THE CEMETERY

The agents spot the goons (**Urban Survival**) surrounding the cemetery with ease. The thugs are loitering near the cemetery's entrances and watching the surrounding streets. They're all wearing concealing clothing or have sports bags nearby to hide their guns. They've also got radios. **Military Science** suggests these are hired muscle, not real professionals. The agents can sneak past with **Infiltration (Difficulty 4)**, or take out the mooks in a fist-fight.

- **Architecture:** There are plenty of tall buildings overlooking the cemetery. The minaret of the mosque is the best vantage point,

but there are other potential sniper nests. A 1-point **Architecture, Military Science** or **Notice** spend lets the agents spot Mr. White's perch, though not Mr. White.
- Spotting Mr. White requires a deliberate scan of potential snipers' nests with some sort of magnifying night-vision optics, and a **Surveillance** test (Difficulty 8).

Once they're in the cemetery, the rows of tombstones offer plenty of cover. Call for an **Infiltration** test **(Difficulty 5)** if they're trying to be stealthy; if they don't, they'll be spotted by Mr. White. Depending on the agents' current relationship with the Third Party, he may start firing, get Mr. Black and some goons to investigate, or just watch them until they get too close to Philby's grave.

THE GUNSHOT

From up ahead, the agents hear a muffled report from a silenced gun. (Give them a Difficulty 2 Sense Trouble test if you don't feel like handing the clue out.) That was Mr. Black shooting Nikolai.

The ideal staging here is for the agents to split up, so some of them investigate the gunshot and find the dying Nikolai, while the rest go to Philby's grave and the Third Party team. You can then intercut between the two groups, so that Nikolai reveals that the Nigredo is gone just before Red opens the box.

NIKOLAI'S LAST WORDS

The agents find the old spy lying against a tombstone, his hands pressed over his stomach. Blood wells up from between his fingers in gory spurts. If the agents encountered him at the Records Office, they recognize him. He beckons them over and tries to talk, but the pain's too great. Using **Pharmacy (Core Clue)** to stick him with a morphine syrette, or **Medic** to treat Nikolai's wounds, lets the old man speak. (Optionally, you can have the agents stabilize Nikolai in the graveyard, and run his confession scene after they escape the horrors unleashed by the Third Party team.)

Through blood-flecked gasps, Nikolai reveals the following:

- When St. John died back in 1960, the owner of the hotel where he was staying paid for his funeral. That owner was a KGB man… they've known about the Nigredo for years.
- Kim Philby hid the Albedo around the same time, and never told the KGB where it was.
- Nikolai is a KGB agent, sent here in 1974 by Arkady Shevlenko. They thought in '74 that Philby was finally ready to put the plan into operation.
- The Nigredo's not in the grave. The Arabs stole it in '75. He doesn't know what happened to it. They left something terrible in its place.
- He loses consciousness at this point. Searching through his pockets turns up a house key and an identity card with his address on it. The agents can find Nikolai's house with **Urban Survival**. See *KGB Beirut* for more.

THE BOX OF DEVILS

Meanwhile, in another part of the cemetery, Mr. Red is exhuming the remains in Kim Philby's grave. As the agents arrive, he's just pulled a shroud full of bones out of the ground to expose a small black iron box. Also present: Mr. Black and a number of thugs equal to the number of agents, plus that troublesome sniper on the rooftop.

- If the agents go in shooting, then Red dodges into cover, with Black and the remaining thugs providing covering fire. White also starts shooting, although he can't distinguish between friendlies and hostiles easily on his night-vision scope.
- If the agents just walk in, then the goons point guns at them. Red apologizes – he's got no intention of needlessly hurting the agents, but he has to get the Nigredo. He won't believe them if they claim that the Nigredo's already gone.
- If they hide and watch, then they see Red pull the box out of the ground and open it…
- **Forensic Pathology:** The bones pulled out of the ground are definitely not those of St. John Philby. For one thing, Philby didn't have a gunshot wound in his skull when he was buried. Those are clearly the bones of a younger, slighter man, not a heavier man in his 60s.

The box was planted by St. John Philby's Arab agents in 1975, to throw other hunters of the Nigredo off the trail. It does not contain the true Nigredo – it's a trap containing a debased form of the Nigredo. When it's opened, it releases something horrible and lethal that's related to the Nigredo. Exactly what it is depends on the nature of the Nigredo and vampires in your campaign, but it should be (a) lethal enough to kill off the Third Party agents and (b) terrifying. This is a big-budget horror moment for your campaign, the vampiric equivalent of opening the Ark. Some ideas:

- ✠ Opening the box unleashes the damnation of the Nigredo without the corresponding spiritual protection of the Albedo. Everyone nearby starts sinking into the ground; those who are pulled into the earth are dragged away to Hell. Effectively, the agents just opened a spiritual sinkhole. The agents need to make Difficulty 6 **Athletics** tests to pull themselves out of the unholy morass.
- ✠ The box contains a blasphemous relic that awakens the dead of the Bashoura graveyard. Zombies claw their way out of the dirt and attack everyone nearby.
- ⊗ The box contains an undead horror like a bhuta (see **Night's Black Agents,** p. 148), which attacks everyone nearby.
- ⊗ The box contains the preserved head of a monster, like an elder vampire preserved

MISSING THE LIGHT SHOW

If the agents stay away from the Bashoura Graveyard, then they'll spot the sirens, the screams and the chaos that ensues when the box is opened. They'll run into a bloody, dying Nikolai as he stumbles through the alleyways, pursued by a murderous Mr. White who blames the Russian interloper for the botched operation.

FORESHADOWING

There's a big betrayal coming in a few scenes (see *Treason in the Blood*, p.129), so make sure you lay the groundwork to justify this. Dropping an unexpected reversal of fortunes on the players without any foreshadowing smacks of GM fiat. A few hints that only make sense in retrospect integrate the reversal into the narrative, so it feels more organic and less like the Director screwing over the players. Throw in shadowy figures, flocks of crows, cars zooming off at high speed, mysterious beeps and clicks on the phone lines, unexplained break-ins, and the feeling of being watched every so often. (Of course, you should be doing such things anyway – salt your game with lots of asides and trivial events that can be woven into the plot retroactively.)

in honey. When exposed to the air, it awakens and hits everyone with a Mental Blast (see p.131 of ***Night's Black Agents***). The head's got Aberrance 10. It keeps screaming until it's destroyed.

- 👽 Inside the box is a fragment of alien hull metal from a crashed flying saucer. When freed from the Faraday cage of the box, it reverses gravity around it, causing everyone nearby to float into the air. The goons find themselves falling into the sky; the agents can use **Athletics** (Difficulty 6) to grab onto something solid like a gravestone. The unfortunate goons, along with the metal fragment, vanish into the night sky.
- ☢ **Chemistry** or **Astronomy** spots the telltale blue flash of Cherenkov radiation as the box is opened. It contains an extremely powerful radioactive isotope that blasts the Health of everyone around. Everyone nearby loses 1d6 Health instantly, and another 1 point per round. Getting closer to the box drains more Health. The alien metal – one that doesn't fit on the periodic table – vanishes after the box is closed, decaying into a shower of exotic particles.
- 🧛 Opening the box releases a variation of the vampire virus, triggering intense uncontrollable bloodlust in those infected. The agents must make **Stability** tests at Difficulty 5 to avoid succumbing to the disease. Those who are infected (at least half of the NPCs) attack everyone around them with Hand-to-Hand attacks, clawing and biting like rabid beasts. The virus boosts the Hand-to-Hand of the infected by 4 points.
- ☣ Inside the box is a swarm of mosquitoes pumped full of vampire blood extract. When they feed, some of the blood is transferred to their hosts, causing the victims' skin to swell up into black, oozing boils. This not only inflicts nasty damage (1d6 Health lost per round while the agents are in the cloud of insects), but also injects the victims with the same trace vampirism that St. John Philby used on the Saudi royal family. If the Rubedo is activated, the agents will become slaves of the vampires.

If the agents are knocked unconscious by whatever's in the box, they're rescued and brought to Bell's island – skip onto *Old Ghosts*. If they manage to survive, then ideally there should be no trace of Mr. Red so you can bring him back as a villain later in the operation. If Red's killed, have Mr. White step into his role.

KGB BEIRUT

SCENE TYPE: Core
LEAD-INS: The Exhumation, Old Ghosts
LEAD-OUTS: The Arab Boy (if you haven't run Old Ghosts), King Saud's City

Nikolai spent the last thirty-plus years living in a small apartment in central Beirut. It's a sad, lonely testament to misplaced duty. Photos on the wall speak of a tangential existence, forever on the fringe of life. No family, no close friends. A meticulous set of accounts (**Accounting**) shows that he was paid monthly by international money transfer; the amount varies slightly every month due to international exchanges, and hasn't been increased since the 1980s. A radio sits on the table next to a notebook and pen. It's tuned to UVB-76, a Russian numbers station.

Human Terrain notes the presence of several Russian orthodox religious icons on the walls – and above all the entrances. Optionally, you can hint at the existence of a Block here – Nikolai might have smeared juniper berry paste across the windowsill, or have an incense burner with a filter-tip cigarette in it.

Notice (Core Clue) finds a false panel inside the air conditioning vent. Inside are papers and documents relating to Nikolai's career as a spy – terrible tradecraft, but forgivable humanity. He spent more than thirty years out in the cold, so it's little wonder he kept a few tangible reminders of his duty. If the agents never spoke with Nikolai, then they find enough evidence here to confirm he's a KGB agent.

Notably, there's a photograph of him arm in arm with **Arkady Shevlenko**; once the agents identify the other man in the photo with **Research**, they can investigate Shevlenko (a trail that leads them to Vienna and *Out of the House of Ashes*.)

DOWN & OUT IN BEIRUT

If any of the agents get knocked out in Beirut (either by the box in the graveyard, or by Third Party attacks), then that gives the Director an alternate way of getting them to Cyprus. Falluh grabs their unconscious bodies and drags them to the boat. The agents wake up when they're halfway to Cyprus.

NIGHT'S BLACK AGENTS – THE ZALOZHNIY QUARTET

Another document traces Kim Philby's movements in the days just before he left Beirut and defected to Moscow in '63. Most of the information in the document is common knowledge among spies, conspiracy theorists and Kremlinologists, but one item was discovered by Nikolai himself and is an important clue. On the evening of January 23rd, 1963, Kim Philby visited the Beirut branch of the Koernersbank just before it closed for the night. Investigating the Koernersbank sends the agents to Zurich and *The Boxmen*.

Finally, there's a strip of photographic negatives in an envelope. According to notes on the envelope, they were taken in 1975. When developed with **Photography,** (or just studied through a bright light) they show a group of young Arab men digging in the Bashoura graveyard, and removing a shrouded object that can only be Philby's remains. **Photography (Core Clue)** lets the agents develop and blow up the image enough to get a good look at the Arabs; **Human Terrain** identifies them as members of the Al-Murrah tribe of southern Arabia from their dress. **Research** then points the agents at the Sheikh of that tribe, Haroun al-Murrah.

THE ARAB BOY

SCENE TYPE: Alternate
LEADS-IN: The Exhumation, KGB Beirut
LEAD-OUT: Old Ghosts

At some point after the Bashoura graveyard, the agents find themselves under surveillance. This scene might happen after the agents visit Nikolai's house, or while they're fleeing the graveyard, or as blowback when they're at their current base.

The agent with the highest **Urban Survival (Core Clue)** spots that he's being followed. The tail is a teenage Arab boy. At first glance, he looks like just another kid on the streets: he's wearing unremarkable clothing and pretends to be focussed on his phone and his MP3 player. However, the trained eye notices that one of the earpieces from his MP3 player is hanging loose, and that he keeps casually snapping photos of the agents with the phone.

Luring the boy into a trap with an **Urban Survival** spend or a **Surveillance** contest is easy – the boy's got **Surveillance** 4. Once the agents grab him, they can **Intimidate** him into talking. Another approach for more cautious agents is to tap into his radio communication with **Electronic Surveillance** and track him that way. He's in direct radio contact with his handler, who orders him to keep the agents in sight and determine if they have the Nigredo.

If the agents don't capture the boy, then he contacts them after observing them for some time. *"Forgive me for being so… intrusive, but I must ask you to accompany me."*

The boy's name is **Falluh.** He's working for someone he knows only as "Katun" (**Languages:** roughly, "queen" in Arabic). She sent him to Beirut to spy on the agents. Katun wants to talk with them. He will bring them to her – she lives in Cyprus. He has a boat in the harbor. Come. Come.

GETTING TO CYPRUS

Falluh's got a boat in the docks. He opens the throttle up as soon as they're clear of Beirut's harbor, heading northwest across the blue waters of the eastern Mediterranean. There are medical supplies in the boat if the agents are injured, as well as food and water. Falluh only answers the most basic questions about his employer; she will explain everything, he promises.

The boat heads to the southeast coast of Cyprus. Off in the distance to the west, the agents spot warning buoys marking the approach lanes to the British naval base at Dhekalia. The boat skirts the coast, then docks at a small private pier at the base of a chalky cliff. A narrow stone stairs leads up to the top of the cliff, where the agents find themselves outside an old mansion with peeling red-painted walls. Falluh escorts them in to meet some *Old Ghosts*.

OLD GHOSTS

SCENE TYPE: Alternate
LEADS-IN: The Arab Boy, (if they were knocked out: The Exhumation)
LEADS-OUT: KGB Beirut, King Saud's City.

The agents pass through an archway into a shady courtyard. Waiting there for them is a figure dressed in a black burqa, sitting on a marble bench. Cushions and seats surround a low table and a map of Saudi Arabia.

The figure gestures for the agents to sit down. She addresses them in a British accent. *"We have a great deal to discuss. Please, sit."*

KATUN

Katun's true identity is up to the Director. Whoever she is, she's got some ties to British Intelligence and is opposed to the use of the Rubedo. She's also clearly trading on Gertrude Bell's reputation. Some possibilities:

- She's Gertrude Bell. She faked her death in 1926 and became undead (using the same techniques that St. John Philby used to create the Nigredo). She's no longer human, but isn't as monstrous and malignant as the other vampires.
  - She's just as monstrous and malignant – she wants the Rubedo for herself.
  - She's not a vampire, but she's prolonged her life using vampire blood.
- Gertrude Bell secretly gave birth to a child late in life. The father was King Faisal of Iraq. For diplomatic reasons, the child's existence was hidden from the world. Katun is Bell's daughter (or granddaughter, or great-granddaughter), continuing on Gertrude's work of nation-building and espionage. She fled Iraq after the revolution in 1958 and took refuge in Cyprus.
  - Faisal wasn't the father – it was a vampire. Katun is a *dhampir*. Her father's blood was used by Philby to infect the Saudi royal family, so she's vulnerable to control by the Rubedo. Ensuring that the Conspiracy never get the Rubedo is a matter of self-preservation for her.
- Several mysterious incidents in Bell's life hint at the existence of a double. Her lover Doughty-Wylie reported a dream where he was attacked by a *"shadowy woman thing that swept and swept across my bed like a hawk"* while staying at the Bell family home of Rounton. Later, in 1915, a veiled woman walked across the war-torn beaches of Gallipoli during a brief gap in Turkish artillery fire to lay a wreath on Doughty-Wylie's grave. Gertrude herself demonstrated almost superhuman powers of endurance and organization.
  - Bell was haunted by an undead entity that took her form after she died (her suicide was a last, desperate attempt to escape it). The creature absorbed much of her personality and memories, and became Katun.
  - Bell was attacked and infected with vampirism during her mountaineering exploits in Europe. She was able to suppress her hunger with drugs, but sometimes her vampiric nature would come to the fore. After her death, her vampiric shadow became Katun.
- Gertrude Bell is long dead, and had no connection to the supernatural. Katun is an MI6 cut-out; they're using the agents as pawns to capture the Rubedo and close out the Philby case.

Whoever Katun is, she knows a great deal about the vampires, the Conspiracy, and the Philby plot.

PLAYING KATUN

- Be polite, but forthright and commanding. You're in charge here.
- Interrogate the players methodically. Make sure they explain events in order. Approach questions with the zeal of a historian.
- Keep as still as possible. No body language, no gestures. Be a statue of a sphinx.

THE DEBRIEFING

Katun's goals in this conversation are:

- Determining whether or not she can trust the agents.
- Learning what happened in Beirut.
- Determining how close the Conspiracy are to acquiring both the Albedo and the Nigredo.
- Forcing the agents to decide what they will do with the Albedo and Nigredo should they find them.

She'll only give the agents as much information as she has to in order to achieve her goals. She'll try to avoid questions about who she is and her connection to the Philby plot if possible. She'll claim to be restricted to this house, which may or may not be true depending on what she is, which is why she has to work through intermediaries like Falluh.

- **Bullshit Detector** doesn't work on Katun. A 1-point spend

lets the agent pick up on hints that she has a personal stake in the Philby plot – this isn't about power for her, it's about survival.
- **Human Terrain** confirms she's English-educated, with a faint hint of a Yorkshire accent.
- **Tradecraft:** Definitely influenced by old-school British Intelligence.

When discussing the Beirut incident, she'll put the Third Party in the worst possible light, calling them another part of the Conspiracy or fools who don't understand what they're getting into. She's quietly amused if the agents mention the Bell diary, and is completely familiar with its contents, suggesting she either wrote it or studied it in depth.

- If the agents never followed up on Nikolai, then she can identify him as a KGB spy based in Beirut. The agents can return to his house en route to their next destination and search it (see *KGB Beirut*).
- She knew the Nigredo was in Philby's grave, and hoped it was still there. If told about the Arabs who dug up the grave in 1975, she identifies them as members of the al-Murrah tribe – the same tribe who visited her in Baghdad in 1922. They were always close friends to Philby, ever since his earliest expeditions in Arabia.

Ask the players what they would do with the Albedo and Nigredo (if this operation comes early in the **Quartet**, then couch the question in vague terms, like "*what would you do if you were the secret kings of the world*"). If they don't know, then Katun offers to take it from them (or help them destroy it, if it is possible to destroy your take on the Albedo and Nigredo). The agents should use either **Reassurance** or **Tradecraft** here to prove themselves; alternatively, invoking a Symbol or Solace might work. Once convinced that the agents are not part of the Conspiracy, then Katun suggests **(Core Clue)** that the best place to start inquiries in Riyadh would be with **Qadeer al-Murrah** in Riyadh, the sheikh of the tribe. He is a settled Bedouin, but may still know what is afoot in the deep desert. See *King Saud's City*, p. 125.

AFTER DEBRIEFING

Fattuh can bring the agents back to Beirut if they have loose ends to tie up there, like Nikolai. Alternatively, they can catch a flight from Cyprus to Riyadh easily. If the agents need cash/covers/guns/other supplies, then Katun can provide them with what they need.

RIYADH: QUICK AND DIRTY

Capital of Saudi Arabia. There's been a settlement here for centuries, but Riyadh's rise to prominence really began when the Ottomans razed the old Saudi capital at Diriyah. One of ibn Saud's ancestors chose Riyadh as a replacement.

POPULATION
5,200,000 (bigger than any American city except New York)

CONFLICT
The Saudi state began with an alliance between the cleric Muhammad ibn Abdel Wahhab and the warlord Muhammad Ibn Saud, fusing Ibn Saud's military and economic strength with the fierce determination of the fundamentalist Wahhabi sect, who believed that Islam should be purified by a return to strict traditions. This strained alliance still shapes the culture of Riyadh. On one side, Islamic law is strictly observed in the city, and religious police (Mutaween) patrol the streets to ensure that Sharia is enforced. On the other, 40% of Riyadh's population are foreign workers or immigrants, many of the princes are corrupt, and resentment towards the theocracy is growing.

BACKDROPS
THE KINGDOM CENTRE: 41 storeys of steel and glass and ambition. The twin spires of the centre are a common symbol of the city; the skybridge that runs between them is a popular tourist attraction.

MASMAK FORT: A clay and mud-brick fort in the centre of the city, the Masmak Fort was the site of a historical battle between Ibn Saud's forces and those of the rival Ibn Rasheed tribe. This battle gave the Ibn Saud tribe control of Riyadh and cemented the Wahhabi's preeminence in the region.

THE MINISTRY OF THE INTERIOR: The Ministry of the Interior runs the Saudi police, passport control, and civil defense. Its headquarters is a huge inverted pyramid. It's referred to as "the Spaceship" or "The Flying Saucer" by Westerners.

THREE HOOKS
- With its ultra-hard-line on religious orthodoxy, practising any sort of occultism is dangerous in Riyadh. There's even, supposedly, a dedicated Anti-Witchcraft Unit in the secret police. One alleged witch, Amina bint Abdulhalim Nassar, had "glass bottles of an unknown liquid used for sorcery" in her possession before her arrest. Vampire blood, maybe? Or should player characters with Occult Studies watch their backs?
- In 2012, the Saudi government announced a plan to survey and electronically tag every grave in the city. Ostensibly, it's to create an up-to-date register of burial places in Riyadh, and has nothing to do with anything crawling out of the earth...
- A traditional medical technique called *hijama* is practised widely in Riyadh. The physician makes a small cut with a surgical lancet, then places a glass cup on the skin. A small vacuum in the cup causes it to adhere to the skin and suck out the blood. The agents might run into *hijama* practitioners anywhere in the city, and smell fresh blood in their glass cups.

Katun's role in the rest of the **Quartet** is up to the Director. Pick from the following options:

- **KEEPER OF THE RUBEDO:** Once the agents get both the Albedo and the Nigredo, they can give them to Katun. She'll put the artifacts out of the Conspiracy's reach, removing them from the campaign. The agents can focus on other fronts against the Conspiracy, instead of the whole game revolving around one MacGuffin. Use this option if you want to wrap up the whole Philby plot neatly.
- **MYSTERIOUS ENIGMA:** Not every mystery needs to be explained. Katun can simply vanish after helping the agents. Who was she? What was she? They'll never know. This approach may frustrate the players who want to know everything, but it's a nice mysterious note to end on. You can always bring Katun back if you need to.
- **DOOMED PATRON:** Katun helps the agents for a few game sessions. She might provide information and backing, reveal vital clues about how to fight vampires, and maybe even put the agents on the trail of a clue that leads to Odessa, Vienna or Zurich. Then, as a result of some disastrous Blowback, the Lisky Bratva trace Katun's position and wipe her out. If this is the last operation in the **Quartet,** then you can even up the stakes by having this happen while the agents are in Cyprus. Just as they're finishing their conversation with Katun, a helicopter gunship descends and opens fire on the house; the agents have to escape the Lisky Bratva assassins and flee the scene. This option works especially well for DUST mode games.
- **TREACHEROUS PATRON:** Katun helps the agents, as above, but she's really after the Rubedo for her own ends – she intends to beat the Conspiracy at their own game and rule Saudi Arabia. Or, alternatively, she's part of the Conspiracy. This approach works best if she's the one who puts the PCs on the trail to the Koernersbank in Zurich to get the Albedo. She can also replace the Vampire Lord in Riyadh.

KING SAUD'S CITY

SCENE TYPE: Core
LEADS-IN: KGB Beirut, Old Ghosts
LEADS-OUT: Hajj Shaitan

Riyadh is the beating heart of the Philby plot. Nearly a century ago, Harry St. John Philby tainted the House of Saud with something monstrous, and it is here that the Rubedo will seize control of their blood. Creating the Rubedo requires both the Albedo and the Nigredo, and the Nigredo is lost.

The city crawls with servants of the Conspiracy. Ever since the vampires learned that the Rubedo could give them control over the oil of Arabia, they've made Riyadh one of their strongholds. Their assets include some Lisky Bratva thugs, as well as local strongmen and security forces. Notably, all air travellers coming through King Khalid Airport are watched by the Conspiracy.

Call for **Cover** tests (Difficulty 3, or 4 if the agents have Heat 2 or more) as the agents pass through the airport. If the test is failed, the Conspiracy's assets at the airport (P police officers) spot the agents and tail them. They'll also stall the agents at immigration with added bureaucratic checks and questions.

- **Notice:** The agents spot the Conspiracy officers tailing them.
- **Bureaucracy (2 point spend):** Not only do the agents fast-talk the customs officials into letting them through quickly, they also spot the customs officials glancing towards the Conspiracy goons, giving the enemy away.

The Conspiracy police officers try to intercept the agents on the road from the airport. The agents can escape with a **Driving** contest (the police have **Driving** 4), give them the slip at the airport, or stop and try to talk their way out.

- **Conceal** tests (possibly retroactive ones) may be needed if the agents have weapons in their car.
- **Cop Talk** picks up that one of the police is nervous and hesitant. He knows he's doing something illegal, and the bribes from the Conspiracy aren't enough to completely smother his conscience. If the agents separate him from the others, they can convince him to do the right thing and let them go (and maybe **Filch** his radio as they go, so they can monitor police movements with **Traffic Analysis**).

Once alerted to the Conspiracy's presence in Riyadh, the agents can break into their communications with **Electronic Surveillance** and then use **Traffic Analysis** to spy on them. Notably, they learn that a major player in the Conspiracy is coming into Riyadh soon. From the chatter, it has to be a top-tier member of the Conspiracy, maybe even a vampire.

THE BEDOUIN

Katun's intel was good, but years out of date – Qadeer al-Murrah is dead. His son, **Haroun al-Murrah**, is the agents' next best candidate for finding the Nigredo.

Research: The al-Murrah tribe's traditional territory is in the south and east of Arabia. They've become rich working with oil firms on the harsh expanse of the Rub' al Khali, the fabled "Empty Quarter" of the desert. Qadeer al-Murrah died two years ago of a heart attack; his young son Haroun took over the family affairs.

Getting a meeting with Haroun requires either **High Society**, **Negotiation**, an introduction from a **Network** contact in the oil industry, or a suitable **Cover**.

Haroun is in his mid-thirties, the prime of his life. He's an Arab playboy prince – as the older oilfields of Arabia are sucked dry, the ever-thirsty oil industry is forced to move deeper into the forbidding Rub' al-Khali, and that is the ancestral domain of the al-Murrah tribe. Every new well in the deep desert enriches Haroun. He still maintains the appearance of a traditional Bedouin nomad, and spends one month each year touring the encampments and tents of his cousins, but he's much more at home in air-conditioned hotels than on horseback.

He knows next to nothing about the Philby plot. His father never initiated him into Philby's conspiracy. As far as he's concerned, names like St. John Philby belong to the history books, and have no bearing on modern Saudi Arabia.

Asking about the Nigredo, St. John Philby or vampires gets a polite smile and an imperceptible gesture towards his security guards to remove the crazy people from his presence.

- **Bullshit Detector** confirms that he's genuinely mystified – he doesn't know anything about the Philby plot.
- **Negotiation** can keep the conversation going by hinting that there's something valuable hidden in the desert.
- **Human Terrain (Core Clue):** If the agents describe the events in the Bashoura cemetery in '75, then Haroun recalls a strange event in his childhood. When he was a young boy, his father took him to a cave in the deep desert, and said that it was the "other Kaaba." The Kaaba is the most sacred site in Islam; it is a building in the heart of Mecca that contains a black stone said to have fallen from Heaven.

A profane Kaaba could contain a profane "black stone" – the Nigredo. Haroun even remembers one of the Bedouin riders who accompanied them laughing and calling their journey "Hajj Shaitan" (Devil's pilgrimage). See *Hajj Shaitan*, p. 127.

The next step is convincing Haroun to reveal the location of this cave. If he believes that the cave contains something valuable, he'll want to claim it for himself. Haroun is an ambitious man, so telling him that he's got the key to controlling Saudi Arabia *and* immortality in one handy bundle means he'll mount his own expedition to the cave. Possible tactics:

- **Cop Talk:** Hinting that it's something dangerous or illegal like a cache of weapons smuggled out of Iraq. Qadeer al-Murrah had many secrets that he never told his son.
- **Intimidation:** If the agents can convince him they're representatives of the CIA or some other black operations outfit, Haroun may decide it's not worth interfering. (For that matter, taking out Haroun's guards with a surprise attack and then pointing a gun in his face works too).
- **Flattery** or **Human Terrain:** Appealing to Haroun's sense of honor by invoking the name of his father. They came to call in a debt owed by Qadeer al-Murrah; surely Haroun al-Murrah will listen?

PLAYING HAROUN AL-MURRAH

- Be magnanimous. Entertain these foolish petitioners.
- Anything in the deep desert belongs to you and your tribe. Do not let anyone take what is yours!
- Adopt a proud, regal bearing. Rule the room.

OTHER TALES OF THE CAVE

Alternatively, the agents can find another member of the al-Murrah tribe with

LEVERAGE OVER HAROUN

Paranoid agents might prefer to have something over Haroun before visiting him. Potential threat/blackmail material includes:

- **Research (1-point spend):** Digging into Haroun's family reveals that his maternal grandfather was part of Ibn Saud's retinue. He was at the feast of Eid ul-Fitr in 1931, which means that Haroun must be infected with the same vampiric curse. If the Rubedo is immanentized, then Haroun will be just another blood slave to the vampire king.
- **Human Terrain (1-point spend):** Haroun is unpopular in the al-Murrah tribe. Many of the older members see him as weak, corrupt and venal. He needs to fortify his reputation – and keeping to his father's oaths to Philby would do so.
- **Accounting (1-point spend):** Haroun's invested a lot of cash with the Black Sea Bank. Revealing the bank's questionable business dealings could spook Haroun.

Human Terrain and get the location of the cave. Only a few members of the tribe know exactly where it is, but once the agents have a rough idea of its location, a few hours poring over satellite images with **Data Recovery** lets the agents pin down the cave with **Archaeology (Core Clue)**.

Doing so also turns up a curious story (**Human Terrain** or **Occult Studies**). An old tradition speaks of a cave in that region where a ghul dwells. According to the tale, the ghul tries to lure travellers into its cave by promising them wealth and power, and by claiming to share their faith. If a traveller succumbs to the ghul's tricks, it devours them.

HAJJ SHAITAN

SCENE TYPE: Core
Leads-in: King Saud's City.
LEADS-OUT: Treason in the Blood

There are few places on Earth more forbidding than the hyper-arid wastes of the Empty Quarter. Hundreds of kilometres of dunes stretch across the border from Saudi Arabia into Oman, the United Arab Emirates and Yemen. Only the Bedouin live here, and they only travel along the fringes. The deep desert is empty and trackless. St. John Philby crossed it in 1932 – one of the first Occidentals to do so in history.

The agents can catch a train or plane to one of the oil towns on the edge of the Rub' al Khali, but from there they must arrange their own transport. They can hire 4x4s easily, but must make a **Cover** test (Difficulty 3) to do so without drawing the attention of the Conspiracy. Alternatively, the agents can travel by horse and camel in the traditional fashion, which drops them off the Conspiracy's radar but means that everyone must spend a point of **Outdoor Survival** (or have a point of **Outdoor Survival** spent on their behalf; a kind GM may let them use **Preparedness** instead). Anyone who doesn't spend a point suffers greatly from the heat and counts as Hurt.

If Haroun sponsors their expedition, then he can provide them with a *rafiq* (guide/ambassador). He may even accompany them personally if circumstances warrant. Otherwise, they can hire a guide with **Human Terrain** or **Network**. The guide's name is **Rasheed**.

THE LABYRINTH OF SAND

Endless dunes. Daytime temperatures up to 51° C (124° F). No water, no roads, nothing but the winds and the sand. The agents are alone as few people are ever alone.

Outdoor Survival (Core Clue): The agents navigate across the wastes of the Empty Quarter, travelling around 200 kilometres south-east of the city of Al-Kharj.

This is an excellent opportunity for an introspective scene. For the first time in several weeks (or longer), the agents are not under attack, running from Lisky Bratva thugs, or dodging surveillance cameras. They've got a chance to talk.

Finally, the agents come to a rocky outcrop that rises from the surrounding sands like a half-buried monster. Searching around, they find a steep-sided shaft like a well that plunges into the darkness. The sides of the well are worn smooth – maybe by the endless abrasions of the desert sands, or maybe by long years of labor. Climbing up that shaft would be impossible without specialized equipment (**Preparedness:** who brought rope?).

Shining a light down the shaft illuminates a cave at the bottom. Skulls grin back at the agents. There are several exits from the cave; it must be a labyrinth down there.

Archaeology: The shaft itself is ancient, dating back hundreds of years, but there are signs of recent repair. It reminds the agent of a prison, an oubliette where you'd dump a condemned man.

Forensic Pathology or **Outdoor Survival:** Some of those bones are those of camels and goats, not human. No such animals live nearby (very little lives in the furnace of the Rub' al Khali), so they must have been deliberately thrown down there. Sacrificing an animal, or dropping a bag of blood (**Preparedness**, Difficulty 5 or a 1-point **Vampirology** spend to have one to hand) can attract the monster in the cave.

THE THING IN THE CAVE

Beirut, 1960. Harry St. John Philby dies of a heart attack. He's buried in haste. Every observer – Arkady Shevlenko of the KGB, Nicholas Elliot of MI6, Miles Copeland of the CIA, whoever the vampires had in the shadows – believed that St. John died before he could activate the Nigredo. The old man had the keys to the kingdom, a passage to immortality. If he *didn't* use it during those three days in Beirut, then it must have been hidden elsewhere.

Only a handful of people, among them Kim, knew the truth about St. John's death. The explorer intended to fake his death – or, rather, he intended to die a very real and public death, and then rise again. He was buried with the Nigredo, and over the years, the dark artifact remade St. John Philby, transforming him into a vampire. His transformation was watched over by Kim. According to his original plan, dictated to his son in a Beirut hospital room that stank of disinfectant and death, Philby would slumber for more than a decade while Saudi Arabia grew stronger and stronger on American oil money. He was convinced that this "purdah" was needed to ensure that his human soul came through the transformation unblighted. When the time was right, his Bedouin allies would take him in secret to his new kingdom, while Kim brought the Albedo to seize control of the family of Ibn Saud.

St. John miscalculated. The Nigredo transformed his body, but it also drove him insane. Kim Philby never revealed the location of the Albedo or the Nigredo to his KGB handlers because he feared the same fate would await him.

The vampiric *thing* – feral, vicious, monstrously powerful – that was once Harry St. John Philby was taken by his Bedouin allies in 1975. They brought it to Arabia as promised, but then threw it into this ancient prison. Qadeer al-Murrah hoped that his father's friend would eventually return to sanity, but as the years went by and the vampire remained feral, he lost hope.

The thing in the cave is still there, and still hungry. It looks like a filthy sack of bones and fangs, with chalk-white skin pulled tight over a misshapen skull. There isn't a trace of humanity or sanity in its eyes. In game terms, it's something like a really tough feral vampire.

NIGHT'S BLACK AGENTS – THE ZALOZHNIY QUARTET

Strength (tests mandatory for feats of strength; see p. 137 ***Night's Black Agents***), Vampiric Speed
BANES: standard vampiric banes for campaign, *may do more damage faster*
BLOCKS: standard vampiric blocks for campaign (+2 to Aberrance test Difficulty to pierce). Furthermore, it is completely terrified by sunlight, even if vampires in your game are normally unaffected by daylight.
COMPULSIONS: drink fresh blood.
DREADS: standard vampiric dreads for campaign (+2 to Aberrance test Difficulty to confront)

HUNTING THE DEAD

The feral monster's lair consists of a half-dozen caverns linked by narrow passageways. The steep shaft is the only exit, although **Explosive Devices** could blow a hole in a thin rocky wall if the agents need a back door. The caves are completely lightless, so the agents need torches or night-vision goggles.

The agents can tool up with **Preparedness** if they've gone vampire hunting before. Optionally, a **Vampirology** spend lets the agents find traces of a block/bane/dread left here by Qadeer all those years ago (a silver crucifix, some magnetic dust, a palindrome carved around the lip of the well shaft).

The feral vampire is starved to the point of death – its Health score reflects its deranged tenacity, not its physical condition. Any smell or taste of blood drives the vampire wild. The agents can pick up on this irrational bloodthirst with **Vampirology**; the creature is thirsty enough to risk licking a live grenade that's been dipped in blood. It can make **Health** tests to overcome its bloodlust, but the Difficulty is always 6 and it costs 3 Health points for every +1 bonus to the die roll.

The Nigredo is still around Philby's neck (or buried in the cave). Optionally, the agents can grab the Nigredo with **Filch** (Difficulty 6) and escape, leaving Philby to his eternal hunger.

(If this operation takes place early in your campaign, or if the agents are terminally unprepared, you may want to drop the vampire's Health down to a more manageable level.)
GENERAL ABILITIES: Aberrance 12, Hand-to-Hand 15, Health 18.
HIT THRESHOLD: 5
ALERTNESS MODIFIER: +2
STEALTH MODIFIER: +1
DAMAGE MODIFIER: +1 (talon), +0 (bite; extended canines), -1 (fist, kick)
ARMOR: -1 (tough skin); firearms and projectiles do only half damage after armor
FREE POWERS: Drain (to Health cap of 24), Infravision, Regeneration (all damage refreshes next sunset), Unfeeling
OTHER POWERS: Extra Attacks (see ***Night's Black Agents*** p. 74; first extra attack is free, further attacks in a round cost 2 Aberrance or Hand-to-Hand points each),

TREASON IN THE BLOOD

SCENE TYPE: Antagonist Reaction
LEADS-IN: Hajj Shaitan
LEADS-OUT: Last Train to Istanbul (or Capstone: The Alchemical Wedding)

The agents may have been the first to find the lost Nigredo, but that doesn't mean they get to keep it. The vampire lord who arrived in Riyadh around the same time as the agents stretches forth his dark hand, and snatches the Nigredo away from them. This betrayal can take many different forms – pick the one that suits the current situation best.

THE TRAITOR

The Conspiracy found out about the agents' expedition into the Empty Quarter through a traitor. Potential candidates for that traitor include:

- **MR. RED:** The old mentor barely survived the horrors of the Bashoura Graveyard. Wounded and scarred, he blundered blindly through the alleyways of Beirut until the Conspiracy found him and recruited him. He knew his old friend's habits and movements, and was able to track the agents into the desert. Ideal for **DUST** or **MIRROR** mode games.
- **MR. WHITE:** White blames the agents for the disaster in Beirut. He followed them to Nikolai's house, and learned about the al-Murrah connection from there. This option works well if the players already hate Mr. White.
- **KATUN:** The mysterious woman was working for the conspiracy all along. The Al-Murrah tribe would never have revealed Philby's hiding place to a vampire or one of their minions – the Conspiracy had to use the agents as their pawns to find the Nigredo.
- **HAROUN AL-MURRAH:** The Saudi wants power, and by offering the Nigredo to the Conspiracy, he ensures that he will be one of the secret rulers of the world. The vampires promised that once he becomes one of them, he will no longer be subject to the curse of the House of Saud.
- **A GUIDE:** If the agents hired a guide, then they've put their lives into the hands of a stranger. The Conspiracy could be one step ahead of them all along…
- **A SOLACE:** One of the agents' close friends or family was turned by the Conspiracy. Make sure that this is a Solace who's already appeared in the game and has interacted with several of the agents – a Solace who was only ever a line on a character sheet won't do.
- **ONE OF THE AGENTS:** The vampires got to one of the player characters and used mind control on them. They've been under the control of the Conspiracy for weeks. The vampires erased the agent's memory of any tampering. Lead the players through a series of flashbacks where he remembers the vampire's brainwashing him. Discuss this option before springing it on a player (or aim it at an agent with a suitable Drive, like Mystery or Programming).
- **NO TRAITOR:** Maybe there isn't a traitor. The Conspiracy could have spied on the agents in some other way like a bugged phone, blood magic, high-flying drone reconnaissance, or a strix or murony spy. However, the Conspiracy agents should still claim there's a traitor in the group, to fan the players' paranoia.

Once you've decided on who the traitor was, you need to take the Nigredo away from the agents. Choose from one of the following scenes, each of which concludes with near-certain death for the agents.

WHAT WAS BRIEFLY YOURS IS NOW MINE

The team crawls out of the cave in the desert – to find an Overwatch Security team waiting for them. There are Px2 soldiers, all armed with assault rifles that are pointed right at the agents. The Overwatch squad is commanded by Lt. Col. Weddle (see p. 109). Any troops who aren't already working for the Lisky Bratva have been told that the agents are dangerous terrorists.

Weddle demands the agents hand over the Nigredo. If they refuse, one of them gets shot and he asks again. Once the agents give him the Nigredo, they're thrown back down into the cave to be eaten by the vampire. The Overwatch team cut the ropes, trapping the agents at the bottom of the shaft. He leaves them for dead, assuming they'll be trapped in the same prison that held Philby for years.

Preparedness or **Filch** (Difficulty 4) can grab a grenade just before the team are thrown down the shaft; **Architecture** can identify a breakable wall, and **Explosive Devices** (Difficulty 4) blows open a hole for the agents to crawl out of.

From there, the agents have to cross two hundred kilometers of desert with only minimal food and water. **Outdoor Survival** lets the agents survive this crossing, but only barely – all the agents arrive back in civilization at 0 Health. A kind Director might let **Outdoor Survival** spends be used to reduce the damage, or allow other abilities to be used (**Preparedness** to have a cache of supplies or extra water, **Human Terrain** to find some Bedouin, **Network** to have a buddy send out a rescue party when the agents don't arrive back on schedule).

This is the high-octane, *Indiana Jones* approach to depriving the agents of the Nigredo. It works best if the agents all went down into the cave; if some of them stayed outside, then the ambush can get complicated.

DESERT AMBUSH

As the agents make their way back across the desert from the cave, they're intercepted by an Overwatch Security team in a helicopter gunship (a Bell 212 Military with rockets and a machine gun). The helicopter descends on them out of the desert sky, leaving them with no chance to escape and no place to hide in the desert. Lt. Col. Weddle is on board – he gives the agents a chance to surrender. **Military Science** confirms that the helicopter has enough firepower to wipe the agents out easily – if anyone fights back, then they're almost certainly dead (the pilot's got **Shooting 8** and **Driving 10**).

If the agents do surrender, then Weddle is "merciful" – he takes the Nigredo (and brings the Traitor with him, if there's a Traitor), then blows up the agents' jeep/kills their horses and leaves them to die in the desert – use the same dying horribly of exposure rules as outlined above in *What Was Yours Briefly Is Now Mine*.

Use this approach if your players are the kind who try to outthink every obstacle – there's no way to outthink a gunship when you're in the middle of the desert.

NO SURRENDER, NO NIGREDO

On the off chance that the agents doggedly hang on to their prize and keep the Nigredo despite the overwhelming odds, then you've got two options.

Firstly, the Conspiracy can try again. If the agents dodge the desert ambush, then run with the Mount Doom gambit. If they try hiding the Nigredo in an unsafe place, then the Conspiracy can pick it up just like they grab the Albedo (see p. 133). Alternatively, if the agents already have the Albedo, the conspiracy can steal that instead and you can run *Last Train to Istanbul* with a different MacGuffin.

Secondly, if this is the last operation in the **Quartet** and you want to run the Capstone, the Conspiracy can create or find a new Nigredo. They've tracked the agents all through the quartet, and the agents led them to Philby's cave. They may not have the true Nigredo, but they learned enough to guess where Philby obtained it. The Conspiracy might dig up a Nigredo substitute in the ruins of Wabar, or create a copy from a mix of river clay and vampire blood, or just try to use the Albedo on its own – a stopgap Rubedo won't increase the user's power, but it would still gain control over the House of Saud.

RIYADH ARREST

In this scenario, the agents arrive back in Riyadh with the Nigredo – and then get hit with more Heat than they can handle. The Conspiracy has planted evidence that the agents are part of an ultra-right-wing Christian sect here on a mission of retaliation for 9/11 (or are part of an extremist eco-warfare cell who intend to wipe out the oil industry, or a crypto-Zionist terror group, or whatever flavor of international terrorist fits the agents). Every cop and soldier in Saudi Arabia is looking for the agents – and the Traitor has already given them their location. The Conspiracy works through a *Mahabith* supervisor, **Usman Bousaid**, who's reporting to Overwatch Security.

The arrest kicks off with Department of Public Safety police officers backed up by *Mahabith* secret police special forces surrounding wherever the agents are in Riyadh, or else intercepting their car/plane/train as they return to the city. A 2-point **Urban Survival** spend or **Sense Trouble** test (Difficulty?) gives the agents a brief advance warning of the ambush, allowing them to run if they want. The Traitor, if present, will try to "accidentally" impede the agents' escape (stalling the car, attracting attention, twisting an ankle, blocking exits).

If the agents do run, then you've got a city-wide chase that stops only when the Nigredo is found. **Cop Talk** or **Traffic Analysis** lets the agents find out they're being hunted on trumped-up charges, and suggests that the Conspiracy is expending a lot of effort to capture them. **Urban Survival** and **Streetwise** coupled with **Human Terrain** lets the agents survive on the streets of Riyadh (if they're not familiar with Riyadh, emphasize the cultural differences and the size of the city – this is not a good place to be lost).

Captured agents are arrested, brought to a *Mahabith* interrogation centre and questioned about their alleged terror crimes. The Nigredo is confiscated if found.

Once the Nigredo is in police possession, the agents will be released… eventualy. The *Mahabith* can hold them for months without trial, although a **Law** spend can speed the process along if the agents drop the right names. It's more likely that the agents choose to escape. The interrogation centre is in the basement of an anonymous government building, and the agents are kept in brick-walled cells with nothing but a blanket and a single lightbulb. **Military Science** lets the agents work out guard movements, **Filch** lets them palm objects or weapons to aid in an escape, and **Human Terrain** picks up that the *Mahabith* are under pressure to deliver results. If an agent promises to confess, then he'll be brought out of the cell and into a room with Usman Bousaid. A quick **Hand-to-Hand** contest likely lets the agents flip the tables, take Bousaid hostage, and then fight their way out.

Alternatively, **Human Terrain** lets them identify the Conspiracy's mole in the *Mahabith*. **Bullshit Detector** reveals that the police interrogators are increasingly doubtful about the allegations; if the agents play on these worries, they can turn the interrogators against Bousaid and escape in the confusion.

This is a more subtle way to intercept the players, especially suitable to DUST games.

THE MOUNT DOOM GAMBIT

In this scenario, the Traitor claims to have a way to destroy the Nigredo, or take it somewhere that the Conspiracy will never find. For example, if Haroun al-Murrah is the traitor, then he might offer to use his Bedouin to smuggle the Nigredo across the desert; if it's Mr. Red, he contacts his friend after they return from the desert, claiming that the Third Party left him for dead after the Bashoura cemetery in Beirut and that he now wants to help the agents.

If the agents take the deal, the Traitor leaves with the Nigredo – and then you segue into *Riyadh Ambush* as the police arrive outside wherever the agents met with the Traitor.

TRACKING THE TRAITOR

Once the agents escape whatever death-trap you dumped them in, they need to find the Nigredo and get their revenge on the Traitor.

If this is the last operation in the *Quartet,* skip to the Capstone: *the Alchemical Wedding.*

Otherwise, the Conspiracy intend to extract the Nigedo from Saudi Arabia until they've got the Albedo too. They've sent a courier to pick it up. If Josef Lisky is still alive, use him. Otherwise, use Benjamin Weddle. Either way, **Traffic Analysis (Core Clue)** shows that a private jet left King Khalid Airport a few hours ago, en route to Baghdad.

The courier has a lead of several hours on the agents. The agents need to get to Baghdad as quickly as possible to catch up. It's about 16 hours by road; flying is faster, but if the agents have Heat, they'll need to use **Cover (Difficulty Heat +2)** to get past airport security at King Khalid International Airport to catch a commercial flight.

From Baghdad airport, the Nigredo is transferred by road to the railway station.

- **Bureaucracy** or **Traffic Analysis (Core Clue)** lets the agents find out about the transfer to the railway.
- **Accounting:** The rail journey is booked under the name of Baldak Shipping.
- **Vampirology** (1-point spend): There must be a reason that the Conspiracy is using a train. Maybe there's something guarding the Nigredo that can't be moved by air.

LAST TRAIN TO ISTANBUL

SCENE TYPE: Core
LEADS-IN: Treason in the Blood

Mile by mile, the Nigredo comes closer and closer to the Lisky Bratva's heartland in Russia. Instead of flying it directly there, the vampiric masters of the Conspiracy ordained a slower but safer route. The old Baghdad-Istanbul railway line is no longer in service, but the line exists and is still traversable. Using a railway also allows the Conspiracy to set one of their most powerful and trusted servants to guard the Nigredo – a camazotz (see p. 149 of *Night's Black Agents*).

THE TRAIN

In addition to two Baldak shipping freight cars, there are three other freight cars and three passenger cars on the train. The first Baldak shipping freight car contains the Nigredo along with other smuggled goods (hidden inside Overwatch Security crates). The second car contains the camazotz. There's a concealed hatch in the roof of this freight car, allowing the monster to fly out of the train and patrol the surrounding area for danger – or prey.

There are one hundred and fifty civilian passengers on board (although only 148 will get off the train in Turkey – the camazotz is hungry), as well as Px2 Lisky Bratva thugs. Most of the train staff are working for the Lisky Bratva.

CATCHING THE TRAIN

If the agents made it to Baghdad quickly enough, they can get on the train there. The railway station is under surveillance by Lisky Bratva thugs. **Surveillance (Difficulty 3)** spots them; **Disguise (Difficulty 4)** gets past them without a fight. Otherwise, it's fisticuffs and **Athletics (Difficulty 4)** to leap onto the train as it pulls out.

If the agents didn't make it to Baghdad in time, they've got to intercept the train en route. The train goes from Baghdad to Mosul, then across the border into Syria, then northwest to Turkey. It's a slow train due to the degraded condition of the line, so the agents can overtake it on the roads. All they need to do then is get on board – it's not scheduled to stop anywhere, but the agents could force a stop by blockading the tracks.

ON THE TRAIN

Once on the train, the agents need to find the Nigredo.

The train passengers are a mix of Iraqi migrant workers heading for Turkey, and tourists intrigued by the potential rebirth of this historic train line. Conditions and amenities on the train are poor; the rolling stock hasn't been used since the 1980s.

If the camazotz hasn't shown up already, then **Languages (Arabic)** lets the agents overhear whispered conversations among the migrant workers about sightings of a huge bird or bat.

Lisky Bratva thugs have the exits from the passenger cars under surveillance. The agents need to either distract the guards or else climb onto the roof of the train and make their way along the tops of the cars (leaving themselves wide open to camazotz attack). If the agents try leaving without distracting the guards, then they'll raise the alarm and draw the Lisky Bratva thugs down on them.

The first freight car is locked (**Infiltration, Difficulty 4** to open) and crammed with crates similar to the ones the agents saw in the Overwatch Shipping/Turkish warehouses/in Odessa (see p. 21). Optionally, one of the crates contains gold stolen from Saddam's hoard that's bound for the

Black Sea Bank. Following that leads to the bank deal in Zurich (*The Boxmen*, p. 80).

FIGHTING THE CAMAZOTZ

The flying monster is the end-of-operation boss for this part of the **Quartet,** and it's a doozy. Try to spring it as a horrible surprise on the agents.

- As mentioned above, anyone who tries the classic running-along-the-top-of-the-train routine gets a giant Man-Bat in the face. Trying to keep your balance on top of a train lowers your Hit Threshold by 1.
- The camazotz patrols the area around the train at night (or under cover of bad weather), looking for potential threats to the Nigredo. If the agents set up an ambush, or chase the train in a car, or try dropping onto the train from a handy bridge, then the camazotz attacks as they're about to intercept the train.
- The camazotz slumbers in the second Baldak shipping freight car, right next to the car containing the Nigredo. If the agents break in, it awakens and starts battering at the walls. Soon, it starts battering *through* the walls.
- The camazotz needs to feed regularly. It usually sates its hunger by grabbing sheep or goats from the farmlands near the railway, or else by snacking on unfortunate farmers. However, it may also pick off passengers — there's a small open platform at the rear of one passenger car, and anyone who goes out there to escape the smoky interior or in search of a breath of fresh air is a potential victim.

FINAL CURTAIN

Grabbing the Nigredo from the train and escaping from the camazotz completes this operation. Optionally, you can seed the freight car with clues leading onto other operations in the **Quartet.**

EXIT VECTORS

This operation uncovers leads pointing to the other operations in this book. Depending on how things go, and how the agents handle themselves, Katun could put the agents on the trail of other Conspiracy activities.

THE ZALOZHNIY SANCTION

- The Baldak shipping freight was due to be transferred to a different train, heading for the Turkish port of Samsun. Digging around with **Bureaucracy** or **Traffic Analysis** puts the agents on the trail of the smuggling route to Odessa.

- **Criminology:** The Lisky Bratva is known to be headquartered in Odessa.
- Mr. Red might recommend the agents see Donald Caroll about "an Odessa job related to this Overwatch thing." This is most likely an attempt to point the agents at the Lisky Bratva as a diversion from the Third Party's plans.

OUT OF THE HOUSE OF ASHES

- Nikolai's documents point the agent towards Arkady Shevlenko, who's currently (**Research**) due any day in Vienna for a trade conference.

- Katun can send the agents off in search of Arkady Shevlenko.

THE BOXMEN

- Again, Nikolai's done the groundwork here — his notes tie Kim Philby to the Koernersbank. A little **Accounting** or **History** traces the Beirut branch back to the Swiss mother bank in Zurich — and flags the rumors about the impending Black Sea Bank takeover.
- Optionally, the train to Istanbul also carries stolen Iraqi gold that ends up part of the shipment bound for the Koernersbank in Zurich.

CAPSTONE: THE ALCHEMICAL WEDDING

LEADS-IN: Treason in the Blood

This capstone kicks in after *Treason in the Blood*. Instead of shipping the Nigredo off for safe keeping, the Conspiracy bring it to Riyadh to activate Philby's long-delayed plan. To bring about the Rubedo, of course, they need the Albedo.

- If the Conspiracy already has the Albedo, then there's nothing stopping them.
- If the agents had the Albedo on them when they're ambushed in *Treason in the Blood*, then take it off them and smack them with a rolled-up newspaper for bad tradecraft.
- If they've stashed it somewhere that the Conspiracy can find, then the vampires go and get it. The agents stagger out of the desert to find that their hiding place was burned, their allies killed or turned, and the Albedo taken. Be unforgiving – if there was ever the slightest opening for the Conspiracy to find the location of the hiding place, use it. Remember to apply the Stability loss for a burnt Solace/Safety, if appropriate.
- If the players stashed the Albedo somewhere where the Conspiracy could never find it, or if they've destroyed it, then the Conspiracy decides to cut its losses. While the full Rubedo would give them control over the House of Saud, the Nigredo on its own can still transform a human into a vampire – or massively increase the power of an existing vampire.

THE VAMPIRE KING

The vampire chosen to receive the Rubedo is an elder member of the Conspiracy. If you've a vampire lord in mind, or if the agents have already tangled with a named villain who deserves an encore, use that bad guy. Otherwise, use an ancient vampire, one that has long since abandoned any pretense of humanity.

THE RITUAL SITE

Al Mamlaka Tower, better known as the Kingdom Centre, is the best-known landmark in Riyadh. It's nearly a thousand feet tall, and its distinctive twin spires glitter in the sunlight. Make your way through the shopping arcades, the offices and the staggeringly expensive apartments and you climb to the skybridge that runs between the two spires, giving an unparalleled panorama of the city. Stand on that skybridge, and all of the Kingdom of Saudi Arabia spreads itself out below you.

The skybridge is normally open to the public, but it can be rented for private functions – say, by an expanding financial concern, the Black Sea Bank. The Kingdom Centre Skybridge offers the vampires more than just a dramatic backdrop – it also has practical advantages. It's highly secure. It's right in the middle of Riyadh, thus maximizing the area of effect of the ritual. Its position, suspended high in the air, insulates it from spiritual/occult/psychic/electromagnetic influences.

FINDING THE RITUAL

Locating the Ritual site is easy.

- **Interrogation:** Beating up any of the Conspiracy's minions can point the agents towards the Kingdom Centre.
- **Traffic Analysis:** Chatter goes off the charts as the Conspiracy gathers at the Kingdom Centre.
- **Accounting:** Renting the skybridge is a high-profile transaction; if the agents are watching for movement by the Black Sea Bank, they'll spot this.
- **Occult Studies:** Omens come thick and fast in advance of a ritual this potent. Oil turns to blood in the wells. Sensitives dream of vampires. Compasses point towards the Kingdom Centre. Something is coming.

VAMPIRE SLAYING WITH AN APACHE HELICOPTER

The agents can just walk into the lower levels of the Kingdom Centre as long as they're not obviously packing heavy weapons – it's a shopping mall for the moneyed elite of Riyadh. In addition to building security, there are Lisky Bratva guards mingling with the crowds. Sneaking past them requires **Infiltration** or **Disguise** (both at **Difficulty 6**). Once past the public levels of the 99-storey building, it may be time to go *Die Hard* and sneak/fight past the security teams. The Black Sea Bank controls the top five floors of the building, but they'll send smaller teams to sweep the lower floors if they suspect trouble.

If the presence of the agents is confirmed, then a zalozhniy is dispatched to deal with them. The monster tries to use its ability to mimic voices to split the agents up. It might tap into their radios and give false orders, or pretend to be a prisoner (maybe a Solace) who needs rescuing. If any key friendly NPCs (or even player characters) died untimely over the course of the campaign, then you could bring them back as a zalozhniy, assuming Dr. Dorjiev could have got his syringes into them in time.

The real challenge comes when the agents make it to the skybridge, where they're up against:

- P bodyguards
- Half a dozen senior figures in the Conspiracy – they're on the same tier as Dorjiev or Weddle. If it fits your campaign, some of them may be candidates for transformation into a vampire.
- Optionally, a murony guardian-spirit. The creature's body is kept in a metal coffin near the south entrance to the skybridge.
- The vampire lord.

Inside, the skybridge looks like an ancient temple drawn in glass and steel.

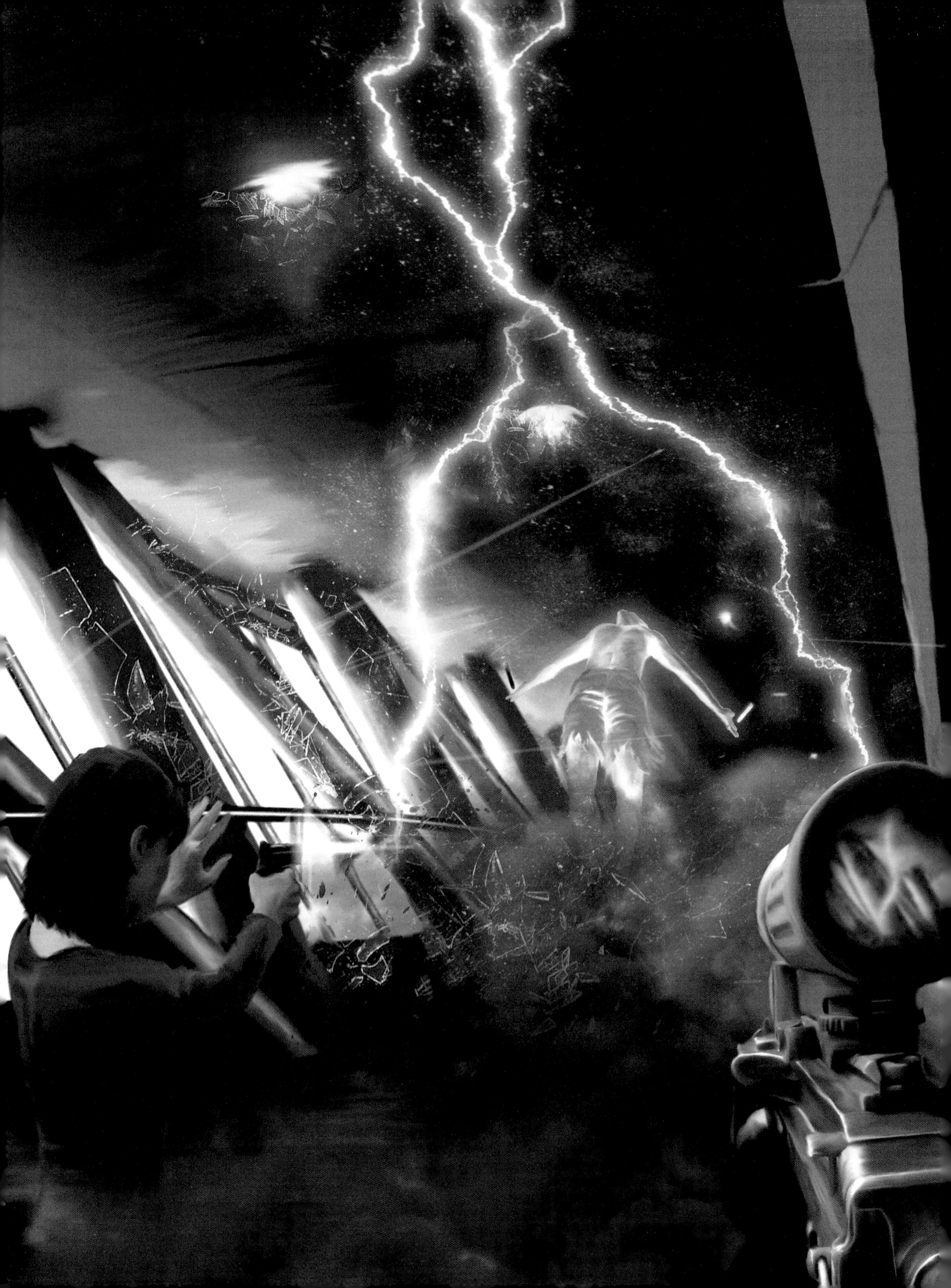

The curved floor gently arcs across the 150-foot gap between the two spires. Steel struts jut out at strange angles over the cityscape below. The Conspiracy ritual has whatever trappings fit your vampires. If you've got occult vampires, then they've brought in flaming torches and inscribed magic circles onto the floor. If it's alien vampires, then the stars over Riyadh wheel into patterns never before seen on Earth, and strange lights shoot over the city.

The ritual takes place at the very centre of the bridge. Two supplicants bring the vampire lord the Albedo and the Nigredo so that he may transform them into the true Rubedo.

How do the players stop it? Some possible options:

- The most direct route – head into the building, start climbing and keep beating up mooks until they hit the vampire. The agents can tool up on stakes, garlic and blessed grenades before heading into the Kingdom Centre.
- The agents can bypass the climb if they can get hold of a helicopter, and drop onto the skybridge from above. This high-octane approach does abandon the element of surprise, and also means they'll need to deal with a murderous murony-spirit eating their pilot at an inopportune moment.
- If the agents want to end up international fugitives for the rest of their lives (and don't mind killing some unknown number of civilians below), they can try blowing up the skybridge. Even if the vampire survives a thousand-foot fall, it'll be severely wounded when it lands and the agents have a chance to take it down before fleeing.
- To create the Rubedo, the vampire must consume part of the Nigredo and attune itself to the Albedo. If the agents tampered with one of the components before the Conspiracy stole them, they may be able to trick the vampires. They'll still have to go to the Kingdom Centre and distract the vampires to stop them spotting the sabotage before the ritual.

The defeat of the vampire lord and the loss of the Rubedo is a significant blow to the Conspiracy. Identifying the other senior figures present at the ritual can lead the agents to half-a-dozen new nodes that are ripe for takedown.

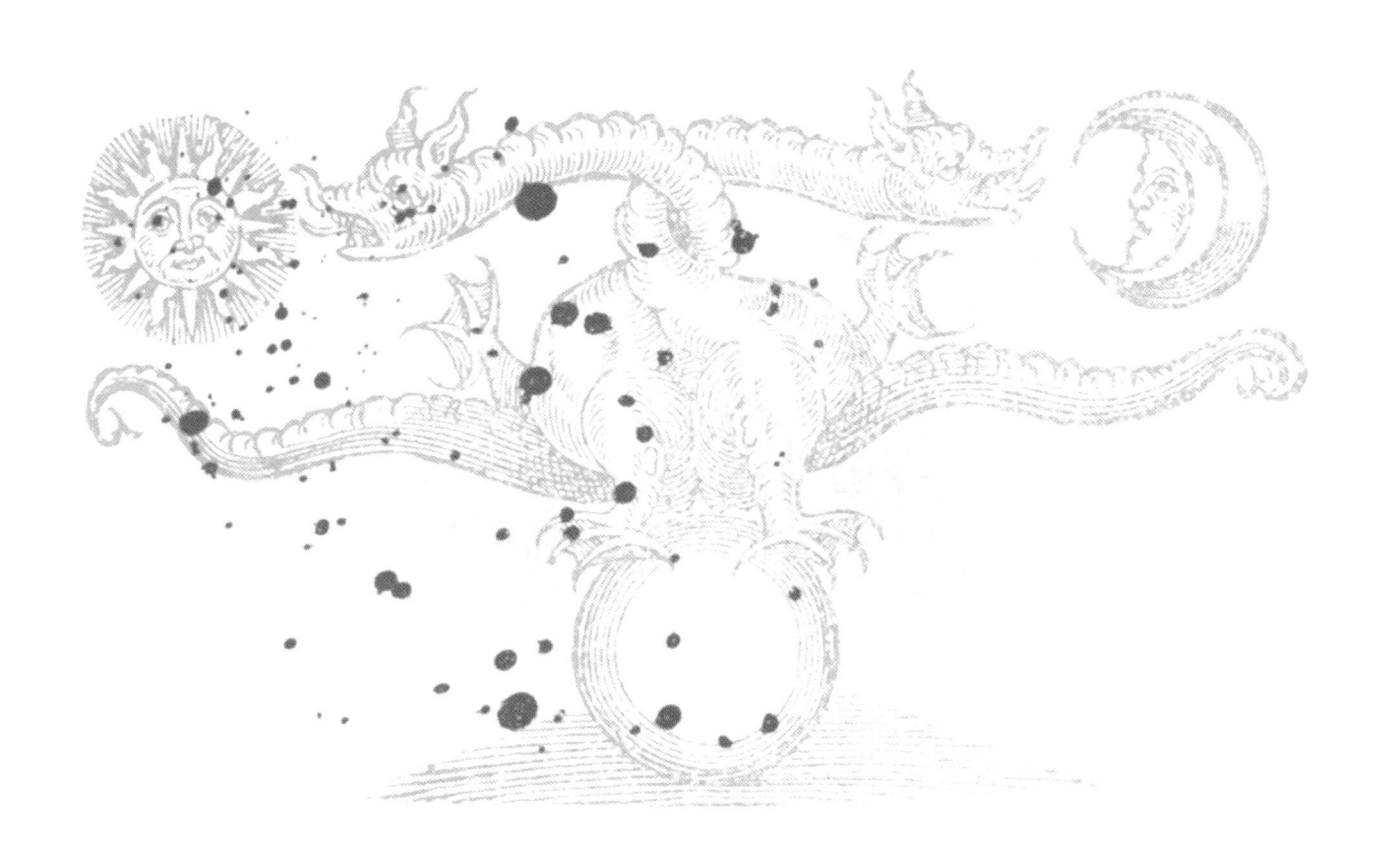

AGENTS

This chapter presents six example player characters for a *Night's Black Agents* campaign. None of them are complete, but the missing pieces can be finished in a matter of minutes, letting a player jump into the game with a minimum of fuss. All the prospective agents are out on their own, but start with no knowledge of vampires or the existence of the supernatural. Gender isn't specified for any of them, and their personalities are lightly sketched out to be developed further in play.

ROSTER

O'LEARY (MUSCLE/WHEEL ARTIST): Former Irish special forces soldier with an abiding Catholic faith.

TANNER (INVESTIGATOR/WATCHER): British journalist from a wealthy background.

WHITMAN (BAGMAN/ASSET HANDLER): American HUMINT specialist; ex-CIA.

SAVINE (BLACK BAGGER/WIRE RAT): French burglar and freelancer.

CAULDEN (HACKER/ANALYST): American NSA analyst.

MALACH (WET WORKER/CLEANER): Ex-Mossad assassin.

# OF PLAYERS	INVESTIGATIVE BUILD POINTS
2	15
3	7
4	5
5+	3

TO DO LIST

For each agent…
- Spend Investigative Ability points, depending on the number of players
- Spend 20 General Ability Points (remember to boost Health and Stability!)
- Choose MOS
- Buy Tag Team Benefits
- Determine how the agents met

SWITCHING MODES

◉ If you're playing in **DUST** mode, then drop O'Leary's Health to 10 and give him Weapons 5 instead.

◉ Don't forget to allocate Trust between the agents.

O'LEARY

Former Irish Special Forces, you were sent on peacekeeping duty to Chad in Africa. There was something behind the tribal wars, something that fed on the blood and suffering. No good Christian could stand aside and do nothing when there's such evil in the world. It must be destroyed.

SAVINE

With your talents, you could have been anything – a movie star, a politician, a spy – but you craved adventure. You're a jewel thief and a freelance industrial espionage agent, stealing from the rich for the equally rich. You're in it for the adrenaline and the sense of danger. And the money.

TANNER

You studied journalism in Cambridge, and spent several years as a political correspondent for various broadsheets. Your family disagree with your politics, but you've kept to your convictions.

CAULDEN

You worked in the green-lit dungeons of the NSA, spying on internet traffic and blocking cyberwarfare attacks. One night, you started chatting to a rival hacker who went by the handle Ghost and over the months you became emotionally involved with your mysterious counterpart. Ghost vanished, leaving only a cryptic note for you. You've got to find out who got them.

WHITMAN

After 9/11, the Company needed HUMINT in the Middle East. You were part of a team sent to recruit assets. One of your team screwed you over, selling the CIA out to the enemy and pinning you with their crimes. You're out on your own, and you know there's a mole in the Company…

MALACH

You were a Mossad wet-work specialist, eliminating those who deserved death – or so you thought. Too late, you learned your superiors were following a very different agenda, and many of those you killed were innocent. Now, you've turned on your former employers.

NIGHT'S BLACK AGENTS — AGENT RECORD SHEET

AGENT NAME O'Leary
BACKGROUND Muscle / Wheel Artist
DRIVE Slayer
PREVIOUS PATRON Irish Army Ranger Wing
SOURCES OF STABILITY
- SYMBOL Crucifix
- SOLACE Your old army priest
- SAFETY Mother's house in Galway

HEALTH
-12	-11	-10	-9
-8	-7	-6	-5
-4	-3	-2	-1
0	1	2	3
4	5	6	7
8	9	10	11
[12]	13	14	15

STABILITY
-12	-11	-10	-9
-8	-7	-6	-5
-4	-3	-2	-1
0	1	2	3
4	5	6	7
[8]	9	10	11
12	13	14	15

ACADEMIC ABILITIES
- Accounting ___
- Archaeology ___
- Architecture ___
- Art History ___
- Criminology ___
- Diagnosis ___
- History ___
- Human Terrain ___
- Languages 1
  - •
  - •
  - •
  - •
  - •
  - •
- Law ___
- Military Science 2
- Occult Studies 1
- Research ___
- Vampirology ___

COVERS
- •
- •
- •
- •
- •
- •

NETWORK CONTACTS
- •
- •
- •
- •
- •
- •

INTERPERSONAL ABILITIES
- Bullshit Detector 1
- Bureaucracy ___
- Cop Talk 2
- Flattery 1
- Flirting ___
- High Society ___
- Interrogation 1
- Intimidation 1
- Negotiation ___
- Reassurance ___
- Streetwise 3
- Tradecraft 1

TECHNICAL ABILITIES
- Astronomy ___
- Chemistry ___
- Cryptography ___
- Data Recovery ___
- Electronic Surveillance ___
- Forensic Pathology ___
- Forgery ___
  - •
  - •
- Notice 1
- Outdoor Survival 2
- Pharmacy ___
- Photography ___
- Traffic Analysis ___
- Urban Survival 2
  - •
  - •
  - •
  - •
  - •

GENERAL ABILITIES
- Athletics 6
- Conceal ___
- Cover 10
- Digital Intrusion ___
- Disguise ___
- Driving 10
  - • ___
  - • ___
- Explosive Devices 2
- Filch ___
- Gambling ___
- Hand-to-Hand 8
- Infiltration ___
- Mechanics 4
- Medic 2
- Network 15
- Piloting 4
  - • ___
  - • ___
- Preparedness ___
- Sense Trouble ___
- Shooting 4
- Shrink ___
- Surveillance ___
- Weapons 3

HIT THRESHOLD [3]

TAG-TEAM BENEFITS

SPECIAL WEAPONS TRAINING

TRUST
- • •
- • •
- • •

NIGHT'S BLACK AGENTS — AGENT RECORD SHEET

AGENT NAME Tanner
BACKGROUND Investigator / Watcher
DRIVE Transparency
PREVIOUS PATRON Fleet Street
SOURCES OF STABILITY
- **SYMBOL** Your battered notebook
- **SOLACE** Your sister
- **SAFETY** Family estate in England

HEALTH
-12 -11 -10 -9
-8 -7 -6 -5
-4 -3 -2 -1
0 1 2 3
4 5 6 7
[8] 9 10 11
12 13 14 15

STABILITY
-12 -11 -10 -9
-8 -7 -6 -5
-4 -3 -2 -1
0 1 2 3
4 5 6 7
[8] 9 10 11
12 13 14 15

PORTRAIT

ACADEMIC ABILITIES
- Accounting ___
- Archaeology ___
- Architecture ___
- Art History ___
- Criminology 1
- Diagnosis ___
- History ___
- Human Terrain 1
- Languages ___
  - •
  - •
  - •
  - •
  - •
- Law 1
- Military Science ___
- Occult Studies ___
- Research 1
- Vampirology ___

COVERS
- •
- •
- •
- •
- •
- •

NETWORK CONTACTS
- •
- •
- •
- •
- •
- •

INTERPERSONAL ABILITIES
- Bullshit Detector 1
- Bureaucracy 1
- Cop Talk 1
- Flattery 1
- Flirting ___
- High Society 1
- Interrogation 1
- Intimidation ___
- Negotiation ___
- Reassurance 1
- Streetwise 1
- Tradecraft 2

TECHNICAL ABILITIES
- Astronomy ___
- Chemistry ___
- Cryptography ___
- Data Recovery ___
- Electronic Surveillance 1
- Forensic Pathology ___
- Forgery ___
  - •
  - •
- Notice 2
- Outdoor Survival ___
- Pharmacy ___
- Photography 1
- Traffic Analysis 1
- Urban Survival 2
  - • •
  - • •
  - • •

GENERAL ABILITIES
- Athletics 5
- Conceal ___
- Cover 10
- Digital Intrusion ___
- Disguise 4
- Driving 4
  - • •
  - • •
- Explosive Devices ___
- Filch ___
- Gambling 4
- Hand-to-Hand 6
- Infiltration 4
- Mechanics ___
- Medic ___
- Network 15
- Piloting ___
  - • •
  - • •
- Preparedness 4
- Sense Trouble 2
- Shooting ___
- Shrink 2
- Surveillance 10
- Weapons ___

HIT THRESHOLD [3]

TAG-TEAM BENEFITS

SPECIAL WEAPONS TRAINING

TRUST
- • •
- • •
- • •

138

NIGHT'S BLACK AGENTS
AGENT RECORD SHEET

AGENT NAME Whitman
BACKGROUND Asset Handler / Bagman
DRIVE Restoration
PREVIOUS PATRON CIA
SOURCES OF STABILITY
- **SYMBOL** Your actual passport
- **SOLACE** Your old mentor in the Company
- **SAFETY** Your ex's apartment in Amsterdam

HEALTH
-12 -11 -10 -9
-8 -7 -6 -5
-4 -3 -2 -1
0 1 2 3
4 5 6 7
8 9 [10] 11
12 13 14 15

STABILITY
-12 -11 -10 -9
-8 -7 -6 -5
-4 -3 -2 -1
0 1 2 3
4 5 6 7
[8] 9 10 11
12 13 14 15

PORTRAIT

ACADEMIC ABILITIES
Accounting	2
Archaeology	1
Architecture	
Art History	
Criminology	1
Diagnosis	
History	1
Human Terrain	1
Languages	1
•	
•	
•	
•	
•	
•	
Law	
Military Science	2
Occult Studies	
Research	
Vampirology	

COVERS
-
-
-
-
-
-

NETWORK CONTACTS
-
-
-
-
-
-
-

INTERPERSONAL ABILITIES
Bullshit Detector	2
Bureaucracy	1
Cop Talk	1
Flattery	
Flirting	
High Society	
Interrogation	
Intimidation	1
Negotiation	2
Reassurance	1
Streetwise	1
Tradecraft	1

TECHNICAL ABILITIES
Astronomy	
Chemistry	
Cryptography	
Data Recovery	
Electronic Surveillance	1
Forensic Pathology	
Forgery	
•	
•	
Notice	
Outdoor Survival	
Pharmacy	
Photography	
Traffic Analysis	
Urban Survival	
•	
•	
•	
•	

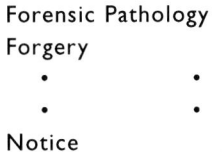

GENERAL ABILITIES
Athletics	
Conceal	4
Cover	13
Digital Intrusion	3
Disguise	2
Driving	
•	
•	
Explosive Devices	
Filch	
Gambling	
Hand-to-Hand	
Infiltration	
Mechanics	
Medic	
Network	15
Piloting	
•	
•	
Preparedness	
Sense Trouble	10
Shooting	3
Shrink	4
Surveillance	10
Weapons	

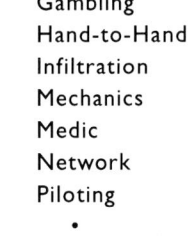

HIT THRESHOLD [3]

TAG-TEAM BENEFITS

SPECIAL WEAPONS TRAINING

TRUST
-
-
-
-

NIGHT'S BLACK AGENTS — AGENT RECORD SHEET

AGENT NAME Savine
BACKGROUND Black Bagger / Wire Rat
DRIVE Thrill-Seeker
PREVIOUS PATRON Varied
SOURCES OF STABILITY
- SYMBOL Diamond ring
- SOLACE Your fence and supplier, Jacques
- SAFETY Your retirement villa in Switzerland

HEALTH
-12 -11 -10 -9
-8   -7   -6   -5
-4   -3   -2   -1
0   1   2   3
4   5   [6]   7
8   9   10   11
12   13   14   15

STABILITY
-12 -11 -10 -9
-8   -7   -6   -5
-4   -3   -2   -1
0   1   2   3
4   5   6   7
[8] 9   10   11
12   13   14   15

PORTRAIT

ACADEMIC ABILITIES
Ability	Rating
Accounting	
Archaeology	
Architecture	1
Art History	1
Criminology	1
Diagnosis	
History	
Human Terrain	
Languages	
•	
•	
•	
•	
•	
Law	
Military Science	
Occult Studies	
Research	
Vampirology	

COVERS
-
-
-
-
-
-
-

NETWORK CONTACTS
-
-
-
-
-
-

INTERPERSONAL ABILITIES
Ability	Rating
Bullshit Detector	
Bureaucracy	
Cop Talk	
Flattery	
Flirting	
High Society	
Interrogation	
Intimidation	
Negotiation	
Reassurance	
Streetwise	2
Tradecraft	1

TECHNICAL ABILITIES
Ability	Rating
Astronomy	
Chemistry	1
Cryptography	
Data Recovery	2
Electronic Surveillance	2
Forensic Pathology	
Forgery	1
•	
•	
Notice	1
Outdoor Survival	
Pharmacy	
Photography	2
Traffic Analysis	
Urban Survival	2
•	
•	
•	

GENERAL ABILITIES
Ability	Rating
Athletics	9
Conceal	8
Cover	10
Digital Intrusion	2
Disguise	2
Driving	4
•	
•	
Explosive Devices	2
Filch	6
Gambling	
Hand-to-Hand	
Infiltration	10
Mechanics	
Medic	
Network	15
Piloting	
•	
•	
Preparedness	2
Sense Trouble	2
Shooting	
Shrink	
Surveillance	
Weapons	

HIT THRESHOLD [4]

TAG-TEAM BENEFITS

SPECIAL WEAPONS TRAINING

TRUST
-
-
-

140

NIGHT'S BLACK AGENTS — AGENT RECORD SHEET

AGENT NAME Caulden
BACKGROUND Hacker / Analyst
DRIVE Revenge
PREVIOUS PATRON NSA

SOURCES OF STABILITY
- **SYMBOL** Your print-out of the last chat
- **SOLACE** Your childhood friend Mark, who's dying of cancer
- **SAFETY** The family's holiday home

HEALTH
-12 -11 -10 -9
-8 -7 -6 -5
-4 -3 -2 -1
0 1 2 3
4 5 6 7
[8] 9 10 11
12 13 14 15

STABILITY
-12 -11 -10 -9
-8 -7 -6 -5
-4 -3 -2 -1
0 1 2 3
4 5 6 7
[8] 9 10 11
12 13 14 15

PORTRAIT

ACADEMIC ABILITIES
Accounting	1
Archaeology	
Architecture	
Art History	
Criminology	1
Diagnosis	
History	1
Human Terrain	
Languages	
•	
•	
•	
•	
•	
•	
Law	
Military Science	1
Occult Studies	
Research	1
Vampirology	

COVERS
-
-
-
-
-
-

NETWORK CONTACTS
-
-
-
-
-
-

INTERPERSONAL ABILITIES
Bullshit Detector	
Bureaucracy	1
Cop Talk	
Flattery	
Flirting	
High Society	
Interrogation	
Intimidation	
Negotiation	
Reassurance	
Streetwise	1
Tradecraft	1

TECHNICAL ABILITIES
Astronomy	
Chemistry	
Cryptography	1
Data Recovery	3
Electronic Surveillance	2
Forensic Pathology	
Forgery	
•	
•	
Notice	1
Outdoor Survival	
Pharmacy	
Photography	1
Traffic Analysis	2
Urban Survival	2

GENERAL ABILITIES
Athletics	5
Conceal	2
Cover	10
Digital Intrusion	10
Disguise	2
Driving	
• •	
• •	
Explosive Devices	
Filch	
Gambling	
Hand-to-Hand	
Infiltration	2
Mechanics	4
Medic	2
Network	20
Piloting	
• •	
• •	
Preparedness	4
Sense Trouble	5
Shooting	
Shrink	
Surveillance	7
Weapons	

HIT THRESHOLD [3]

TAG-TEAM BENEFITS

SPECIAL WEAPONS TRAINING

TRUST
- •   •
- •   •
- •   •

NIGHT'S BLACK AGENTS — AGENT RECORD SHEET

AGENT NAME Malach
BACKGROUND Wetwork / Cleaner
DRIVE Atonement
PREVIOUS PATRON Mossad

SOURCES OF STABILITY
- **SYMBOL** Your silenced pistol
- **SOLACE** Your daughter
- **SAFETY** Your cousin's place in Seattle

HEALTH
-12 -11 -10 -9
-8 -7 -6 -5
-4 -3 -2 -1
0 1 2 3
4 5 6 7
[8] 9 10 11
12 13 14 15

STABILITY
-12 -11 -10 -9
-8 -7 -6 -5
-4 -3 -2 -1
0 1 2 3
4 5 6 7
8 9 [10] 11
12 13 14 15

ACADEMIC ABILITIES
Accounting	
Archaeology	
Architecture	1
Art History	
Criminology	2
Diagnosis	
History	
Human Terrain	
Languages	1
•	
•	
•	
•	
•	
•	
Law	
Military Science	1
Occult Studies	
Research	
Vampirology	

COVERS
-
-
-
-
-
-
-

NETWORK CONTACTS
-
-
-
-
-
-

INTERPERSONAL ABILITIES
Bullshit Detector	
Bureaucracy	2
Cop Talk	1
Flattery	
Flirting	
High Society	
Interrogation	
Intimidation	2
Negotiation	
Reassurance	
Streetwise	2
Tradecraft	1

TECHNICAL ABILITIES
Astronomy	
Chemistry	
Cryptography	
Data Recovery	
Electronic Surveillance	
Forensic Pathology	1
Forgery	
•	
•	
Notice	1
Outdoor Survival	
Pharmacy	
Photography	
Traffic Analysis	1
Urban Survival	2
•	
•	
•	

GENERAL ABILITIES
Athletics	8
Conceal	6
Cover	10
Digital Intrusion	
Disguise	2
Driving	4
• •	
• •	
Explosive Devices	2
Filch	
Gambling	
Hand-to-Hand	4
Infiltration	
Mechanics	
Medic	
Network	15
Piloting	
• •	
• •	
Preparedness	3
Sense Trouble	
Shooting	10
Shrink	
Surveillance	4
Weapons	

HIT THRESHOLD [4]

TAG-TEAM BENEFITS

SPECIAL WEAPONS TRAINING

TRUST
-
-
-
-

NIGHT'S BLACK AGENTS

MAP – EUROPE

NIGHT'S BLACK AGENTS
MAP – ODESSA

NIGHT'S BLACK AGENTS — MAP – VIENNA

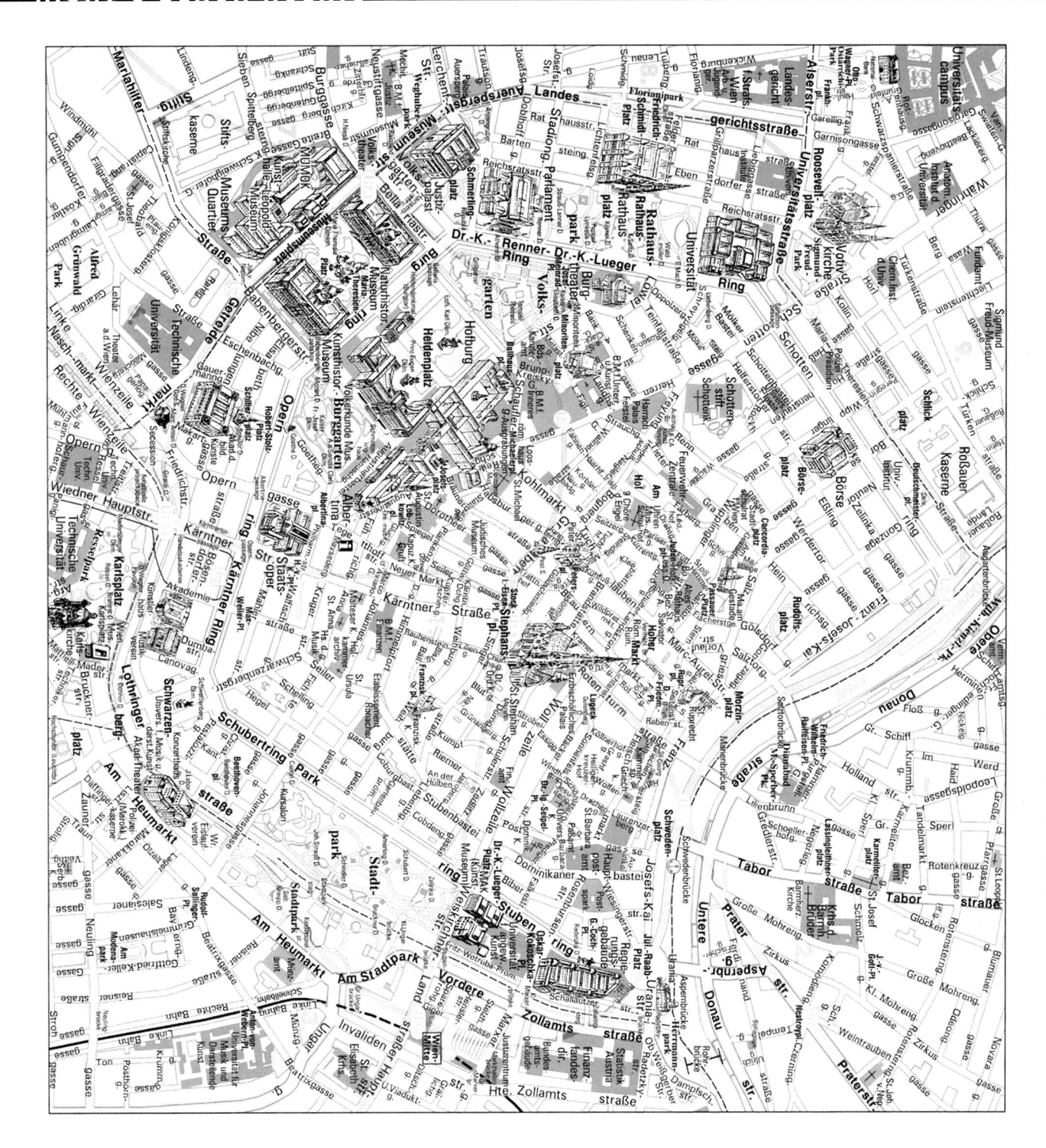

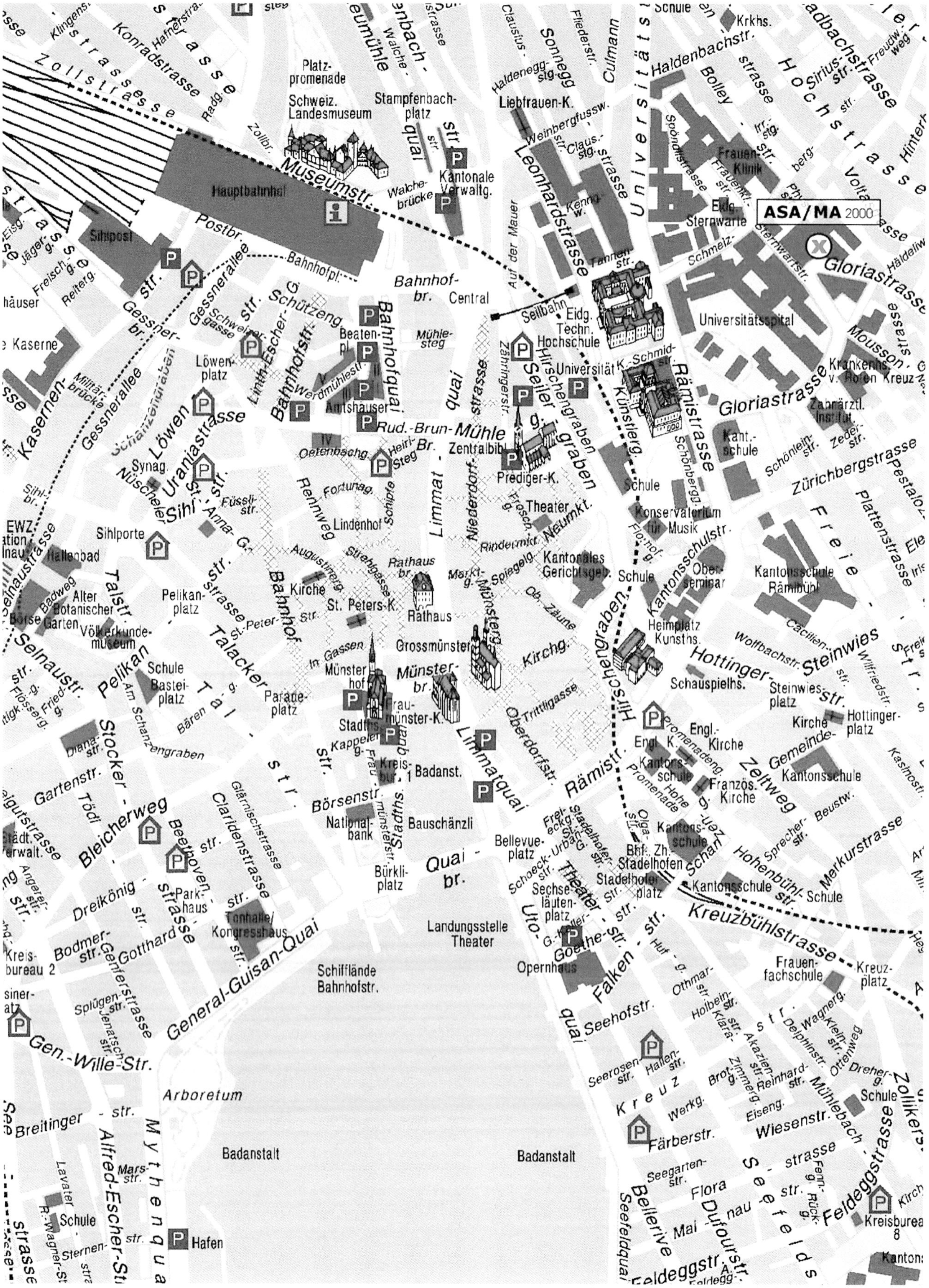
ASA/MA 2000
Hauptbahnhof
Sihlpost
Museumstr.
Schweiz. Landesmuseum
Platz-promenade
Stampfenbach-platz
Kantonale Verwaltg.
Walche-brücke
Bahnhofpl.
Bahnhof-br.
Central
Seilbahn
Eidg. Techn. Hochschule
Universität
Universitätsspital
Gloriastrasse
Zürichbergstrasse
Leonhardstrasse
Universitätstrasse
Haldenbachstr.
Hochstrasse
Frauen-Klinik
Eidg. Sternwarte
Krrhs.
Liebfrauen-K.
Sonnegg
Culmann
Weinbergfussw.
Zollstrasse
Konradstrasse
Postbr.
Gessnerallee
Kaserne
Kasernen-strasse
Löwen-platz
Löwenstrasse
Uraniastrasse
Bahnhofstr.
Bahnhofquai
Beaten-pl.
Amtshäuser
Rud.-Brun-Mühle
Mühlesteg
Limmatquai
Niederdorf-strasse
Hirschengraben
Seilergraben
Rämistrasse
Künstlerg.
Prediger-K.
Zentralbibl.
Theater
Neumarkt
Rindermkt.
Kantonales Gerichtsgeb.
Schule
Konservatorium für Musik
Kantonsschulstr.
Ober-seminar
Kantonsschule Rämibühl
Heimplatz Kunsths.
Schauspielhs.
Hottingerstr.
Steinwies-str.
Steinwies-platz
Hottinger-platz
Kirche
Engl.-Kirche
Französ. Kirche
Zeltweg
Kantonsschule
Gemeindestr.
Synag.
Sihlporte
Hallenbad
Alter Botanischer Garten
Börse
Völkerkunde-museum
Pelikan-platz
Pelikanstr.
Talstr.
Talacker
Schule Bastei-platz
Selnaustr.
Stockerstr.
Bärengasse
Schanzengraben
Paradeplatz
St. Peters-K.
St.-Peter-str.
Rennweg
Lindenhof
Rathaus
Rathausbr.
Grossmünster
Münsterbr.
Münsterhof
Fraumünster-K.
Stadths.
Kirchg.
Oberdorfstr.
Trittligasse
Badanst.
Börsenstr.
Nationalbank
Bauschänzli
Bürkliplatz
Quaibr.
Bellevue-platz
Stadelhofen
Bhf. Zh. Stadelhofen
Stadelhofer-platz
Sechseläuten-platz
Theaterstr.
Utoquai
Opernhaus
Falkenstr.
Goethestr.
Kreuzbühlstrasse
Kreuzplatz
Frauen-fachschule
Hohenbühlstr.
Merkurstrasse
Seehofstr.
Kreuzstrasse
Färberstr.
Wiesenstr.
Seefeldstrasse
Feldeggstrasse
Florastrasse
Dufourstr.
Mainaustr.
Bellerive
Seefeldquai
Kreisbureau 8
Schule
Landungsstelle Theater
Schifflände Bahnhofstr.
General-Guisan-Quai
Tonhalle/Kongresshaus
Claridenstrasse
Gotthardstr.
Dreikönigstr.
Beethovenstr.
Bleicherweg
Parkhaus
Tödi
Gartenstr.
Bodmerstr.
Genferstrasse
Kreisbureau 2
Gen.-Wille-Str.
Arboretum
Breitingerstr.
Alfred-Escher-Str.
Mythenquai
Badanstalt
Hafen
Schule
Lavaterstr.

146

NIGHT'S BLACK AGENTS — MAP - BEIRUT

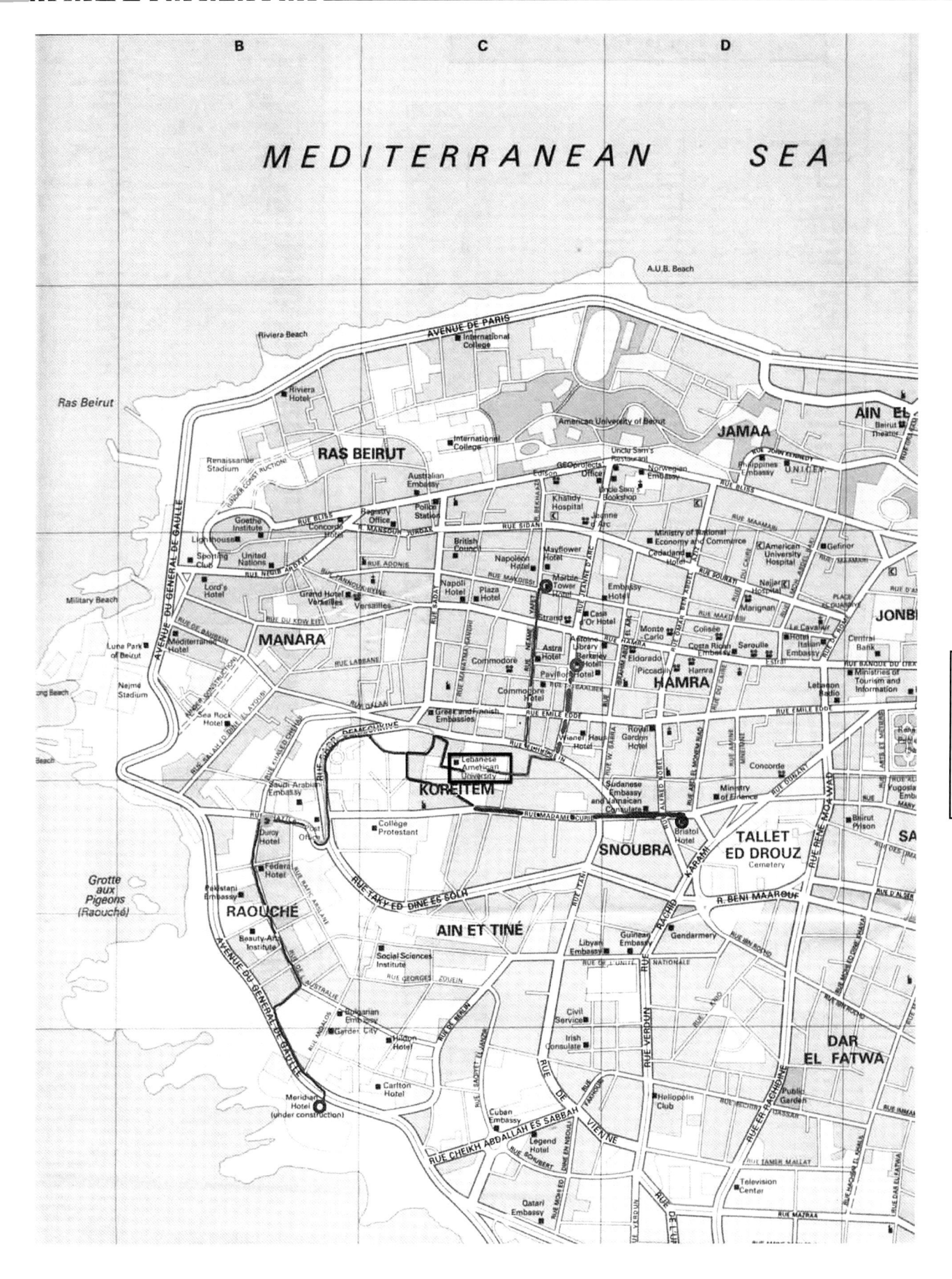

NIGHT'S BLACK AGENTS — MAP - BAGHDAD

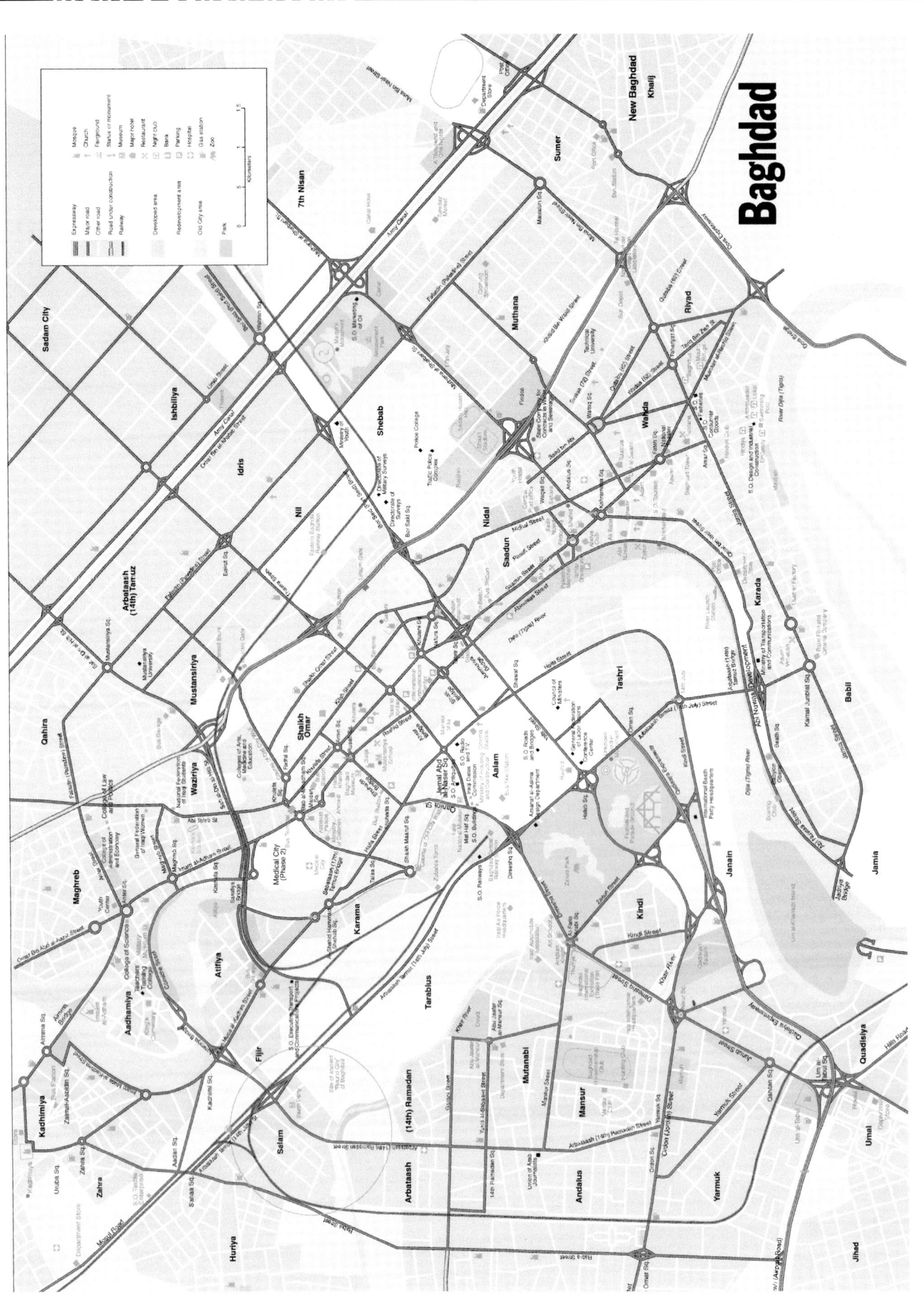